MARKETING
TO THE
MIND

MARKETING
TO THE
MIND

Right Brain Strategies
for Advertising and Marketing

◆

Richard C. Maddock
and
Richard L. Fulton

QUORUM BOOKS
Westport, Connecticut • London

Library of Congress Cataloging-in-Publication Data

Maddock, Richard C.
Marketing to the mind : right brain strategies for advertising and
marketing / Richard C. Maddock, Richard L. Fulton.
p.   cm.
Includes bibliographical references and index.
ISBN 1–56720–031–1 (alk. paper)
1. Advertising—Psychological aspects.   2. Motivation research
(Marketing)   3. Marketing.   I. Fulton, Richard L.   II. Title.
HF5822.M33   1996
659.1′01′9—dc20   95–50743

British Library Cataloguing in Publication Data is available.

Library of Congress Catalog Card Number: 95–50743
ISBN: 1–56720–031–1

First published in 1996

Quorum Books, 88 Post Road West, Westport, CT 06881
An imprint of Greenwood Publishing Group, Inc.

Printed in the United States of America

The paper used in this book complies with the
Permanent Paper Standard issued by the National
Information Standards Organization (Z39.48–1984).

10 9 8 7 6 5 4 3 2

Dedicated to the memory of Dr. Roland L. Frye,
teacher, professor, businessman, psychologist, scholar and friend.

Contents

Illustrations

Acknowledgments

The authors wish to acknowledge and thank the following friends for their help and assistance: Dr. Ray Sexton, who uncovered the motive of spiritual survival, and Dr. Paul Fleischman, who made it operational. They are both pioneers and visionaries.

We also wish to express thanks to those who assisted in specific areas: Larry Percy in qualitative to quantitative; Jim Mecredy in food and beverage; Dave Swearingen in communications and creative strategies; Dave Fulton for his legal assistance; Max Maddock for his help with Elvis; Tim Martin for assistance with automotive; Jim Lumpp for his insight into the left side of the brain; and Steve Puckett in health-care.

We also want to offer special thanks to Eric Valentine of Quorum Books and Greg Patterson of Richard D. Irwin Publishing, for their assistance on the manuscript, and to Becky, Vicki, and Taylor.

Preface

CONSIDER:

On March 16, 1989, under the cover of darkness, Mark Stone quietly slipped out of his bedroom, picked up the duffel bag he had prepacked the night before and went to the garage. After rolling his BMW down the drive with the engine off, he drove slowly away, leaving his wife of 17 years and three beautiful children behind. His was a good marriage by any objective standard. The kids were bright, loving, and doing well in school. Mark's brokerage job gave him a six-figure income and a big promotion was just weeks away.

Five years later, Mark's wife, Susan, first heard of her missing husband by accident. Glancing through the Sunday travel section of the newspaper, she spotted a photo of Mark with the following caption: "Solo captain drops in at Tahitian port on a trip around the globe."

OR, CONSIDER:

Karen Whitehead is the production manager at *Globe* magazine. Her boss, Jim Williams, is the assistant editor. They both are waiting at Midway Airport for the corporate jet from Print Services Corporation to pick them up and take them to Lubbock—a two-hour flight. They board the jet, have a smooth flight, and are met at the airport by the plant manager, Fred Rogers, and the customer service representative, Jill Baker. The four of them have an excellent lunch at the country club, then take a plant tour. Later that afternoon they discuss closure on their account: a 2.5 million print order six times a year. For Print Services Corporation this represents their largest single account to date. Everything goes well at the meeting, and dinner follows. The next morning they board the jet for the trip back to Chicago.

All details and loose ends seem to have been settled. The first issue of *Globe* is scheduled to be printed on May 1.

Three weeks later the plant manager, Fred, goes to Jill's office to see what the follow-up to the meeting has been. To his dismay, he learns that despite Jill's attempts to follow up, there has been no response. Jill is as puzzled as he is. "They politely take my messages at *Globe*, but they never return my calls." She did not have an answer. But Fred, who had been in the business for 18 years, knew the answer. Despite the assurances that were given at the meeting three weeks ago, they had decided not to move their account to Print Services Corporation. Why? What happened? Fred knew from experience that he would probably never know the answer.

Why do people make the decisions that they make? Can you predict who will stick with their decisions, and who will not? Why do people change in midstream, despite their assurances, promises, and pledges? What percent of our choices in life are based on rational vs. emotional considerations?

WHY?

These two brief examples are meant to illustrate the essential elements and the importance of emotion and motivation in decision making. All too often the real agenda is underneath, hidden or obscured. Customers, co-workers, and even our loved ones act on emotion. "The mind is like an iceberg," we have been told, "with two-thirds beneath the surface." As a result, all of us on a daily basis confront decisions that we just do not understand or comprehend. How can we predict or plan for the future when the world around us appears to be so irrational, so emotional?

Psychologists, psychiatrists, management, and marketing experts have generally failed to assist us in these understandings. We are told that most of these irrational behaviors lie in the unconscious mind, but the unconscious is never fully described or delineated. We are given rational guidelines to deal with these irrational behaviors, but often that will not work either. The goal of science is prediction, but in the arena of marketing and customer service, prediction and control rely on unconscious as well as conscious determinants.

MARKETING AND MOTIVES

Prior research into the unconscious motives and emotions of the consumer has been clouded by failed attempts, misguided methodologies, and "hype." Most have heard about subliminal methods, and about the importance of sexuality. Some human factors psychologists, engineers, and designers have concentrated on the external rather than the internal persuaders: lighting, petitions, displays, etc. Market research has done an excellent job of describing the parameters, but market researchers need to say more about motive; the issue of why consumers and customers do what they do. The unconscious, we believe or we are told, is like a "black box," and there are certain things that are just better left unexplored or unexamined. Some professional psychologists even doubt the existence of the unconscious.

Despite all this confusion about motivation and emotion, one thing is clear: the marketer must have this information if he/she is to effectively do the job. The job of marketing is to motivate the consumer. In police science and law enforcement, there is no solution to a crime until a motive is established. Similarly, the marketer has to know the motives, which often account for over 80 percent of decisions that are made in consumer and business contexts.

BACKGROUND

In an area where "the harvest is plentiful but the laborers are few," what makes us qualified to enter? To begin with, we have over 15 years of experience in research with consumers in over 200 different product areas. Each one of the projects that we undertook involved a unique form of market research, where we relied upon "visualization" rather than paper-and-pencil techniques or verbalization. This was employed because visualization is a "right brain" methodology and as such uncovers the emotions and motivations rather than the rationalizations and excuses that people often give for their behaviors. This is the unconscious side of advertising and marketing. It is the side of the decision-making process that is often unheard, unexplored, and unexamined. Likewise, it has seldom been researched. We are about to reveal some secrets.

What can the marketer hope to know when he/she becomes familiar with the Silent Side? To begin, he/she will learn why consumers do what they do. The marketer will discover what motivates consumers and why they make the decisions that they do. The marketer will find out what makes consumers loyal to a product or service, and what makes them switch. The unconscious side of the mind reveals the real reasons for consumer decisions, versus the ones that are fed back to us so often in numerous research projects. Most of all, Marketing to the Mind uncovers what consumers are looking for in products and in services: what they like and what they do not like.

When we think of advertising and marketing, we usually think of it being loud. Indeed, it is the conscious side that is usually heard. But just as important to marketing is the unconscious side. In this book we will demonstrate that the unconscious is the power side, the dominant side, the forceful side, and the Silent Side. When the unconscious side speaks, the marketer needs to listen!

MARKETING
TO THE
MIND

Introduction

The unconscious side of marketing neither replaces nor removes the motivational systems that are already in place and in use in predicting consumer behavior. Instead, the unconscious side adds a new and exciting dimension, a third dimension that opens up a perspective in consumer motivation that has not been seen before. Marketing to the Mind addresses what is going on inside the consumers' minds and what they are thinking, as they make purchasing decisions, affirm loyalties, and respond to advertising. It is the emotional/affective dimension.

In a paper that won the 1993 Award for Distinguished Professional Contribution to Consumer Psychology at the annual meeting of the American Psychological Association, Krugman (1994) addressed the need for such an approach. Krugman suggested that none of the core subdisciplines of psychology have studied the likes and dislikes of people in general. He added that the everyday data of consumer research is the perfect forum for such a focus, presumably because the consumer psychologist is studying people when they spend their money. The unspoken implication of his paper is that American psychology in general and consumer psychology in particular have taken a limited approach. Much of it has relied upon Pavlov's research, which assumes that all behavior can be conditioned. Krugman concludes that "consequently, their research has investigated every other stimuli except the stimulus directly related to the response being studied."

Unfortunately, when such a narrow approach is taken to the study of behavior, it becomes more and more difficult to make predictions. Therefore, to broaden the scope of consumer psychology, advertising effects are now measured by taking into account the *intervening variable*, which intervenes between the simple stimulus (S) and the simple response (R). Hansen (1994) refers to this as the S—O—R model, where S represents the stimulus (advertising); O represents the intervening variables; and R represents the response (buy-no buy). The example that Hansen gives of an intervening variable is attitude. Other examples of intervening variables may be interest (on the part of the consumer) and likability (Stapel, 1994). Rossiter & Percy (1983) in their summary, "Visual Communication in Advertising," note that there are two important intervening variables. These consist of (1) the initial processing of the advertising stimuli and (2) the stored communication effects. These two intervening variables in turn break down into attention, coding and decoding, beliefs, attitudes, intentions, and choice rules.

BACKGROUND—THE IMPORTANCE OF VARIOUS DIMENSIONS OF CONSUMER BEHAVIOR

It is tempting to apply the experimental approach to all psychology, and thus to isolate the variables. In social psychology, it is not always possible to do this, and other methods such as field studies and observation often have to be employed. Rigorous laboratory studies in which there are plenty of structure always lead to problems with the ability to generalize findings. On the other hand, field studies, which lack rigor, may be more generalizable, yet may be open to criticism and conjecture.

The present approach, based on 15 years of research with consumers, relies on a less rigorous approach but one which addresses most of the crucial issues Krugman addressed: What do consumers like; What do they dislike; and, more importantly, Why? To answer the why, we must first address three basic approaches to consumer motivation (of which we will provide a broad overview).

The first dimension of consumer motivation may be referred to as the *rational side*. This is the side of the consumer that is appealed to the most often. Rational decisions account for a large percentage of variance in consumer behavior and motivation, and include decisions that are made on the basis of value, habit, price, immediacy, speed, and product features, such as user friendliness, that eliminate anxiety, hard work, and other negative emotions on the part of the consumer or the end user. The rational side of the consumer is appealed to in terms of rationalizations and justifications. We will refer to this as *left brain advertising*. This is because the left brain is the more rational, logical, and sensible side of the consumer; decisions reached using the left brain are made on the basis of facts rather than emotion. But most product and service decisions are not made on the basis of reason and logic. Many are made on the basis of emotion and passion. They are made on the unconscious side. This is especially true of products in fields that involve recreation, fashion, cosmetics, and other areas where discretionary income accounts for the largest share of purchases.

A second major approach to consumer motivation is *behavior modification*. This approach sits midway on a continuum between the left brain and right brain approach. This approach straddles the fence, in that it deals with both logic on the left side and emotion on the right side of the brain. Behavior modification works, when executed correctly. Behavior modification will increase consumer interest and motivation at the point of sale.

Examples of behavior modification are frequent-flyer and frequent-traveler rewards or reinforcements and contests, games coupons, and other incentives or rewards that are contingent upon using or buying the product. Unfortunately most of the approaches to behavior modification that work rely on consumer behavior that is already occurring, since the behavior modification approaches tend to reward behavior that is already in progress. Therefore, behavior modification may keep consumers loyal, but it does not always work to bring in new customers.

An exception to this rule is outlined in *Positioning: The Battle for Your Mind* (Reis and Trout, 1981). Positioning is a strategy of advertising and marketing that relies upon a behavior modification method called *stimulus generalization.* Positioning was developed by Reis and Trout. Stimulus generalization is a way of getting the respondent or consumer to generalize from one stimulus to another, as in the small child who associates the word dada with his father and then generalizes this to all men whom he/she sees (at least during a brief period of his/her development). In positioning, a unique use of behavior modification in marketing, the intent is to get the consumer to *generalize* from one stimulus (product or service) to another (product or service). Reis and Trout illustrate this concept using the example of Avis positioning itself as Number Two, a move that was effective in moving former Hertz customers into the Avis driver's seat. There are many different examples where a competitor may "identify with the aggressor" and use the adversary's superior marketing position to his/her own advantage. This is stimulus generalization, a technique well researched and supported by those who practice and extol the merits of behavior modification.

The rational approach can work because everyone likes to think that they make all their decisions on a rational, logical basis. The behavior modification approach works because it deals with both the logical and the emotional sides of the consumer. But there is a third approach that works just as effectively, if not even more so, and that approach is the unconscious approach to advertising and marketing.

The unconscious encompasses the emotional side, yet may also be referred to as the *cognitive side.* It is the side of advertising and marketing that addresses what is going on in the consumers' minds. This approach gets inside their heads. Within the realm of consumer activity there is both thinking and emotion. This is the Silent Side, and this is the third dimension of consumer behavior. In Hansen's terminology, it is an intervening variable, operating between the stimulus and the response. However, it is one that has been addressed only very tangentially, even though it accounts for a very substantial part of consumer behavior.

The primary reason for the study of the unconscious is to address the issue of consumer emotion, a right brain activity. This is the study of emotion, and is important because most consumer decisions are based on emotion, not reason. Marketing to the mind addresses the issues of how to motivate consumers and keep them loyal. Marketing to the mind explains how to get consumers to use your products or services rather than the competitors', all the while satisfying their emotional as well as their rational needs.

When asked, consumers cannot tell how they really feel, or what they want emotionally. Rather than trying to discredit the rational side or the strategies of behavior modification, marketing to the mind complements them, giving the marketer more insight and more direction in a very large area of consumer motivation that has been overlooked and ignored: the emotional side.

One may add, how is it possible to explore the emotions when they have been overlooked for so long? Other methods of marketing and marketing research have gathered information from the left side of the brain, because it is the side of the brain that communicates. Marketing to the mind also goes through the left side of the brain, but this is done only to get into the right side of the brain. And it is this side—the right side—that holds the keys to the powerful emotional needs that influence and control consumer decisions. It is the right side that addresses the question of why consumers do what they do. The right side enhances the marketers' power to make predictions about what consumers will do because it does more than describe behavior—it explains it.

MARKETING TO THE MIND AS A DIAGNOSTIC METHOD OR TOOL

Marketing to the mind stands out from all other market research techniques in many ways. As stated earlier, it goes to the right side of the brain, including the right hemisphere. Secondly, marketing to the mind provides a motivational structure against which all advertising can be weighted, measured, and interpreted. Finally, this approach provides a diagnostic method to be used in advertising, marketing, and business in general.

As a diagnostic method, marketing to the mind is not the same as other research methodologies. Since marketing to the mind evolved partly from a medical setting, the emphasis is on diagnosis. Marketers may want to know why their product is not selling, why people are not using it, or why they are switching to another brand. The research and diagnostic technology presented in *Marketing to the Mind* will provide the answers to these questions. More importantly, it will also provide viable solutions. As such, marketing to the mind may be used productively along with other market research methodologies, but it stands alone as an effective diagnostic tool. This is because it looks at the whole situation—rational and emotional—not just at the rational side. It has been used not only by marketers but by many others who have encountered problems in their businesses that seem to have no answer. Up to now the problem has been not that there is no answer, but that the answer cannot be found on the rational side of the brain. Answers are found on the emotional, unconscious side as well as on the rational side of the brain. And that is where marketing to the mind comes in.

REFERENCES

Hansen, F. (1994, June 2). Recent developments in the measurement of advertising effectiveness: the third generation. *Working Paper.* Copenhagen, Denmark: The Copenhagen Business School Marketing Institute.

Krugman, H. E. (1994). Pavlov's dog and the future of consumer psychology. *Journal of Advertising Research, 34* (6), 67–71.

Percy, L., & Rossiter, J. R. (1992). In a model of brand awareness and brand attitude advertising strategies. *Psychology and Marketing* (Vl 4 (9), pp. 263–274). New York: John Wiley and Sons, Inc.

Reis, A., & Trout, J. (1981). *Positioning: The battle for your mind.* New York: McGraw Hill.

Rossiter, J. R. & Percy, L. (1983). Visual communication in advertising. In R. Harris (Ed.) *Information processing research in advertising* (pp. 83–126). Hillsdale, NJ: Lawrence Erlbaum Associates.

Stapel, J. (1994). A brief observation about likability and interestingness of advertising. *Journal of Advertising Research, 34*, 79–80.

1

Advertising Past and Present

EFFECTIVE ADVERTISING WITH A LASTING MESSAGE

Fifty years ago, when radio was at its peak and radio advertising was at a premium, the way to create a memorable and motivational spot for a product was to develop a pitch or jingle. Advertisers would hire professionals to compose and record the lyrics that accompanied the pitch.

During the long, sunny days that our family spent each summer at the Jersey shore, my brother and I memorized no fewer than 100 different commercials for various products, anything that was advertised on WNEW, New York. We would spend hours singing them in the car, while on the beach, or out on the boat. It was one way we dealt with idle time.

I can still remember my mother, who I now realize was somewhat of a marketing whiz herself, saying to a friend: "I just can't understand how these kids can memorize these commercials in one sitting, but have so much difficulty memorizing their multiplication tables."

What is even more impressive is that after 50 years, we can still recall at least 90 percent of those jingles.

Does anyone remember:

My beer is Reingold the dry beer
Think of Reingold whenever you buy beer
It's not bitter, not sweet
But a dry flavor treat
Won't you try Extra Dry Reingold beer.

Or:

Skip the bother, skip the fuss
Take the Public Service Bus
Public Service sure is great!
Takes you right up to the gate
(Of Palisades Amusement Park)

These lyrics, along with the music and lyrics of dozens of others, are still imbedded in the preconscious minds of my brother and me, and probably will be forever. They are, in a way, immortal.

THE ROAD TO EFFECTIVE ADVERTISING

During the fifties, with the advent of television and the still burgeoning radio business, psychologists and creative directors tried to chart the course to effective advertising. Humor was tried. It seemed to work. In the late fifties, a series of spots for Piel's beer featured two brothers, Bert and Harry Piel, who hit an all time high for popularity in advertising with their humorous approach. But the beer did not sell, and eventually the company floundered, due mainly to a marginal product, not because of the ads. But the question about humor was: Does it really work? Does it enhance memory and recall? In the case of Bert and Harry, there was no question that it enhanced brand recognition, but no amount of effective advertising could sell a product that consumers did not embrace.

The role of humor in advertising, in particular in the sale of services and products, is still being debated. This subject will be looked at in much more detail in chapter 5, where it is re-interpreted and re-examined in an entirely new light in a discussion of "absurdities."

SUBLIMINAL ADVERTISING

It was also during the fifties that work with subliminal messages in advertising was carried out. The words "Eat Popcorn" were flashed on the screen in several movie theaters at the speed of a single frame. There was quantifiable evidence that consumers did buy more popcorn. But psychologists specializing in perception and sensation argued over whether this technique really worked and, more specifically, whether it was ethical. Whether a consumer could actually perceive a message that could not be seen or processed at the conscious level was, and still is, very questionable. This dilemma has never been resolved. Eventually the FCC declared the subliminal method unlawful.

Even though unlawful, the controversy is not resolved. Many textbooks still give examples of words that were imbedded in ice cubes in print ads for gin and vodka, words that could barely be made out, but with conscious effort became recognizable. Other examples of ads exist where "subliminal" messages are carved into fabrics or background sets in print and television advertising. The coercive effects of all this are doubtful. In fact, the pursuit of the "double message," or conscious/unconscious delivery of advertising, has not been dropped. Even though conclusive proof of its usefulness does not exist, Key (1973) attempted to convince the public that advertisers were implanting subliminal messages of death, sex, and other taboos through their visual communications. Books such as this create a storm of controversy, presumably because people like to believe that they have complete control over what goes into their own minds.

It is interesting that even today, when marketers address the issue of the unconscious mind, they often will revert back to these examples, perhaps in deference to the famous book that was written on this subject, *The Hidden Persuaders* (Packard 1957). Despite research and four decades of advertising, not a whole lot more attention has been given to the role the unconscious and the emotions exert in advertising and marketing. Experienced advertising people and marketers still believe that there is a pot of gold somewhere at the end of the marketing rainbow. It is just that it cannot—or has not—been found. Or has it?

THE APPROACH TO THE UNCONSCIOUS MIND OF THE CONSUMER

In 1952 Dr. Ernst Dichter, a consumer psychologist, caught the attention of the advertising world when he came to the rescue of Chrysler Corporation. The automobile manufacturer was struggling to survive against growing American competition. Dr. Dichter told Chrysler sales executives to position their convertible on the showroom floor in such a way as to draw men into the dealership. Moreover, he counseled Chrysler to have the salesman deal with the wife, who would make the ultimate (and realistic) decision. It worked, and Dichter went on to become an international consultant to a variety of consumer product industries (Dichter, personal communication, 1984).

Dichter's work (1964, 1971) has lasted for several decades. Another example is his ad campaign "Have it your way" for Burger King. One recommendation he made to home builders was to put a large, 12"-16" dish-type doorknob in the middle of the door of every home so homeowners could "hug" their home. The rationale behind this was that a home is the largest purchase that most people ever make and there should be some way that they can "hold on to it." The dish-style doorknobs were popular during the early sixties but have just about disappeared. The corresponding rationale also has been forgotten.

Dichter also recommended that home builders use wall-to-wall carpeting. The idea was brilliant. The wall-to-wall concept is still used extensively in new and existing houses. His rationale was that wall-to-wall gave the home an "in uterine" ambience. This was a difficult concept for ad executives and creatives to integrate into their copy. They wisely chose to sell the concept and not the rationale.

Dichter was a psychoanalytically trained psychologist whose recommendations often revolved around sexuality and had no real practical applications or significance. More importantly, his techniques were largely intuitive, and in the advertising world more and more pressure was being placed upon developing quantitative advertising techniques. Consistent with our previous observations about scientific procedures that employed the experimental method, many of these quantitative techniques were sharply criticized. This was due to their insensitivity to the creative process. One in particular, the Schwerin test, became available in London in the early sixties. In Europe and Great Britain many of the advertising measurement techniques remained qualitative rather than quantitative, with the emphasis on in-depth interviewing and focus groups rather than measurement (Hansen 1994).

Many products do not lend themselves to sexual interpretations or conclusions. But, on the other hand, Dichter was perhaps on the right track when he looked at the unconscious for cues and lessons about consumer behavior and consumer motivation. That is what we have been examining for the last 15 years. We have found buried treasure. This is treasure that is buried in the unconscious part of the mind and when employed to affect consumer decisions, may change or alter the direction of advertising and marketing in the future. What we have found is that the unconscious mind has much to offer to advertising and marketing. Understanding the unconscious requires a deep knowledge of motivation, which is imperative if the concepts are to be effectively applied.

MARKETING TO THE MIND IN ADVERTISING
AND MARKETING

Marketing to the mind refers to the unconscious mind. This is the side of the brain that has been explored by few, and misunderstood by many. Yet, it is the motivating side. It is the emotional side. It is the visual side. It is the passionate side. In consumer behavior, it is the side that makes the initial ("gut") and final ("spend money") decision. The Silent Side is, or should be, to the advertising executive, the "sell to" side. Also, for the advertising person and the marketer, access to the unconscious will address and answer the question of *why* consumers do what they do. It explains, rather than just describes.

SEARCHING FOR THE UNCONSCIOUS

The unconscious has been the subject of continuing debate since it was first introduced by Freud (1952). The main controversy has been the inability to measure or define this construct of the mind in operational, scientific terms. Scientists who have set out to prove or disprove the existence of the unconscious have been very skeptical. Interestingly, in recent years, researchers have been finding substantial and convincing evidence that the unconscious does indeed exist. Consider the following experiments.

Patients under anesthesia were told that during a postoperative interview they would pull at their ears. When the interviews were conducted, nine of the 11 subjects did pull at their ears, but none of them remembered having heard any instructions to do so. Of the 21 in the control group (who had no instructions) only nine pulled their ears (Bennett 1985).

In a series of experiments by Libet (1985) it was found that when a weak electrical pulse was delivered to the skin, about a half second of brain activity was required for the patient to become conscious of it. In another set of experiments Albert, Feinstein, and Libet (1967) note a similar finding when the brain is stimulated directly with a weak impulse during brain surgery on conscious patients. The conclusion is that the brain needs about one-half second of processing time before a sensation reaches consciousness. They stated that "if you have a delay before perceptions or decisions become conscious, it allows time for unconscious mechanisms to come in and make changes."

Because of these and other results, neuroscientists are beginning to rethink the whole idea of the unconscious mind. Erdelyi (1985) suggests that perception is related to a whole series of processes, with the conscious experience being only the end point in a complex chain. Erdelyi also believes that in the future scientists will be able to identify unconscious processes with specific parts of the brain.

DISCOVERING THE SILENT SIDE OF ADVERTISING AND MARKETING

When the unconscious is understood, or at least considered, it brings to light many consumer activities that advertising people, creative directors, and consumer psychologists have heretofore ignored. For instance:

- Why do people pay over $200,000 for a yacht that they may only visit or use two or three times a year?
- Why are gamblers willing to take a second mortgage on their homes in order to "stay in the game"?
- When a theme park encounters an accidental death on a thrill ride, why does subsequent attendance go up rather than down?
- Why does Graceland Mansion (Elvis Presley's home) now attract thousands of visitors from throughout the world when it attracted very few when he was alive?

Questions such as these cannot be answered from a strictly logical approach. Yet surprisingly, most market research approaches are logical. As such, they only scratch the surface, or what we refer to as the rational side. They fail to embrace the unconscious side of the consumer.

A basic assumption and the controlling proposition for our approach is that the unconscious mind is continually striving for expression. Bryan (1985) has described this silent behavior in terms of its origin in the lower centers of the brain:

The first point to be remembered is that the only way human beings can move a muscle is if a nerve impulse causes those muscular fibres to contract. This is as true in the complex manner of speaking as it is in the blinking of an eyelash. If the individual is conscious of the movement he is making, the impulse is known to have proceeded from the cerebrum, the center of conscious motor activity. There are many movements that we make, however, of which we are completely unaware; hence the generation of these nerve impulses must come from the lower brain centers—that is to say, lower than the cerebrum, where the thinking part of the mind resides. These impulses must come from the thalamus, where the subconscious mind and all of its emotions reside, or originate even further down in the reflex centers of the medulla oblongata; or in some cases, such as the deep tendon reflex of the knee, in the spinal cord itself. (p. 155)

Further examination of the action and re-action of the brain centers, both "conscious" and "unconscious," will be examined in chapters 2 and 11.

For the marketer, the ultimate expression is the purchase decision, and its resulting action. However, the reason that the unconscious is often overlooked is because its voice has not been heard. It is drowned out by the conscious mind and other "noise." It is crowded out by rationales, clutter, logic, alibis, and excuses. This is true in all kinds of human behavior, but especially in consumer behavior. After all, even the perpetrator of the most heinous and unspeakable crime will offer excuses, alibis, and rationalizations for what has taken place. Throughout such a criminal's trial the unconscious rarely speaks and is seldom heard.

THREE-DIMENSIONAL MARKETING AND ADVERTISING

Another component of advertising within the framework of the unconscious mind is that its approach should be three dimensional. The three dimensions that must be addressed are:

1. the rational or logical reasons for purchase
2. the mnemonic or memory aspects of the message (which explains things like the 50 year retention of the Reingold jingle cited earlier)
3. the emotional or motivational reasons for purchase (the unconscious side)

Although marketers and creative directors may be thoroughly familiar with the rational approach and may have learned much about mnemonics and long-term memory, many are still in the dark regarding the unconscious side and motivation. What is presented here is the integration of all three aspects of advertising, leading to a totally integrated three-dimensional approach to advertising and marketing.

REFERENCES

Albert, W. W., Feinstein, B., & Libet, B. (1967). Western electroencephalography and clinical neurophysiology: Electrical stimulation of "silent" cortex in conscious man. *Electroencephalography and Clinical Neurophysiology, 22, 293.*

Bennett, H. L. (1985). Behavioral anesthesia. *Advances, 2*, 11–21.

Bryan, W. J. (1985). *The chosen ones: The art of jury selection* (spec. ed. p. 155). Glendale, CA: Westwood Publishing Co.

Dichter, E. (1964). *Handbook of consumer motivations: The psychology of world objects.*

New York: McGraw Hill.

Dichter, E. (1971). *Motivating human behavior*. New York: McGraw Hill.

Erdelyi, M. H. (1985). *Psychoanalysis: Freud's cognitive psychology*. New York: Freeman Press.

Freud, S. (1952). The unconscious. In *Britannica great books* (Cecil M. Baines, Trans.). Chicago: Encyclopedia Britannica, Inc.

Hansen, F. (1994, June 2). Recent developments in the measurement of advertising effectiveness: thethird generation. Working Paper. Copenhagen, Denmark: The Copenhagen Business School Marketing Institute.

Key, W. B. (1973). *Subliminal seduction*. Englewood Cliffs, NJ: Prentice-Hall.

Libet, B. (1985). Unconscious cerebral initiative and the role of conscious will in voluntary action. *Behavioral and Brain Sciences*, 8, 529–66.

Packard, V. O. (1957). *The hidden persuaders*. New York: D. McKay Co.

2

Advertising to the Right and Left Sides of the Brain

THE SPLIT BRAIN THEORY

Krugman (1977), Mariani (1979), and others have rendered accounts of hemispheric specialization that, although popular, may not be anatomically correct. The two hemispheres of the brain are specialized, but there is by no means a complete dichotomy. Whereas the left hemisphere appears to be more specialized in linguistic processing, it is known that the right hemisphere is more adept at processing musical, emotional, and visual information. Nevertheless, the actual functioning of the brain is much more complicated than this. Furthermore, differences in processing have been found between men and women and between left handers and right handers (McGee, 1979). But even though recent research into the emotional aspects of the brain has found a much more sophisticated and differentiated operation, there is still a lot of truth to the popular theory of the split brain.

It has only been in the last few years that researchers have begun looking at the process of emotionality in the brain. Because of a traditional, overriding interest in the neural basis of memory and perception, the brain's role in emotion has been virtually overlooked.

In contrast to the split brain approach, LeDoux (1992, 1994) has described two separate routes that are involved in emotional learning and that work in tandem with one another. One is subcortical and the other is cortical. He observes that the thalamus, in the case of a startle reflex, activates the amygdala at about the same time that it activates the cortex, or right hemisphere. The thalamic pathway is particularly useful in situations that require an emotional response, as in life-threatening scenarios. If one detects the smell of gas and imminent explosion, it is not necessary to go through a detailed analysis of what is happening. Instead, it is only imperative to respond. In such a situation the right hemisphere may be only tangentially involved. However, other situations involving emotion may require that we bring back some earlier, conscious experience. In this case, it has been determined that declarative memory is mediated by both the hippocampus (mid brain) and the cortex (right brain). The removal of the hippocampus has little effect on fear conditioning.

The two hemispheres not only receive and send information to different sides of the body, but they also have definite specializations of function. Based on recent research, it has been suggested that the left hemisphere actually operates more logically, analytically, and rationally than the right hemisphere (Hellige, 1990), although it has been somewhat difficult to demonstrate these differences. On the other hand, the right hemisphere specializes in visual and spatial tasks, nonverbal imagery (such as visual images, music, art), and face recognition, as well as in the perception and expression of emotion (Kalat, 1988; Hellige, 1990; Semrud-Clikeman & Hynd, 1990).

Springer and Deutsch (1989) tell of "right brain movements" that encourage left brain executives to make use of their right brain skills. Although they said such techniques may be useful in organizational management, there is still much that has not been proven in terms of the specialization of function. Nevertheless, this dichotomy has been proven useful, and the research that is continuing in this area has not only resulted in startling new discoveries of pharmaceuticals that are used for emotional control, but has also tended to support the hemispheric specialization theories.

THE LEFT SIDE OF THE BRAIN

The Reingold beer lyric, with its "staying power," is an example of how advertising can access long-term memory. In order to create effective and memorable advertising and marketing campaigns, it is important to understand how the brain works. Simply put, the marketer is trying to access the brain!

The cerebral cortex, which consists of two large, multiconvoluted lobes beneath the top of the skull, is what makes man unique over all other animals. It is here that thinking goes on. Generally speaking, reasoning, logic, language, and other intellectual activities take place on the left side of the brain. For advertising purposes we can say that the left side is the rational side. The left brain processes rational and logical information. This "division of labor" has been intuitively known for many years, because when a person had a stroke that was localized in the left cerebral hemisphere, he/she could still "think" but had difficulty expressing thoughts through language and through logic, the roadway on which the vehicle of thinking travels.

For the most part, information that is processed by the left brain accesses short-term memory. For example, when studying for a test in anatomy of physiology, hundreds of terms have to be memorized. Shortly after the test this information is usually forgotten. Short-term memory is also more "fragile" than long-term memory. In cases of Alzheimer's disease or senile dementia, short-term memory is one of the first casualties. Everyone has had experiences with elderly people who repeat stories from 50 or 60 years ago, but cannot remember what they had for breakfast.

THE RIGHT SIDE OF THE BRAIN

As discussed above, the right side of the brain is believed to be involved in processing emotion, feeling, creativity, and intuition. Although everyone is not "artistic," almost everyone has an appreciation of or is able to acknowledge music and art. These activities are processed by the right brain. Hence, an advertisement or spot that is set to music or rhyme will have a better opportunity of penetrating the right brain—because of the emotional aspects of music. Print ads that feature eye-catching artwork have the same effect. These ads appeal to the right (artistic) side of the brain.

Why is it important to reach the right brain? It is important because this is where long-term memory is processed. Scientists and researchers are presently studying short-term and long-term memory with the use of electroencephalography (EEG), PET and CAT scans, and magnetoencephalography (MEG). This has made it possible to study brain activity during various states of sleep and consciousness. Although they have not really determined the actual site of long-term memory, they feel strongly that it is accessed through the right side of the brain, since the right brain processes emotion, which is long term. By linking these findings with subjective reports, it will soon be possible to make tremendous strides in our understanding of brain activity in various states of consciousness.

Advertising people have an inherent interest in the right brain because of its association with emotional activity, long-term memory, and motivation. Emotions, by definition, are tied to motivation. And the primary purpose of most advertising is to motivate a purchaser and to do it in the least expensive way!

Recently there has been considerable research into the neuroanatomical centers of emotion. Although most of this research is somewhat technical and scientific, it does indicate that the emotional centers of the brain are usually associated with structures in the mid brain, particularly the hypothalamus and the amygdala. Being in the mid brain, they are more difficult to access, and therefore more difficult to reach. And they should be. We are—for the most part—a rational society or community. But when dealing with motivation, it is essential that the emotional centers of the brain be reached. These mid brain structures are usually accessed through the right hemisphere, or right brain.

HOW PEOPLE MAKE DECISIONS

It is very important for marketers to understand the way in which people make decisions. There are three steps in decision making that directly affect advertising and marketing. This assumes that the advertiser or marketer has already been able to get the consumer's attention. The three steps are:

1. The consumer must have a logical and rational reason to make a purchase.
2. The consumer must remember what he/she saw (long-term memory) based on the mnemonic aspects of the message.
3. The consumer must have the motivation to purchase the product (emotional, right brain-generated emotion).

This synopsis of how the consumer decision-making process progresses is given in sequence—Rationalization • Memory • Motivation. These are the three essential steps of the three-dimensional advertising. If these three steps are not involved, advertising and marketing will only be one or two dimensional and lack impact, power, and direction. Of course, the intensity of each step may vary with the product. Recreational products, such as golf, casino gambling, fine dining, theme parks, etc., will involve much more emotional input from the right brain, but will also require more left brain logic and rationalizations for the purpose of justifying the purchase, or the activity.

THREE-DIMENSIONAL ADVERTISING

It is imperative to examine three-dimensional advertising and marketing in detail, especially with reference to the second dimension: motivation. Once the basic concepts are explained, examples from some of the extensive research carried out over the last 15 years will be examined in later chapters.

The First Dimension of Advertising and Marketing:
Logic, Rationalizations, and Justifications

Logic and rationalization are the first dimension of advertising and the one that is the most familiar. They also are the most exploited dimension in advertising. That is because most marketing approaches are based upon traditional market research, and traditional market research asks people logical questions. Hence, consumers respond accordingly: with logic and the left side of their brain. Since humans want to appear logical and rational, they give logical and rational answers. They respond not only to other people, but also to themselves. Typical of the answers and rationalizations that are given are:

*   "I bought it because I'll never see it at that price again."
*   "When these are all gone, there won't be any more."

- "These coupons cut the price nearly in half."
- "I really needed it."
- "The salesman offered me a deal I couldn't resist."
- "I bank at First because it's so convenient."
- "I like the people at the Apple Tree Restaurant; they're friendly and go out of their way to please."
- "Even though I have a two-hour commute to the city, the taxes are much lower out here."

These are *rationalizations*. They may be true or untrue. They are what the consumer wants to believe, and they are what the consumer wants others to believe. Rationalizations are the most common form of advertising. They work either on the front end or as reinforcers, after the decision has been made. Rationalizations influence the emotions. They are obvious, and they are powerful. They are motivating.

The problem is that at some point before the sale is made the consumer has to deal with emotion. Also, rationalizations do not feed into brand loyalty, positioning, unique selling, and marketing propositions. That is why people buy ABC instead of XYZ, and what has to be done to change them. Consumer decisions are based primarily on emotion and not reason. Even so, rationalizations are an important part of the purchasing process.

Kowata and Buck (1995) illustrate the relationship between rationalizations and emotions (affect) in a cross-cultural study. According to these investigators, all products and services (including business-to-business) involve emotion. There are no choices in the marketplace that are unemotional. As we move from the left side to the right side of the product continuum illustrated below, affect remains stable as rational thinking becomes more important. An example of a product or activity at the left side of the scale would be the Elvis Presley phenomenon. An example on the right side would be the choice of a broker or a subcontractor on a solid rocket fuel project.

Figure 2-1
Relationship of Reason/Affect on a Product Continuum

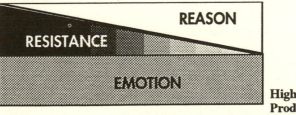

Low Rational
Product
Involvement

High Rational
Product
Involvement

(From Kowata and Buck, 1995)

These investigators, using the CASC Scale, compared several products in both India and the United States and showed that there was a very close relationship between the ratio of emotion and reason in them. This would suggest that the hypothesis of the relationship between emotion and reason in certain products holds up cross-culturally.

The Second Dimension of Advertising and Marketing: Memory

How is advertising made memorable? In the past memorability in advertising has been carried out through suggestions, repetition, and jingles. Music and artwork access the right brain very effectively. Today, however, there is too much competition, visual and musical, for the attention of the right brain. It may be referred to as clutter. Also, repetition is expensive. But there are other new methods.

Suggestions are brief (three to five word) declaratory statements, usually worded in a positive direction. An example of a suggestion is "It's the real thing." A suggestion does not have to be logical or based on fact. It is a simple statement. It is not complex and logical, since the unconscious mind—which does not process logical and rational thinking—reacts to simple, positively worded suggestions.

Suggestions should not be negatively worded—for example, "don't smoke cigarettes"—because the Silent Side, the right brain, is unable to process reverse logic. Negatives involve logic, since they are the reversal of positives, and the right brain does not deal in logic. Suggestions should always be worded in a positive direction.

Another way in which advertising is made memorable is through repetition. Repetition is intimately bound up with suggestions, because suggestions need to be given on a repetitive basis, over and over again. Simple suggestions, like "We try harder" or "It's the real thing" or "Gimme a Lite" or "Hello, Federal," do not have much of a chance of penetrating a consumer's unconscious mind unless they are repeated over and over again. But repetition is very expensive, and it creates even more clutter in the marketplace. The fact is that most marketers do not have the budget for the kind of repetition that it would take to make an impact. Repetition is too expensive.

But there is another way to create memorable advertising that gets around the requirement and the expense of repetition. This alternative is more exciting because of the possibilities that it presents. It is based upon the fact that the right brain thinks in pictures, not words! Medical students have known this for years. Unlike law school or other graduate schools, medical school requires the commitment to memory—much of it to short-term memory—the names of hundreds of organs, procedures, facts, lists, muscles, bones, etc. Medical students quickly become familiar with mnemonics, or methods of converting the subject matter from verbal to visual. It works because everybody has a photographic memory. Most people do not use their photographic memories, but everyone has one.

The most well known mnemonic that is used in medical school is "On old Olympus' towering top a fat aging Greek poured some hops." This mnemonic, which paints a rather unusual or even absurd picture in the mind, serves as a reminder of the 12 cranial nerves: olfactory, optic, oculi, trochear, trifacial, abducent, facial, auditory, glosso-pharyngeal, pneumogastric, spinal accessory, and hypoglossal. The chances that all of this will be recalled at the crucial time—on a test—improves 200 percent with the mnemonic picture of the fat, old Greek pouring hops.

Advertising recall improves when messages are visual, not just verbal. As stated above, this is true because the right brain thinks in pictures, not words. However, television has created a situation where there is visual clutter, so the problem that marketers face is to make the visuals stand out from the clutter.

Advertising can be made memorable when the medium of absurdities is introduced. Absurdities will be examined in chapter 5. They are the key to the second dimension of three-dimensional advertising: memorability and recall.

The Third Dimension of Advertising and Marketing: Emotion

Consumers cannot tell you about their own motivation. They cannot tell you why they do what they do. In fact, motivation is the most puzzling subject in all human behavior. Why do people smoke, take drugs, continue to fail over and over again, or commit crimes when they know that they will be punished? Conversely, why do people succeed, become great leaders, or dedicate their lives unselfishly to others? The whole area of human motivation, the *why* of human behavior seems to be clothed in secrecy. Not only are consumers unable to explain why they do what they do, but the psychologists and the psychiatrists who study human behavior have been at a loss to explain many facets of behavior. So just how does an approach to the unconscious mind differ?

About 20 years ago we were treating patients in a clinical setting. These patients had serious problems. To resolve these problems it was necessary to go into the past, sometimes into childhood, to find out what the causes were so that the cure could be worked out and be effective. But most people could not remember the things that happened to them in childhood. We began using visualization. In other words, instead of addressing the left brain we addressed the right brain, because the right brain "thinks" in pictures. In doing this, we found the reasons behind problems that patients presented that had happened many years before, often in childhood. Incest, abuse, abandonment, surgical trauma, all of these things that had been covered up (repressed) by the left brain began to come up out of the unconscious or Silent Side with the assistance of the right brain and visualization.

There was nothing complicated about these clinical interventions. People were simply told to close their eyes and visualize what may have been happening to them under certain circumstances. Unlike the use of hypnosis, sodium amytal, sodium pentothal, or other accepted but complicated procedures, visualization is very simple. The patients close their eyes and make pictures in their minds. Instead of trying to describe what they think happened or what they remember, they simply describe what they see. This method has also been used for the recovery of evidence at a crime scene or in other situations where remote memory must be accessed. It works!

About five years later, we applied this same technique to consumers. Individuals were recruited and, using trained clinical interviewers, were asked to close their eyes and visualize experiences: their first roller coaster ride; their first new automobile; a trip to the supermarket; a memorable fine-dining experience; the first time they saw Elvis; a trip to a banking institution; a time when they learned to water ski, etc. What emerged from these in-depth interviews with consumers was a lot of rational and logical information (which was expected) but also, over time, a significant amount of emotional and motivational information that was vital to brand choice, brand loyalty, positioning, increasing market share, etc. Of course the interviewers had to be trained. They had to know what approach to use. The interviews were often quite lengthy. But since there are only 11 basic motives involved in the unconscious mind, it became acceptable to use very small samples to get this information. This research and how it was carried out is covered in detail in chapter 8.

This marketing-to-the-mind approach is different because it deals with the actual causes and motives that drive consumers to do what they do and make the choices that they make in the marketplace. Motivation has been a very mysterious and mystical issue. Behavioral scientists, from whom we might expect to get assistance, have not really been that helpful. Creative directors have done their own thing and have been more on target than anyone, but the creative approach is based upon trial and error. What marketing to the mind offers is a system, a methodology and strategy that puts the marketer and creative director on target every time. This is the third dimension of advertising: motivation and emotion. More specifically, the emotion that grows out of motivation. Emotion and motivation are what advertising and marketing are all about. Most consumer decisions are based upon emotion, not reason.

Consumers cannot tell you *why* they do what they do. What they can tell you is either why they think they do what they do or what they would like you to hear. Both of these kinds of answers are from the left side of the brain. Marketing to the mind goes beyond all of this and looks into the right brain responses and motives. Motives are not things that consumers ordinarily think about—but they are significant in motivating them to make the choices that they make. Chapter 4 will detail all 11 of these Silent Side motivations.

WHAT ABOUT POSITIONING?

Reis and Trout (1981) in their classic, *Positioning: The Battle for Your Mind*, define positioning as an approach to advertising that basically ties a new product or concept to another that already exists in the marketplace—it reties "connections that already exist within the mind." They further assert that, because of marketing clutter, the old strategies are not working like they used to. There are too many products, too many companies, and too many methods of getting the message across. Positioning is a classical "short cut" to getting the message into the mind. But in order to do that, there must be a road map or some kind of taxonomy of the mind. Reis and Trout have observed that marketers cannot just keep coming up with new creative strategies year after year and that many of the old methods do not work. Marketing to the mind allows the marketer to look, for the first time, at the unconscious mind to uncover basic motivations and then to address them directly. When motives are uncovered, marketing and advertising strategies become very, very clear.

A significant difference between positioning and marketing to the mind is that positioning relies on strategies that are external—that is, outside of the consumer, as in tying two products together. Marketing to the mind deals with what is inside the consumer, and then, through research, shows how to address it effectively by tying it directly to human motive and emotion. Marketing to the mind is not necessarily a better technique than positioning; it is simply a complementary addition. It is where creative and marketing directors have been looking all along; they just have not had a road map to the unconscious, or emotional side. The two approaches—positioning and marketing to the mind—complement one another.

MARKETING TO THE MIND

This three-dimensional approach—Rationalization • Memory • Motivation—is the cornerstone to effective advertising and marketing. The following chapters will review each one of these components in detail, with major attention given to the emotional part of consumer decision making. When emotion and motivation are included, advertising and marketing will be more effective and more cost efficient. Advertisers, marketers, and others will understand what is meant by marketing to the mind, and they will understand the unconscious side of advertising and marketing.

REFERENCES

Hellige, J. B. (1990). Hemispheric assymetry. *Annual Review of Psychology*, 41, 55–80.
Kalat, J. W. (1988). *Biological psychology* (3rd ed.). Belmont, CA: Wadsworth.
Kowata, S., & Buck, R. (1995, August). Cross cultural study of product involvement using ARI model Presented at 103rd Annual Convention of American Psychological Association (Division 23-Consumer Psychology), New York.

Krugman, H. E. (1977). Memory without recall, exposure without perception. *Journal of Advertising Research, 17*, 7–12.

LeDoux, J. E. (1992)). Brain mechanisms of emotion and emotional learning. *Current Opinion in Neurobiology,* 2 (2), 191–97.

LeDoux, J. E. (1994a, June). Emotion, memory and the brain, part 1. *Scientific American,* 270 (6).

LeDoux, J. E. (1994b, June). Emotion, memory and the brain, part 2. *Scientific American,* 270 (6), 50–57.

Mariani, J. (1979). Can advertisers read and control our emotions? *TV Guide, 27,*84–6, 8.

McGee, M. G. (1979). Human spatial abilities: Psychometric studies and environmental, genetic, hormonal and neurological influences. *Psychological Bulletin, 86,* 889–918.

Reis, A., and Trout, J. (1981). *Positioning: The battle for your mind.* New York: McGraw Hill.

Semrud-Clikeman, M., & Hynd, G. W. (1990). Right hemispheric dysfunction in nonverbal learning disabilities: Social, academic and adaptive functioning in adults and children. *Psychological Bulletin, 107,* 196–209.

Springer, S. P., & Deutsch, G. (1989). *Left Brain, Right Brain* (3rd ed.). New York: W. H. Freeman.

3

The Secrets of the Silent Side

THE SEDUCTION OF THE SCIENTIFIC METHOD

Perhaps nothing has been more influential and seductive in psychology in the twentieth century than the opportunity to apply the scientific, experimental method to the study of behavior. This paradigm has appealed to psychologists throughout the twentieth century and is expected to last well into the twenty-first century. It has, to say the least, had an overpowering effect. American and British psychologists have led the way in converting this new discipline, psychology, into a science. Their primary contribution has been to rid psychology, "the study of the mind," from any notion about the existence of something as undefinable as the mind.

In the late nineteenth century, when psychology and psychiatry were establishing themselves as respectable disciplines, German psychologists were busily studying perception, sensation, and the "science of consciousness." In the United States, their counterparts were looking at rats, and how they learned. One student, destined to become a leader in American psychology, was John B. Watson. Watson was studying rats at the University of Chicago, and as part of his dissertation he was asked to speculate on the kind of consciousness that rats experienced that, in turn, produced the behavior he observed. Watson was offended by this and believed that it was outrageous to even suggest that rats had states of consciousness. Nonetheless, he did what was expected of him and received his degree. He returned to the laboratory to carry out further experimentation on consciousness.

Ten years after he received his degree, Watson angrily confronted psychologists who were deeply entrenched in the study of consciousness. In his book *Psychology as a Behaviorist Views it* (1919), Watson said that the whole idea of consciousness was absurd, and that attempts to study "mental life" were pretentious and unscientific. He said that "you cannot define consciousness any more than you can define a soul. It cannot be located, weighed or observed." For Watson, psychology was the study of measurable, definable behavior. Anything else bordered on witchcraft.

In 1919, as Watson was campaigning for the presidency of the American Psychological Association (APA), he promised his supporters that, should he be elected, "there would be no discussion of consciousness and no references to terms such as sensation, perception and the like . . . frankly, I don't know what these mean, nor do I believe anyone else can use them consistently." He added that the effective study of mental life could never succeed, because it was an unscientific approach. Behaviorism, first under Watson and with the influence of Pavlov, became the cornerstone of American psychology. Later, under the leadership of B. F. Skinner, psychologists for the most part vowed only to deal with observable and verifiable behavior.

THROWING THE BABY OUT WITH THE BATHWATER

Unfortunately, when the study of anything is confined to only what can be observed, measured, and quantified, there is a lot that is overlooked. One thing that is definitely overlooked is motivation. As a result, there are many situations that psychologists should be addressing that tend to be overlooked. Consider the following examples:

- Why do so many shootings occur at the post office? Is it because of stress? But isn't the post office one of the least stressful jobs that can be had?
- Why did Susan Smith murder her two children on October 24, 1994? Isn't there such a thing as maternal instinct, which keeps such a horrible thing from happening?
- Why do women who are beaten by their husbands remain in such situations or, once they have left, why do they often return?
- What causes grown men to have sex with small children?
- What are the motives behind rape?

These are motivational questions, and for the reasons stated above, psychologists for the most part have not provided answers. When the police are confronted with a perplexing crime (often one that involves impulsive killing or mysterious disappearance), they do not necessarily call a psychologist. They often call a psychic.

Different psychologists have studied various aspects of motivation: aggression (Beck, 1983); achievement (McClelland et al., 1953); power (Winter, 1973); and affiliation (Shachter, 1959; Rofe, Hoffman & Lewin, 1985). However, most of these investigations limit themselves to what can be observed, again overlooking that vast resource of hidden motives that lie beneath the surface, the bottom of the iceberg.

In contrast to psychology, the law has a much simpler definition of motivation. In law, a motive consists of three elements: the behavior itself; the intent to engage in the behavior; and the *mens rea*, or simultaneous occurrence of both at the same time.

In behaviorism, motivation is limited to what can be observed. Within the Pavlovian framework, motivation is brought about by the repetition of a simple reward, after the behavior is generated. Skinner recognized that there is a lot of behavior that occurs before the reward, hence, the operant framework. For behaviorists, the behavior comes first and is then followed by the reward. A perfect example of this is the slot machine, which is programmed in terms of various schedules of reinforcement. These schedules determine the frequency and amount that the programmed machine will deliver. Usually they pay off frequently and in small amounts, and this schedule motivates players to "stay in the game." Frequent-flyer discounts are another example of the operant paradigm at work.

While American and British psychologists refined and reworked both the Pavlovian and operant systems, European psychologists traveled down a different road. Most prominent among them were Sigmund Freud, a neurologist whose major work was done in the early part of the twentieth century. Also, Jean Piaget, a French biologist, studied children using observational methods (Piaget, 1932). In fact, both Freud and Piaget used observational, nonexperimental, and subjective methods of observation. Moreover, their findings regarding motivation and other behaviors, were quite striking and profound when contrasted with what the American behaviorists were doing.

Both Freud and Piaget, working separately and at different times, found that children go through stages as they mature into adolescence. This theory was not favorably received by Americans. Stage theory implies that there will be a gradual unfolding, and that maturation is dependent upon genetics and the vagaries of nature. Americans liked the idea of reinforcement, which basically states that the more you reward your child, the smarter and more well adjusted he/she will become, a lot better. In other words, under the American system a parent has complete control; under the European system, a parent takes his/her chances.

Both Freud and Piaget found that at certain ages, children were incapable of performing certain tasks, regardless of the number of "reinforcers" that were delivered. For example, a four-year-old child is not capable of classification (Piaget & Inhelder, 1956). In "experiments" performed with children, they were shown two 8 1/2" x 11" pieces of construction paper, with eight barns on each piece. The pieces of green construction paper were identified as "pastures." On one piece of paper the barns were clustered in the center of the pasture, and on the other piece of paper they were spread out over the pasture. Children were asked, "On which pasture does the horse have more grass to eat?" Children who were in preoperational stages of cognitive development said that the pasture with the clustered barns provided more grass. Children who had matured beyond this stage gave the correct answer: since the pastures and barns were the same size, there was no difference in the amount of pasture that was available. For Piaget, cognitive maturation consists of the gradual ability to move from concrete, physical observations to abstract conceptualizations, and for Freud this occurs within the domain of emotion.

Not only did these stage theorists look "inside" the person, but they brought into question the whole notion of reinforcement as it may or may not be involved in maturation. In addition, there was depth and explanatory value in their conclusions that could be used to predict a wide range of behaviors. We know, for example, that children under 11 or 12 are not capable of abstract thinking. Therefore, we do not teach them algebra until they are in the seventh grade. On the other hand, they are capable of concrete thinking, which is why they can learn a foreign language easier and with better, more lasting results.

It would appear that there should be some way the rich but less precise findings of the Europeans can be combined with the somewhat superficial but absolute findings of the Americans. And in fact they can be. Today, everyone knows about Pavlov's dogs and Skinner's rats. They caused many professionals to completely deny the existence of a "mind."

But not everyone agreed. There had to be more to decision making than a simple stimulus-response (S-R) equation. Wasn't there a process (O) between these two observable ends? Of course, there was. Moreover, O consists of the many emotional, unconscious nuances, especially those in the human species.

To a behaviorist, the decision to buy a Big Mac occurred because of hunger. It is a case of problem solving. But what about the O factor? What about the elements that motivate that particular decision? Why was it a Big Mac and not a Whopper? In consumer terms, the response (buy it) to the stimulus (hunger) was motivated by unconscious considerations of color, size, value, brand name, exposure, recent advertising, and word of mouth. Since that is the case, some psychologists have had to concede the existence of the mind and have profitably returned to a study of these nuances.

Inevitably our work has focused on consumer behavior because the likes and dislikes of potential buyers are of critical importance to advertisers and marketers. In other words, it makes good business sense to start there. We are sure, moreover, that our work on the unconscious side of decision making will have major implications for psychology in general. Meanwhile, in defining the motivational makeup of the human unconscious and measuring the interplay of these emotions, we may have found a lot of information that will be useful and helpful to the marketer.

For too long we were disturbed that so little understanding of unconscious behavior existed among consumers, advertisers, and marketers. Perhaps some of that can now be brought into focus, particularly because of new research that has centered upon the brain, its role in emotional behavior and in the everyday choices and decisions that we make.

MOTIVATION AND EMOTION IN MARKETING AND ADVERTISING

The physiology of emotion, the mechanisms of the brain involved in mediating emotion, and the relationship between motivation and emotion have been described by LeDoux (1992) and were briefly reviewed in chapter 2. After the general motives that are the key to the Silent Side are reviewed in chapter 4, the specific origins of these motivations within the substructures of the brain will be pinpointed in chapters 5 and 11.

Percy and Rossiter (1992) state that both emotion and cognition are important intervening variables in a consumer's attitude toward a brand. They clearly recognize the importance of emotion. Basically, their model (Rossiter & Percy, 1987) states that an attitude toward a brand is a belief that links the advertised brand to specific motivators. They go on to describe five negative and three positive motivations that provide what they call the "dimensions of motivation." These motives and the subsequent motivating process toward brand attitude are listed in table 3-1.

Table 3-1
Eight Basic Motives

Motivation	Motivating Process
Negative Motives:	
1. Problem removal	Seeking solution to a current problem
2. Problem avoidance	Seeking to avoid an anticipated problem
3. Incomplete satisfaction	Seeking a better product
4. Mixed-approach avoidance	Seeking resolution to a conflict caused by both positive and negative attributes in the same product
5. Normal depletion	Seeking to maintain a regular supply of the product
Positive Motives:	
1. Sensory gratification	Seeking extra physiological enjoyment from the product
2. Intellectual stimulation	Seeking extra psychological stimulation from the product
3. Social approval	Seeking an opportunity for social reward from the product

(from Percy and Rossiter, 1992, p. 268)

The motives defined by Percy and Rossiter account for significant variance in consumer brand attitude. However, they are different from unconscious motives in that they are descriptive rather than explanatory. In fact, the consumer himself/ herself might use one or more of these motives as rationalizations to account for or to explain his/her purchasing behavior. For example: "Even though I live 30 miles from work, my taxes are lower out here" (problem avoidance). Such a rationalization often covers up the real reason for buying a house that is 30 miles or more outside of the city. Such emotional reasons may involve status seeking, inability to get along with neighbors, the need for isolation, etc. Another example is "I had to have a car that I could depend on in order to get to work, so I traded for this Lexus" (seeking a better product). There are many dependable automobiles that are much, much cheaper than a Lexus. This explanation is a rationalization that begs the (emotional) issue as to why the customer would pay $20,000 or $30,000 more for a Lexus than he/she would for a dependable car to get him/her back and forth to work.

In yet another example, a person might say, "The ballet is my whole life" (intellectual stimulation). This may be true. Buy why is the customer totally dedicated to ballet? Why not thrill seeking, or casino gambling, or "surfing the net"? Why does a customer prefer one activity over another?

A number of articles have found that advertising that is especially annoying and irritating, such as Wisk's "ring around the collar" and Charmin's "Mr. Whipple," have earned significant market shares for their respective products. Why? Although Percy and Rossiter (1980) explain this on the basis of low-involvement products, isn't there something *emotional* that is happening with these advertisements? Respondents admitted that these ads were extremely irritating and annoying, and yet they bought more of the product! Although such a phenomenon is not the major focus of this book, it does suggest that there are secrets in the consumer's mind that are yet to be uncovered. It is our contention that these secrets lie on the Silent Side.

REFERENCES

Beck, R. (1983). *Motivation: Theories and principles* (2nd ed.). Englewood Cliffs, NJ: Prentice-Hall.

LeDoux, J. E. (1992, April). Brain mechanisms of emotion and emotional learning. *Current Opinion in Neurobiology*, 2 (2), 191–97.

McClelland, D. C., Atkinson, J. W., Clark, R. A. & Lowell, E. L. (1953). *The achievement motive* New York: Appleton.

Percy, L., & Rossiter, J. R. (1992, July/August). A model of brain awareness and brand attitude advertising strategies. *Psychology and Marketing*, 9 (4), 263–74.

Percy, L., & Rossiter, J. R. (1980). *Advertising strategy: a communication theory approach.* New York: Praeger.

Piaget, J. (1932). *The Moral Development of the Child.* New York: Harcourt, Brace.

Piaget, J., & Inhelder (1956). *The child's conception of space* (F. J. Langon & E. L. Lunzer,

Trans.). London: Routledge & Kegan Paul.

Rofe, Y., Hoffman, M., & Lewin, I. (1985). Patient affiliation in major illness. *Psychological Medicine, 15,* 895–96.

Rossiter, J. L., & Percy, L. (1987). *Advertising and promotion management.* New York: McGraw-Hill.

Shachter, S. (1959). *The psychology of affiliation: Experimental studies of the sources of gregariousness.* Stanford, CA: Stanford University Press.

Watson, J. B. (1919). *Psychology as a behaviorist views it.* Philadelphia: Lippincott.

Winter, D. G. (1973). *The power motive.* New York: Free Press.

4

Marketing to the Mind: How to Market and Advertise Directly to Consumer Motivations and Emotions

UNCOVERING THE SECRETS OF THE SILENT SIDE

Consumers and people in general have never been able to discuss their own motivations, because they do not understand them. Nor do they think about them, which is why this part of the mind is referred to as the unconscious. But although consumers do not think about their motives, they do experience them and they do act on them.

The motivational groups that will be discussed in this chapter are basic and primary to all human behavior. They apply not only to consumer behavior, but to all human behavior in any situation. However, since consumers do not actively "think" about their motives, it is difficult to ask directly about them. For this reason, traditional market research is not an option when studying the emotions. Instead, other methods of discovering these motives have been devised and combined with traditional methods. These methods will be described in chapter 8. Furthermore, researchers do not study the role of emotions in everyday life, since emotions are hard to study, scientifically. In fact, since many researchers have been unable to study emotions directly, they often discredit the whole idea of an unconscious mind and also discredit any attempt to describe behavior on anything but the conscious level. Therefore, research on the unconscious, or Silent Side of the mind has remained rather silent over the years, and not much is known about this vital part of the mind and the role that it plays in consumer motivation. Hence, motivation has remained a mystery.

Advertisers, salespersons, and marketers need to understand motivation to be effective. They especially need to understand the motivation that relates to their product(s) and service(s) so that they can market to the mind. Emotion is the third dimension of marketing.

It is important to remember, while moving through the levels of motivation in this chapter, that these motives are completely unconscious in the mind of the person who is referred to as the consumer or purchaser.

The quadrants in table 4-1 illustrate the blind spots that everyone has. These blind spots are in the upper-right and lower-right segments: "What I don't see that others do see" (blind spot), and "What I don't see and others don't see" (unconscious side). The latter is the unconscious mind. The information within this lower-right segment is not for the public to see or understand, or for the user to see and understand. It is the unconscious, or hidden, side of motivation and, for the most part, it is the side where most major consumer decisions are made. The unconscious side of consumer behavior has not been that well understood or discussed in the past. However, it is the major focus of this book.

The five major motivational groups that we have found on the unconscious side are as follows:

1.   the Orientation Motives (person, place, time, and circumstances)
2.   the Survival Motives (spiritual, physical, sexual, and territorial)
3.   the Adaptation Motive
4.   the Expectation Motive
5.   play

THE FIVE MOTIVATIONAL GROUPS THAT ACCOUNT FOR ALL CONSUMER BEHAVIOR

There are five motivational groups that apply to all consumer behavior and, for that matter, to all human behavior. This relates not only to consumers, but to

Table 4-1
Quadrants of the Mind

	WHAT I SEE	WHAT I DON'T SEE
	OPEN	**BLIND SPOT**
WHAT	Logic	Rationalizations
OTHERS	Explanations	Excuses
SEE	"Shared Reality"	Justifications
		"Features"
	SECRETS	**THE UNCONSCIOUS**
WHAT		**(SILENT) SIDE**
OTHERS		
DON'T		Motives
SEE		Emotions
		"Benefits"

criminals, suspects, people being interviewed for jobs, deponents (in legal deposi-
tions), or just about anyone in any situation. The discussion here is limited to
advertising and marketing, because this is where the theory has been worked out,
and is also where the need is the greatest. A major point to know is that consumers
cannot give this information. This is because they do not "think" about it. They do
"feel" it, but often cannot describe the way it feels. It is based on emotion, not
reason. Another major point is that the unconscious is very simple and does not
rely on complex logical structures to do its thinking. One way in which the Silent
Side works is in terms of visualization, or pictures. Another way in which it works
is in its noncritical acceptance of suggestions (e.g., "the Real Thing"). Another
example of how the unconscious works is when two totally unrelated ideas that are
outside of consciousness come together in the unconscious and form one unique
idea, which then bursts into consciousness and often forms the basis for the solution of an everyday problem, or perhaps an invention or scientific breakthrough.
This is called creativity, or the creative process (Kubie, 1961; Jamison, 1995).

Because the unconscious is simple and straightforward (not complex or devi-
ous), it has a limited number of motives. In fact, five distinct motivational groups
have been identified, two of which consist of four subsets. Individual differences
are not an issue in the unconscious, and although they exist they do not have the
impact that they do at the conscious level. The term "individual differences" refers to the differences that exist between people, such as differences in intelligence, achievement, height, weight, eye color, etc. The properties of the unconscious are universal, and are therefore shared by all. The five motivational groups
that follow are shared by the entire population and vary only in intensity and direction.

These motivational groups are as follows:

1.   The Orientation Motives: Everyone has the need to remain oriented to
external reality and has a mechanism within himself/herself that keeps them oriented, much like the "compass" that keeps a migratory bird on course.

There are four motivational subgroups within the Orientation Motives:

- Orientation to person (OR: Person)
- Orientation to place (OR: Place)
- Orientation to time (OR: Time)
- Orientation to circumstances (OR: Circumstances)

2.   Survival Motives: The Survival Motives are the strongest of all the motives. Like the Orientation Motives, survival is "unnoticed" in the unconscious
mind unless it is threatened by some external force.

There are four motivational subgroups within the survival group, presented in
order of importance (strongest to weakest):

- Spiritual survival (defined psychologically and not theologically)
- Physical survival

- Territorial survival
- Sexual survival

3.   Adaptation Motive: There is a strong motive to adapt to one's climate, culture, group, beliefs, and surroundings. If it is "trendy" to smoke cigarettes, then people will smoke, irrespective of how it effects their physical survival and their health. This motive may be stronger than the Physical Survival Motive, since people will do things that are unwise in terms of their physical survival (health) for purposes of adaptation. Cigarette smoking is the obvious example. Adaptation is the most well established of all the motives. It is even seen in neonates *in utero* on diagnostic ultrasounds as they move their hands to their faces in an effort to *adapt* to that environment. Infants continue this behavior during the first six to seven months of life. In adolescence and adulthood adaptation takes on the form of "imitation" (Bandura, 1977).

4.   Expectation Motive: The Expectation Motive relates to the element of hope and trust and the way that people view the future. There is an overall faith and belief that the future will work itself out in a positive way. This is not false optimism or idealism, but simply a trust that one day will follow the other. It is, in a way, a form of adaptation when it comes to dealing with the future. The Adaptation Motive deals with the past and present, while the Expectation Motive deals with the future.

5.   Play: MacLean (1990) has emphasized three major improvements or developments that characterize the developmental sequence that takes place in the brain as we move up the evolutionary ladder from reptiles to mammals: (1) nursing in conjunction with maternal care; (2) audiovocal communication for maintaining maternal-offspring contact; and (3) play.

Play is one of the 11 major motivations that are found in the unconscious. MacLean in his discussion of play suggests that the exact purpose of this activity is unknown, but it may have evolved originally to ease the tension that develops in a nest or litter, when a dozen or so babies are crowded together and they engage in play to relieve the tension.

The Personal Orientation Motives

The four personal Orientation Motives (person, place, time, and circumstances) as *motives* are unique to this book and have grown out of our research over the past 15 years. In psychiatry, these four orientations have been the cornerstone and the foundation of the mental status examination for many years. No mental status examination would ever be carried out with a patient without including and assessing these four mental states. If there is one standard in psychiatry and psychology, it is the mental status examination (Taylor, 1988). However, the description of these mental states as motives is atypical and unique, with no precedent in either the consumer or the psychiatric literature. Briefly, it adds a whole new dimension to consumer research and persuasion, a dimension that we have encountered in our research over and over again (chapter 8) and which now has empirical support (chapter 11).

Although people in general and consumers in particular are not aware of the motive to remain oriented to reality, this motive is just as well established and functional in the Silent Side as the heartbeat is in the chest cavity. People often refer to it tangentially when they are under stress. They will say: "I don't want to lose it," or "I don't want to come unglued." Conversely, on the positive side, they might say, "I want to hold it together." They are referring, obliquely, to the personal Orientation Motives: orientation to person, place, time, and circumstances.

The Orientation Motives have a similar function in humans as they do in birds. A migratory bird stays on course because of an internal "compass" or finding device. Similarly, humans stay on course because of these four orientation devices. Examples of people who have lost their orientation are the victims of Alzheimer's or senile dementia. When people encounter a relative or friend who has lost his/her orientation, it impacts them in a very negative way, because it acts as a warning or an admonition as to how fragile and tenuous personal orientation really is. Upon encountering a person in this position, some will say, "Gee, I hope I don't live that long," or "I hope I pass away before I get like that." Loss of orientation (permanent) can also occur with chronic and prolonged drug abuse, alcohol abuse (Korsakoff's Syndrome), or head injury.

When personal orientation is lost, confusion sets in. The first Orientation Motive to be lost is orientation to circumstances (OR: Circumstances). The next is orientation to time (OR: Time). The third is orientation to place (OR: Place). The last orientation to be lost is orientation to person (OR: Person). It is important to remember that the OR: Person motive is the strongest of the personal Orientation Motives because it is the last to be lost or destroyed. The four subsets of the personal Orientation Motives will be introduced in the traditional order that they are reviewed: person, place, time, and circumstances. We will examine how these vital personal motives are related to consumer behavior, purchasing, brand loyalty, and every other aspect of consumer motivation and behavior. In fact, they are crucial to everyday human behavior and motivation.

Orientation to Person

OR: Person is the strongest of the Orientation Motives. It keeps a person on target as to who he/she is and what he/she stands for. Even in nocturnal activity (dreams) where orientation may be temporarily lost, the OR: Person Motive generally remains intact. Other people in dreams may be seen in a different light, but usually the self is seen in much the same way that it appears in real life. The fact that OR: Person holds up in dreams testifies to the strength of this motive. This is extremely important in understanding consumer behavior—purchasing, recreational activities, and many other aspects of human behavior.

Figure 4-1
Orientation to Person

WOMAN to WOMAN

"To me, the future is all about personal style, not designer dictates. My role is to offer women the freedom and tools to pull it together in a completely modern, sexy way — with simplified pieces that are timeless, luxurious, and flexible enough to go day into evening. This is not about a season: it's about everything I stand for. Building a wardrobe. Playing with pieces both old and new. The feminine with the masculine. The hip sophistication of New York. And dressing every body type, as well as every style of woman. Inspiring, unique, strong, and real woman. Women of character. Women who wear the clothes and never let them wear her. Because that's what great style is all about. The confidence to be true to yourself. That's why I think of these clothes as a celebration of personal style. From one woman to another."

DONNA KARAN
NEW YORK

(Ad copy courtesy of The Donna Karan Company. © 1994 The Donna Karan Company)

Figure 4-2
Orientation to Place

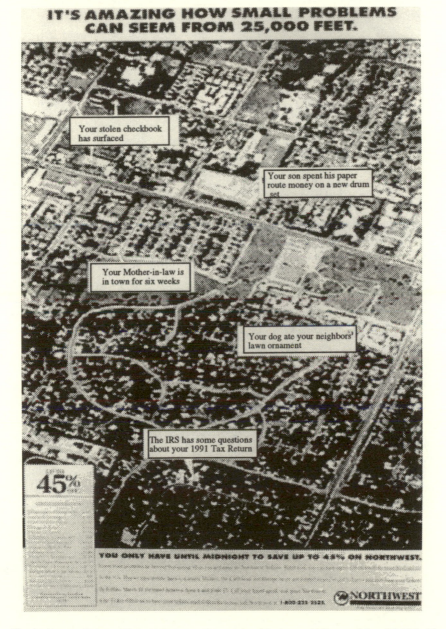

(Used with permission of Fallon McElligott Advertising, Northwest Airlines and Stan McClain Cinematography)

Figure 4-3
Orientation to Time

It seems as if there's never enough of it. And we realize the last thing you can afford to do is run out of it. So to help you make the most of it, Delta Air Lines has a flight leaving every 17 seconds of every day to almost anywhere in the world your business might take you. To London, Frankfurt, Paris, Rome. To Tokyo, Hong Kong, Bangkok, Seoul. And every step of the way, we'll do every thing possible to make sure you not only arrive relaxed and refreshed, but also with plenty of time to spare. Join us on your next business trip. We think you'll love the way we fly.

What You Have The Least Of, We'll Help You Make The Most Of. Time.

▲DELTA AIRLINES
—— You'll Love The Way We Fly™ ——

Based on cities served by Delta and the Delta Connection.® Delta Connection flights operate with delta flight numbers 3000-5999 and 7000-7999. ©1994 Delta Air Lines, Inc.

(Courtesy of Delta Air Lines, Inc.)

Orientation to Place

When orientation is lost, OR: Place is the next-to-the-last Orientation Motive to disappear. Therefore, it is the next-to-the-strongest personal Orientation Motive. Everyone has experienced temporary disorientation to place. It is usually very brief and transient. For example, an overnight flight to Europe or Asia may result in temporary disorientation to place, after the traveler arrives at the destination following a long flight through several time zones.

What is the relationship of OR: Place, or any of the other Orientation Motives, to consumer behavior? It was rumored that one of the world's greatest marketers, Henry Ford, was led into the automobile business because of this motive. Supposedly he had been seriously considering entering the watch business, but at the last moment he changed his mind and went into automobiles. When asked why, he said, "Because everybody wants to get where they ain't, and then when they get there they want to get back home again." In other words, people want to change their orientation to place. The Wright Brothers probably understood the OR: Place Motive, just as Henry Ford did.

Orientation to Time

Everyone has known elderly persons who lose their personal orientation to time. In nursing homes, large clocks are often placed in their rooms to assist them with this Orientation Motive, but they rarely help. This is because the OR: Time device, an internal clock, has been destroyed or impaired by progressive brain disease that is related to the process of aging. OR: Time refers to the fact that a person knows the approximate day, date, and time. This orientation may be lost, temporarily, as in the case of a person who gets so immersed in work that he/she completely loses track of time. In dreams, this Orientation Motive is often obscured when the past is confused with the present, as in a dream where a conversation is taking place in familiar surroundings with someone who has been dead for many years.

In consumer activities such as theme parks, casinos, restaurants, and recreational activities, the marketer does his/her best to remove the constraints of time because this is what the consumer wants. As in all the Orientation Motives, everyone wants to change his/her orientation (temporarily) but no one wants to change it permanently. Simply refer back to the second half of Henry Ford's alleged statement, ". . . and then they want to get back home again."

Many consumer motives can be understood when the personal Orientation Motives are analyzed and then integrated into the context of everyday behavior. Consumers do not think about personal orientation, but they act on it every day!

Orientation to Circumstances

For most people, knowing the day and the date (OR: Time) are not enough. People need to "know" if they are having a good day or a bad day. They need to be able to predict what is going to happen within a reasonable period of time. Circumstances take into account income, health, the family and domestic situation, expectations, and a lot of other variables related to the present and future. Because of the abstract nature of OR: Circumstances, it is the weakest of the Orientation Motives and the very first to disappear when a person begins losing his/her personal orientation.

Since alcohol ingestion will result in a temporary loss of personal orientation to circumstances, this is a primary purpose of drinking. Drinking will usually alter the OR: Circumstances Motive first. Many people, even those who are not heavy drinkers, will agree that a drink or two will "wipe out the circumstances of the day." Some even rationalize that a stiff drink is "just what the doctor ordered." Although some will say that they drink for the taste (rationalization), most drinkers will tell you that they drink for the feeling. That feeling—no matter how you cut it—is the feeling of disorientation.

THE ORIENTATION MOTIVES AND CONSUMER BEHAVIOR

It is important to understand how the Orientation Motive groups affect consumer behavior in many different categories, based upon the findings that have been derived from our research over the past 15 years. In a very general way, people do not want to lose their orientation, although they do want to change it temporarily, for various reasons. Consumer activities, especially within the recreational and discretionary-spending categories, provide the consumer with an opportunity for temporary disorientation in one or more of these four spheres of orientation:

Activity	OR Motive: Disorientation
A trip to a theme park with thrill rides	OR: Person
	OR: Place
A trip to a theme park with crafts and	OR: Time
"old time" theme	OR: Place
	OR: Circumstances
A dinner at a fine-dining establishment	OR: Place
	OR: Person
Cosmetics	OR: Person
Fashion	OR: Person

A theme park with thrill rides will offer temporary disorientation with rides that descend, ascend, whirl, drop, submerge, and immerse into water and darkness. This changes the OR: Person Motive, temporarily. Most thrill seekers are teenagers, and this is the group that is most confused about personal identity, which relates directly to OR: Person. They are going through an age-related identity-confusion crisis, and therefore rides that disorient and reorient in terms of person are popular. This particular group is referred to demographically as "thrill seekers."

Thrill seeking, also described as risk taking, is a well-known phenomenon that occurs within a particular demographic group, namely, males from 12 to 25. Maddi (1994) describes research that has taken place since 1974 on the level of MAO inhibitors, which play a central role in arousal, inhibition, and pleasure seeking. He states that different individuals are "hard wired" in different ways, and this determines their level of risk taking. Others have described this behavior in terms of personality structure, where outgoing or extroverted persons are more likely to take risks than introverted persons (Eysenck, 1970). There is probably some validity to all these explanations, especially when applied to long-term thrill seekers: i.e., those who remain that way for most of their lifetime, versus those who go through a phase. For those who pass through this almost "normal" phase, we believe that the OR: Person Motive explains the need to climb mountains, ride 20-foot waves, or just ride challenging rides in an amusement park. These people are looking for an identity, and once it is established, they generally move on to other pursuits. As one surfer, who had just flown halfway across the world to catch a rumored 60-foot wave, put it, "We do it because, when the ride is over, we feel as if we can conquer anything" (*NBC Dateline*, July 18, 1995). This is consistent with the observations of Fenz and Epstein (1969), who found that among novice parachutists the thrill is in large part the enormous sense of relief at the safe landing that follows the frightening jump or ride.

A theme park with an "old time" ambience, crafts, and entertainment will provide a temporary disorientation in the OR: Place and OR: Time Motives, as the visitor goes back in time and moves away from the present. This also changes OR: Circumstances, at least for the duration of the visit while the mind is focused on life the way that it was lived 100 years ago, rather than on the realities of the present day.

A visit to a fine-dining establishment allows a temporary change in OR: Person, since the staff (waiters and waitresses) are usually trained to treat the consumer as if he/she were special and unique. They are attentive and usually very solicitous. This is effective when the customer has had a trying day and is attempting to reorient in terms of who he/she is. OR: Place is also affected by the ambience and theme of the fine-dining establishment, and the stronger the theme, the more the OR: Place is changed. Hence, the more fulfilling the dining experience. The restaurant that understands the need for a temporary change in OR: Person or OR: Place does much better than the restaurant that does not understand it. This assumes, of course, that the menu, food, and service (rational elements) are the same, or close to the same, in the two restaurants that are being compared. This phenomenon is more closely examined in chapter 15.

For a female, the application of cosmetics in the morning in a fashion that is consistent with her special formula or "mix" allows her to become the "person that she wants to be," or at least the one that she wants to present to the public (OR: Person). Cosmetics are closely examined in chapter 18.

As in cosmetics, women's fashions also allow a change in OR: Person. This is why there are so many different styles and choices of fashions. It is not unusual, particularly for women who are depressed, to go out and buy several outfits in an effort to achieve a change in OR: Person. In a way, she "gets rid of" the depressed person inside of herself and finds someone new; she often finds this "new" person (temporarily) in the way that she dresses and in what she is wearing.

A man fails to understand a woman when she cries out, "But I have nothing to wear!" He explains that her wardrobe, the last he saw it, fills a whole closet with over 50 pairs of shoes. "What do you mean, you have nothing to wear? Are you kidding me?" What she means is that she has nothing to wear that will allow her to present the kind of person she wants to be at that particular occasion! Males do not understand this and probably never will. It is a vital aspect of the motive behind women's fashions, and is the OR: Person Motive. This is examined in chapter 17.

The Survival Motives

Like the Orientation Motives, the Survival Motives operate unconsciously and outside the realm of the consumer's awareness. Also, like the personal Orientation Motives, they become visible and obvious only when they are threatened from some outside source. The results of our research have established four Survival Motives in this group. Spiritual survival is one of the most powerful and motivating of all the motives, and for the purposes of advertising, probably the most persuasive. However, it should be noted that these motives, unlike stages, are not invariant. They change from product to product. Although there may be a "normal" sequence of motivation, our research has not uncovered such a sequence. We have looked at many different products, and the motivational hierarchy changes each time. What does remain constant is the number of motives that have been uncovered: 11. But with each different product or activity, the motivational hierarchy is reorganized.

There are many products that are marketed either directly to the Survival Motives or indirectly via rationalizations and the left side of the brain. Some of the more obvious are health-care products and services (physical survival); fitness (physical survival); sports and office products (territorial survival); and fragrances and fashions (sexual survival). These are just a few. One way to note the power of marketing to the Survival Motives is by adding up the gross revenue from each of these products and calculating it as a percentage of the GNP. Health-care alone accounts for 14 percent.

Maslow's Hierarchy of Needs

Marketers have relied uncritically upon Maslow's hierarchy of needs, and it is frequently cited in marketing textbooks, even though there is no empirical evidence to support Maslow's hierarchy. Soper, Milford, & Rosenthal (1995), in an article entitled "Belief when Evidence Does Not Support the Theory," surveyed a number of exhaustive reviews that conclude that Maslow's theory, which evolved from his own clinical observations, lacks supporting evidence "both conceptually and operationally." In fact, they cite several authors who conclude that "Maslow's theory is of more historical than functional value" (Landy, 1989) and deduce that "there is yet to be discovered compelling evidence that support the high regard in which many marketers hold Maslow's theory."

It is interesting and at the same time enigmatic that scholars and academics in so many different disciplines—psychology, education, marketing, management, human resources management, and communications—hold fast to Maslow's hierarchy of needs when it has no empirical or scientific support. In fact, studies have been carried out that demonstrated that the satisfaction of needs at one level does not necessarily lead to or produce higher-level needs (Beer, 1966). And yet the professionals, researchers, and academics who actively espouse Maslow's theory to explain various phenomena are the same ones who want to advance their disciplines as a science. So it is odd that they hold to a theory that really has the status of a belief, and has no scientific credibility at all. Soper, Milford, and Rosenthal (1995) conclude that the reason for this may be the inherent, intuitive appeal of Maslow's theory, especially within the discipline of humanistic psychology, where everyone is trying desperately to move toward a state of self-actualization. Also, since most of Maslow's work has been carried out within organizational settings, it is easy to teach and use it as a training device, because of its intuitive appeal. These authors summarize all this research and the various criticisms of Maslow's theory by pointing to Rothman (1989), who stated that "the option is not the decades old question, should we have either a science or an art of marketing but, instead, whether to have a science or parascience of marketing." The same thing holds true for psychology, education, management, communications, etc.

The theory presented here has been worked out and applied in both clinical and consumer contexts. Furthermore, it has empirical and sensory support, which will be presented in later chapters. For this reason, it is believed that it will provide a foundation for marketing and advertising in the future that cannot be overlooked. It will become a vital force in research, advertising, marketing, and in any other field that relies heavily upon an interpretation and understanding of human motivation.

Spiritual Survival

If spiritual survival as a motive is compared to Maslow's concept of self-actu-alization (Maslow, 1970), there are some parallels. However, one very important and crucial difference must be considered. For Maslow, self-actualization was attained *after* all the other basic needs were met: food, air, water, shelter, etc., and it will continue to hold up to empirical studies. Conversely, in the unconscious, spiritual survival is one of the most basic motives and most of the other motives come afterward, or build upon it. For our purposes, spiritual survival is basic, not secondary or tertiary as it would be for Maslow. In most cases, spiritual survival is more important than physical survival, and must be satisfied first. This is the only way to explain why people who seem "to have everything" will often sink into despair, and sometimes even take their own lives (suicide). Consumers attempt to fulfill their need for spiritual survival in many different ways, by exercising their purchasing power in hundreds of different product categories.

As the most basic of the Survival Motives, spiritual survival is the strongest in terms of driving motivation. Although not tied to religion, the whole concept of spiritual survival is derived from an unconscious universal belief in the survival and durability of the spirit beyond the survival of the body, and what has to be done to achieve it. This particular belief was derived from early experiences with death, which are universal and have been shared by everyone, usually before the age of seven. This belief is not in the realm of a person's awareness. It lies within the unconscious, labeled in figure 4-1 as "Unknown to self—Unknown to others." The Spiritual Survival Motive has been immortalized in the timeless (never-chang-ing) message of DeBeers: "a diamond is forever." Diamonds and other precious stones are marketed exclusively within the boundaries of spiritual survival.

Spiritual survival is difficult to describe, because it is an abstract concept. It should be regarded as a psychological, not a theological, construct (Maddock & Sexton, 1980). The fact that it is understood even by small children should help to illustrate its simplicity.

In visualization exercises that were carried out in research and in clinical prac-tice (chapter 8), it was found that almost everyone has, before the age of seven, had some kind of experience with death and dying. It may be a close relative, a distant relative, a friend, or perhaps even an animal. The important point is that early experiences with death have substantial impact and remain in the Silent Side of the mind on a permanent basis. Even though these experiences may be forgot-ten at the conscious level, they are readily recalled at the unconscious level through visualization. As a young child, being raised up to a casket and viewing a lifeless body, the commitment of a person to the grave, or the sight of a dead animal lying on the ground exemplifies images that are most meaningful and serves to impact the experiences of childhood. And the experiences remain imbedded in the uncon-scious mind.

What is especially important is the conclusion that children draw from these experiences with death. They conclude that life itself is not permanent or durable but there is something else that is: the life of the spirit. Spiritual death comes more to be feared than physical death, and conversely, more revered and respected. Children, in their typical denial, spend considerable time making fun of physical death (spooks, ghosts, goblins, etc.). Another way of saying this is that when children learn that life is temporary and not enduring, they also quickly come to see and understand that the only thing that does endure in life is the spirit. These childhood beliefs do not go away with maturation; they just become "layered over" with more logical and rational thinking. In time they may also become encoded within the context of a specific religion, and its tenets.

There is very little published material on children's attitudes and beliefs about death. However, Kubler-Ross (1983) recognizes this in what she calls "children's inner knowledge about death." Like Piaget and Freud, Dr. Kubler-Ross uses an observational technique, and then reasons from her observations with an inductive method. In her practice of medicine, she has treated hundreds of dying adults and children, and has observed many of them at the time of their death. In the examples and case histories that she gives, it is clear that children have well-defined and clearly delineated attitudes toward death, even though they are concrete (nonabstract) and unsophisticated (fanciful).

This belief in spiritual survival may or may not be shared in the conscious, rational mind. However, it is imbedded in the Silent Side, even when it is consciously and logically rejected. Loss of life may be frightening, but it is not feared nearly as much as loss of the spirit. People can be trained to accept loss of physical survival (e.g., Marine Corps boot camp) as long as that loss of life is in the service of spiritual survival (e.g., patriotism). Examples of the priority of spiritual over physical survival may be seen every week on the television program, "Rescue 911." Firemen, police officers, EMTs, and even ordinary citizens regularly risk or put their own lives in danger to save the life of someone else—a testimony to the priority of spiritual over physical survival.

Basic elements of spiritual survival are right and wrong. Most people, except for a small, psychopathic stratum of the population, try to follow the basic tenets of right and wrong. Even psychopaths try to follow what they believe is right and wrong in their own minds. The reason people attempt to follow guidelines is because there is something in it for them! Otherwise, common sense dictates that they would not do it. The following of right and wrong in childhood and throughout life is based on the fear of loss of spiritual survival. Spiritual death is worse than physical death.

There are hundreds of examples in every community of people who preferred physical death over spiritual death. The most common example is the depressed person who is dying spiritually because of guilt and subsequent depression. Such people often choose suicide as a way out. If they do not actually choose it, they do seriously consider it. This is how it is known that spiritual survival is more basic and more motivating than physical survival: i.e., the fact that a person is willing to take his/her own life to preserve something greater. Maslow's hierarchy is misleading, since this was not true for him; for Maslow, physical needs were more basic than spiritual needs, or what he calls self-actualization.

If the spiritual were not more essential and more basic than the physical, then people would not be motivated to do the right thing. It may be difficult to believe, but it is not part of human nature to work for something without a reward. Rewards are motivators. Therefore, spiritual survival is achieved by doing the right thing. It is lost by doing the wrong thing, which thereby incurs guilt and spiritual death. Almost all television and motion picture dramas are written around the centralized theme of spiritual survival (right and wrong) with eventual resolution on the side of right. Otherwise, no one would watch, because it would be too boring. Take note, sometime, of the number of TV dramas in which the resolution of right vs. wrong ends in the courtroom.

Fleischman (1990) has defined the various elements of spiritual survival, which are listed in table 4-2. These elements are important, for they assist us in understanding the issues that are involved at the spiritual level for people. According to Fleischman (personal conversation, 1994), conventional religions have not been that successful at resolving spiritual dilemmas. As a result, other activities become "spiritual" pursuits. This is why it is vital to understand the Spiritual Survival Motive as an issue in consumer behavior, wholly apart and detached from any religious or theological considerations. For purposes of research and scoring, Fleischman's system is ideal. These categories allow us to break down the rather unwieldy topic of spiritual survival into operational and observable elements. This is because Fleischman has dealt with spirituality in a psychological context and not in a religious or theological context, making it tangible, operational, and observable.

To understand spiritual survival in consumer behavior, it is important to understand what has to be done to achieve it. People try to achieve spiritual survival in various ways. For example, they may attempt to achieve perfection in sports, in their work, or perhaps in an avocation. In the book *A River Runs Through It* (MacLean, 1992), one of the characters failed miserably in many areas of his life, but managed to eventually achieve perfection near the end of his life in one area: trout fishing.

Love is another important part of the Spiritual Survival Motive, and the loss of love can often lead to the fear of the loss of the spirit and the loss of the desire to live any longer (physical survival) without that love. Love, in all its various facets, is the most important aspect of spiritual survival. These aspects include love of country (patriotism), love of family, brotherly love (philia), sexual love, love of those less fortunate, etc. In chapter 16 where theme park research is reviewed, it is shown how the concept of spiritual survival in the form of patriotism was introduced into the theme park setting. It was dramatic and highly motivating, and had the effect of increasing the overall gate revenue, consumer loyalty, and word-of-mouth advertising, as well as the overall reputation of the park.

Table 4-2
Fleischman's Elements of Spiritual Survival

Element	Meaning
1. Witness significance	Belief that a higher power listens, understands
2. Lawful order	Belief in the basic order of the universe and world that we live in
3. Wholeness	Involves affirmation and acceptance of the person
4. A sense of *calling*	A universal need for importance, to feel like work and life is relevant, connected
5. Membership	Part of a network that affirms, accepts, and legitimizes the person and his/her beliefs
6. Release	Renewal and release of new power
7. Human love	A vital element—love, bonding, and marriage overcome fear, pain, and loss; also includes patriotism, love of country
8. Sacrifice	The ability to go beyond one's self; often used to "bargain" with a higher power
9. Meaningful death	The goal of any spiritual program, organized or unorganized
10. Inner peace	Translating self-centeredness, worry, and responsibility into peace

Spiritual survival is attained by doing the "right thing." But the right thing can often be distorted and misguided. Since right is often equated with words like "clean," "pure," "organized," etc., some unusual stories have surfaced about how people will sometimes try to achieve spiritual survival, especially when morality is equated, on the Silent Side, with cleanliness. One former product manager at Procter and Gamble gave two outstanding examples of this:

1. Women regularly wrote letters to Procter and Gamble acknowledging that they ate Ivory soap. This was related to the Ivory soap signature: "ninety-nine and forty-four one-hundredths percent pure" (spirituality=purity).
2. Procter and Gamble was often named in lawsuits by women who would "practice chemistry" in their home with various cleaning products. No single product would get their homes clean enough, so they mixed separate products together, sometimes causing volatility and explosions.

Obviously these two abberations represent the extreme and not the ideal! Other aspects of spiritual survival include the need to be right, to approach perfection, to acquire knowledge, to speak the truth, to be seen as consistent, etc. Passion, which can be directed either in a positive or negative direction, is an extreme emotion, and as such is associated with spiritual survival. In fact, any excessive and fanatical behavior, positive or negative, is associated with spiritual survival, often with the element that Fleischman refers to as "calling."

One way to know when a person or group has elevated an issue to the level of spiritual survival is when they become extreme or passionately dedicated to an issue. For example, many people feel that the National Rifle Association (NRA) has taken an extreme position on gun ownership and control, way beyond the intent of the Second Amendment. Hence, it can be assumed, when it comes to issues of guns and gun control, that spiritual survival is involved for the NRA and some of its members because they are so passionate about them. Similarly, a man who dedicates himself to his job, 16 to 18 hours per day, seven days per week, with no breaks for vacation or days off is finding his spiritual survival in his job. He is referred to as a "workaholic." He has made a religion or a spiritual ritual out of his work.

Spiritual Survival Made Clear

William Faulkner, when he traveled to Stockholm, Sweden, in 1950 to accept the Nobel Prize for literature, made the motive and quest for spiritual survival perfectly clear. It was in a very brief speech at a state dinner, part of which follows:

I decline to accept the end of man. It is easy enough to say that man is immortal simply because he will endure: that when the last ding-dong of doom has clanged and faded from the last worthless rock hanging tideless in the last red and dying evening, that even then there will be one more sound: that of his puny inexhaustible voice, still talking. I refuse to accept this. I believe that man will not merely endure: he will prevail. He is immortal, not because he alone among creatures has an inexhaustible voice, but because he has a soul, a spirit capable of compassion and sacrifice and endurance. The poet's, the writer's duty is to write about these things. It is his privilege to help man endure by lifting his head, by reminding him of the courage and honor and hope and pride and compassion and pity and sacrifice which have been the glory of the past; of the props and the pillars to help him endure and prevail. (Bennett, 1993)

Spiritual Survival in Advertising and Marketing

To say that spiritual survival is the strongest motive in advertising and marketing is putting it very mildly. In most cases a marketer can easily move up to this level and increase the motivation of the consumer to buy the product, as well as rise above and beyond the clutter and noise that is made by competitors. With the

Silent Side framework in place, and with some creative ingenuity, most marketers will find that it is feasible and economical to devise a campaign that revolves around the whole Silent Side motive of spiritual survival. Consider the following examples.

Michelin does not talk about the features and benefits of tires, but instead about what is riding on your tires. This is an excellent example of an approach at the level of spiritual survival. Family values, love, concern, and parental responsibility are what the consumer is purchasing, not just tires. After all, tires are for sale at most service stations on just about every street corner.

Cadillac does not talk about the features and benefits of an automobile; they talk about creating a higher standard. This is spiritual survival: perfectionism, standards, achievement, excellence, flawlessness, and superiority. Two or three generations of buyers have always understood, intuitively, that when they purchase a Cadillac, they are not just purchasing an automobile. Cadillac has maintained this position, over the years, by positioning its product at the level of spiritual survival and leaving it there. Many other automobile manufacturers have tried to achieve this level, but have fallen short.

McDonald's, unlike Burger King, Wendy's, Arby's, etc., does not sell fast food. It sells family values, standards, and togetherness. Taking the family to McDonald's is the right thing to do. By marketing directly to children and letting the children market to the parents, the product is automatically positioned at the spiritual level.

Similarly, DeBeers does not just sell diamonds. It sells abiding, timeless, and perpetual love. A diamond is forever. Note that a spiritual position such as this does not change from month to month, but remains timeless itself.

Perhaps an even better example of an appeal at the spiritual level is Hallmark's timeless message: "You care enough to send the very best."

Recent examples in the literature of attempts to create a spiritual appeal are weak and superficial when compared to the timeless messages in the examples just listed. But they do support the overall quest for the authenticity of this motive. For example, Rikard (1994) predicts that in 1995 and beyond, there will be a much heavier appeal to spirituality in order to reach "consumers' states of mind." She says that advertising will incorporate spiritual themes in 1995 as consumers are looking for comfort, hope, and spirituality in an era of change. Parfums International is among the companies that are launching products with "other worldly" themes. Coty will launch Ghost Myst (1995), which is designed to appeal to women who want to make a personal statement and to those who are interested in inner, spiritual beauty. In addition, Calvin Klein is introducing Escape, a fragrance that will lay up the spiritual aspects for both men and women (Born, 1994).

In subsequent chapters it will become clear that spirituality as a motive is never addressed directly, but rather indirectly through the ten elements defined by Fleischman and by us (table 4-2), and one element (family values) defined only by us. Similarly, physical survival and the other motives are not addressed directly. A recreational marketer never says, "We'll help you to disorient" (Orientation

Figure 4-4
Spiritual Survival

IF YOU'VE GOT THE CAR, WE'VE GOT THE TIRE.

If you've got a family car, we've got the tire that may last as long as you own it.

Our all-season XH4. Backed by an 80,000-mile treadwear limited warranty. (See dealer for details.) If you've got a luxury performance car, our new MXV4 gives you the kind of comfort and handling that only a Michelin can. Plus all-season technology so advanced we call it Climate Control.

If you've got the kind of car everyone in the world wants, we've got the tire that will make them want it

even more. The XGT Series. With speed ratings from 112 to 149 mph and higher. And the technology to handle it.

And if you've got a light truck, we've got the tire with durability and traction both on and off road. Plus the smooth and quiet ride you expect from us.

We make a lot of different tires. Each one built the very same way. Like a Michelin. Anc if you don't know how important that can be, you will the minute you own

MICHELIN®
BECAUSE SO MUCH IS RIDING ON YOUR TIRES.®

Motives); instead, he/she simply designs an attraction that will accomplish that purpose. In casinos they simply remove all reminders of time (clocks) and cover the windows with curtains. The same thing holds for spiritual survival. This is not to say that the Coty and Calvin Klein productions will fail, but only that they would be more successful if they addressed the spiritual motive more indirectly.

Physical Survival

The Physical Survival Motive is a very strong motivator in consumer behavior. The Physical Survival Motive involves all the basic processes or elements that contribute to life: food, air water, health, and all the basic life-sustaining elements. As noted, Physical Survival, like other motives, is "silent" until it is threatened. In the last few years, the Physical Survival Motive has been seriously threatened by an exponential increase in crime and criminal behavior in the United States. Alarms and security systems have reached new heights in sales.

Crime is a major national issue because of the threat that it presents to physical survival. Since law enforcement agencies and the courts cannot keep up with this explosion of crime, threats to physical survival are imminent. This normally silent motive is now highly visible as people demand that Congress provide the funds for more protection and more police officers. This is an example of how a threat from the outside to the unconscious will cause that motive to emerge from the unconscious into the open. It then has to be dealt with.

Alarms, security services, and devices that protect physical survival are not necessarily restricted to marketing strategies at the level of physical survival. For example, an alarm company could choose to market at the level of spiritual survival. This would be accomplished by repositioning the product from one that protects from physical harm and injury (physical survival) to one that protects loved ones, family, and friends (spiritual survival). In doing this, the alarm marketer accomplishes two things:

1. Achieves distance from competitors and creates a special category in the marketing of alarm systems.
2. Moves to a deeper and more passionate level of motivation (spiritual survival), thereby adding impact to the physical survival message, getting more attention, and thus increasing sales.

Health-care services are usually marketed to the level of physical survival. The exception would be mental health-care services, which are usually targeted toward groups who are having crises and whose spiritual survival is threatened. Health-care services are also heavily dependent upon the Expectation Motive and will be discussed in more detail in chapter 21.

Territorial Survival

Morris (1967) has discussed the importance of the Territorial Survival Motive in animals and has offered a convincing argument as to how this motive extends to organized societies as a function of evolutionary development. Both men and women have territorial instincts and motivations. However, there are some differences in the way the genders manifest the motivation. McClelland (1975), Anastasi (1961), and Bakan (1966) have all concluded that males are more achievement oriented, whereas females are more affiliation oriented. Achievement orientation involves competition, striving, and the drive to accomplish external goals. Affiliation orientation involves concern for other people's feelings, seeking approval from others, and creating nurturing relationships with others. According to Bakan (1966), men are more competitive and women are more communal. The Territorial Survival Motive is more visible than the other motives, because it regularly comes under attack from external forces. This is because of competition, which is a strong element of Territorial Motive. When confronted by competition, territorial survival is threatened and the human reacts. This is seen regularly in business and everyday circumstances. This reaction is predictable, because it threatens security, and security is the strongest emotion involved in territorial survival. The reaction to this threat (the behavior) can take many forms: reorganization, anxiety, agitation, fear, mobilization, etc. It also encourages the competitive spirit.

The wide appeal of sports and sporting events is organized around the motive of territorial survival. Children learn early the value of teamwork in protecting their territory. For many, however, sporting events are much more than territorial survival; they are experienced at the level of spiritual survival. Organized professional and college sports are excellent examples of how an activity can be shifted from the territorial to the spiritual level of motivation. Season tickets, large screen TVs, and special cable channels that feature sports are often marketed to those who have shifted their passion for sports from the territorial to the spiritual level. These fans are fanatics. They are known to experience severe depression when their team loses; they spend up to 20 hours a week watching sports on TV (they never miss a game); they watch all the competitors' games; and, for the most part, they become totally immersed in the game, in sports, and in events that surround the contests. An example of how this allegiance shifted from the territorial to the spiritual level is the Olympics, where patriotism and love of country (spiritual survival) are tied in with the competitive spirit (territorial survival).

Fleischman (personal conversation, 1995) indicated that "for some, I have recognized that there has always been more going on at Fenway Park than baseball." He was referring to the fanatic and dedicated spiritual involvement of the fans, partly because of the stadium's long tradition there. He believed that this was an excellent example of the elevation of a competitive (territorial) element of motivation to a spiritual level.

During the 1994 Winter Olympics from Norway, more people watched the figure-skating championships than any other broadcasted television event in history. The reason was because of the much published Harding-Kerrigan match up. It had become an intensified issue of right vs. wrong or good vs. bad that shifted the whole contest from the territorial level to the highest level of spiritual survival.

Prakash (1992) found that territorial differences in the way males and females process information were important in considerations involving advertising. Because of these differences, he concluded that advertising aimed toward males should include males socializing in large groups, participating in competitive activities (especially sports related) and in scenarios of traditional male-female interaction. He cited the advertisements of Busch, Miller and Miller Lite, and Budweiser, where the viewer sees the territorial elements of self-mastery, self-assurance, self-confidence, and comradery, which appeal to the achievement orientation. In contrast, women should be shown in both competitive and noncompetitive activities, often alone. In addition, women should be given more detailed and complete product information, because of the way that they process information. These findings all suggest that territorial considerations are extremely important in advertising and marketing.

Sexual Survival

The Sexual Survival Motive, which is the least dominant of the survival group of motives, is also the most controversial. It consists of three elements: sexual gender, sexual impulse, and sexual inhibition.

Many consumer products are marketed to the gender issues of masculinity and femininity. Examples of masculine gender products are pickup trucks, guns, cowboy boots, cowboy hats, miscellaneous cowboy gear, after-shave lotion, and some articles of clothing. Other products that are typically marketed to men at the level of sexual survival (impulse) include workout equipment (home gyms), some clothing, weight loss programs, automobiles, and "fast" boats. Examples of feminine gender products are fragrances, cosmetics, wearing apparel, shampoo and other hair treatments, nail treatments, flowers, costume jewelry, etc.

When considering the other two aspects of sexual survival—impulse and inhibition—it is customary for women's products to be marketed to inhibition and for men's products to be marketed to impulse. In the late sixties, Ford marketed the Mustang directly to male impulse when it said, "We made it hot, you make it scream." Automobiles are frequently marketed at the impulse level, particularly if the target audience is male. A picture of a male standing by a car with a provocative and seductive female is an example of marketing to male impulse at the level of sexual survival.

Marketing to sexual inhibition is more commonly seen in women's products. What this means is that when marketing to women at the level of sexual survival, the customary avenue has been through inhibition rather than impulse. One fragrance—Jontue—says, "Sensual . . . but not too far from innocence." The word "but" negates sensual (impulse) and "not too far from innocence" is directed toward inhibition. Similarly, Maybelline recently addressed impulse by presenting an alternative: "Maybe she's born with it . . . Maybe it's Maybelline."

As mentioned above, a number of products are typically marketed at the level of sexual survival for women, including some cosmetics, some fashions, some hair treatments, weight loss programs, shoes, and costume jewelry. Most of these are marketed to sexual inhibition. Exceptions include lingerie (nightwear), which is marketed to women directly at the level of sexual impulse, and diamonds, which are *always* marketed to the level of spiritual survival.

A recent radical "twist" in automotive advertising took place when Hyundai, advertising its 1994 automobile, marketed directly to women's impulses. It was a bold step, and it worked. A sensual man, shirtless, is shown leaning on the hood of a new Hyundai, and four women are staring from an office window with their noses pressed against the glass. They appear to be lusting. One of them asks, "I wonder what he has under his hood?" This bold breakthrough in appealing to women at the impulse level was a significant step, for prior to this attempt appeals to women at the sexual survival (impulse) level had been limited to just a few products. But by most of the measures that are applied to advertising, it worked!

Men and women are very different when it comes to their attitudes about sex. It has been said that "men tolerate love so they can get to sex, whereas women tolerate sex so they can get to love." This is an overstatement, but it emphasizes some of the basic differences. This is why the marketer who chooses to market at the level of sexual survival needs to be careful to stay within the acceptable boundaries of gender, impulse, and inhibition and make use of these research methods to determine which is the most appropriate target for the marketing plan.

Men prefer to think of themselves sexually as virile, potent, masculine, powerful, forceful, and aggressive. Conversely, women tend to conceptualize themselves sexually as more passive, acquiescent, compliant, yielding, and submissive. This phenomenon is socially and not necessarily politically correct. Yet, it exists.

Although it is "politically improper" to emphasize many of the differences in men and women today, within the unconscious these differences still exist and are very real. Some of these differences are cultural and will change as the culture changes, as has happened with the Territorial Survival Motive over the last few years. The Hyundai approach shows that some concepts are already changing.

Sex in advertising is a long-debated, hotly contested subject. In a special issue of the *Journal of Advertising Research* on Ethics in Advertising, Gould (1994) argues that sexuality is a major issue of ethical concern and that very little is known about its overall or lasting effects. His solution is to set up a research agenda on the effects and ethics of sexuality in advertising, and then to develop a set of ethics-based policy guidelines for addressing these issues. In the same issue, LaTour and Henthorne (1994) find in a survey using the Reidenback-Robin multidimensional ethics scale, that regardless of gender, advertisements making strong or overt sexual statements are very offensive and need to be rethought by advertisers, who typically use sex to break through media clutter. In a related article, Elliot (1991) suggests that "Madison Avenue has gone too far" in the use of sexually explicit ads.

Despite this controversy, articles appear each year that indicate that "sex still sells, always has, and always will." Kuriansky (1995) shows that although the use of sex and sexuality waned in the late seventies, it was ignited again in spots for Calvin Klein jeans by actress Brooke Shields. Although the emphasis changes (gender roles, body parts, etc.), sex still sells. Marshall (1994) reflects on the return of the same theme in auto sales, and Lippert (1995) in ads for Diet Coke. The marriage of sex and the emphasis on fitness and being in good shape appears to be a natural alliance.

The Adaptation Motive

The motives that have been discussed—the survival and orientation groups—are acquired. Infants are not born with an orientation to person, place, time, etc., and they do not have sexual, territorial, or other survival motives. As infants, they do not know who or where they are. Instead, these motives "unfold" over time.

The Adaptation Motive is different. Pictures of neonates that appear in diagnostic ultrasound during the third trimester show clear and present movements of the hands to the face. These are known as *adaptors*. Early adaptors consist primarily of hand-to-face movements and they aid the infant in adapting to his/her in uterine environment. Adaptation is a motive that is observable even before birth! Therefore, it is an extremely forceful and robust motive.

The Adaptation Motive appears before birth in hands-to-face movement but goes through certain developmental changes. In pre-adolescence, seven-to-ten-year-old boys have other boys as friends, and girls have other girls as friends. They all want to be *like* their friends. This is adaptation. In adolescence, this Adaptation Motive becomes even stronger as boys and girls desire more and more to be like their friends, and this occasionally accounts for negative behaviors such as smoking, drug abuse, and alcohol abuse or positive behaviors such as excelling in sports or academics. It also accounts for the kind of clothing that is worn, personal appearance, preferences in styles, etc. For example, in the last 20 years (beginning with the Izod alligator) labels have begun to appear on the *outside* rather than the *inside* of wearing apparel for both men and women. Well-known examples are Duck Head, Dockers, Christian Dior, etc. All this is in deference to the Adaptation Motive: the desire to adapt to the environment and to be like other people. After all, a label clearly identifies one person as being like another.

Adults often resort to the primitive hand-to-face adaptors that were seen in infancy when they are tense and anxious (McKinnon, 1984; Maddock & Fulton, 1995). Cigarette smoking, with its hand-to-face movement, is an adaptor. Although it starts as a desire to be like one's friends (adaptation), smoking quickly establishes itself as a reflexive behavior that is difficult to break or extinguish.

Figure 4-5
The Adaptation Motive

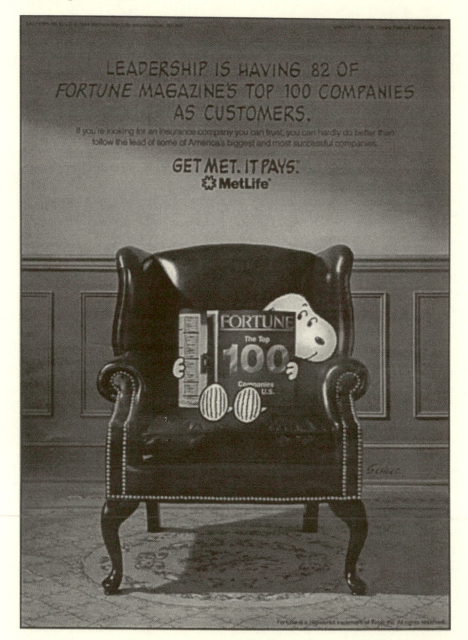

(Used with permission of Metropolitan Life Insurance Co., United Features Syndicate and *Fortune Magazine*)

Figure 4-6
Another Example of the Adaptation Motive

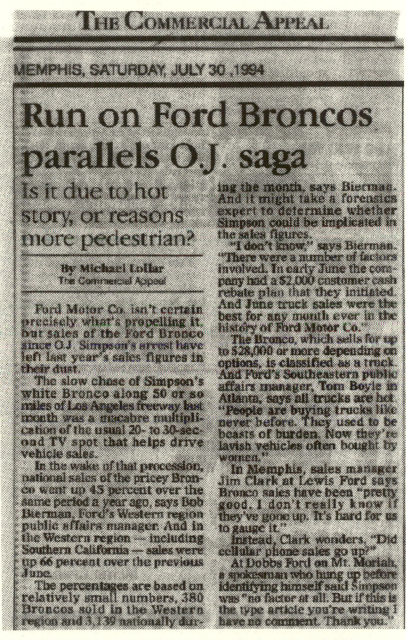

THE COMMERCIAL APPEAL

MEMPHIS, SATURDAY, JULY 30 ,1994

Run on Ford Broncos parallels O.J. saga

Is it due to hot story, or reasons more pedestrian?

By Michael Lollar
The Commercial Appeal

Ford Motor Co. isn't certain precisely what's propelling it, but sales of the Ford Bronco since O.J. Simpson's arrest have left last year's sales figures in their dust.

The slow chase of Simpson's white Bronco along 50 or so miles of Los Angeles freeway last month was a macabre multiplication of the usual 20- to 30-second TV spot that helps drive vehicle sales.

In the wake of that procession, national sales of the pricey Bronco went up 43 percent over the same period a year ago, says Bob Bierman, Ford's Western region public affairs manager. And in the Western region — including Southern California — sales were up 66 percent over the previous June.

The percentages are based on relatively small numbers, 380 Broncos sold in the Western region and 3,139 nationally dur-ing the month, says Bierman. And it might take a forensics expert to determine whether Simpson could be implicated in the sales figures.

"I don't know," says Bierman. "There were a number of factors involved. In early June the company had a $2,000 customer cash rebate plan that they initiated. And June truck sales were the best for any month ever in the history of Ford Motor Co."

The Bronco, which sells for up to $28,000 or more depending on options, is classified as a truck. And Ford's Southeastern public affairs manager, Tom Boyle in Atlanta, says all trucks are hot. "People are buying trucks like never before. They used to be beasts of burden. Now they're lavish vehicles often bought by women."

In Memphis, sales manager Jim Clark at Lewis Ford says Bronco sales have been "pretty good. I don't really know if they've gone up. It's hard for us to gauge it."

Instead, Clark wonders, "Did cellular phone sales go up?"

At Dobbs Ford on Mt. Moriah, a spokesman who hung up before identifying himself said Simpson was "no factor at all. But if this is the type article you're writing I have no comment. Thank you."

(Copyright 1995, *The Commercial Appeal*, Memphis, TN. Used with permission.)

59

This is because the Adaptation Motive consists of reflexes as well as motives, as in thumb sucking. Once broken the sucking reflex will go into remission, but it is never completely extinguished or gone. It can always be awakened. Just as in infancy, the adaptor aids the adult in anxious and tense situations.

Adaptation carries with it, for adolescents and adults, the motivation to be like everyone else. This is another unconscious motivation that works automatically and quietly, within the unconscious, until it is threatened from the outside. An example of a threat may be when the "everyone else" turns out to be the wrong people, and parents, the police, or the courts interfere. This is why children, who are born with the Adaptation Motive, need to be raised properly and with guidance. This is the only way that parents can ensure that the Adaptation Motive will not lead them in the wrong direction. Unfortunately, and as some parents can attest, it often does.

Marketing campaigns designed to appeal to the Adaptation Motive have been carried out ever since advertising was invented. In street language, it is called "keeping up with the Joneses," and it was a very popular marketing strategy during the fifties and sixties. It was brought to light and popularized by Vance Packard during this time, and the impression that was given was that it was the only motive behind major purchases and brand loyalty (Packard, 1957, 1959). It is still around and is still very much in use—a testimony to the power of marketing to the unconscious, or marketing directly to the motives.

Perhaps the most common and frequent appeal to the Adaptation Motive is in testimonials and in sponsoring. Hansen (1994), in an unpublished research paper, reviewed the effects of sports sponsoring and found that sponsoring has marked effects upon recall but is not necessarily that effective in the modification of attitudes. Other findings suggest that sponsoring is most effective in situations where there is a need to generate increased awareness of the product.

The Expectation Motive

The Expectation Motive consists of trust, hope, and conviction about what is likely to happen in the future. Like the Adaptation Motive, the Expectation Motive is present from the very beginning of life. The newborn infant is unable to make it on his/her own, and needs to be taken care of, by someone, for a very long time. The infant comes to expect and knows that someone will be there to perform this task, for as long as it takes. In the last 30 to 50 years, at least since the Great Depression, Americans have looked more and more to their government to fulfill the Expectation Motive.

The Expectation Motive is one of the five motivational groups that make up the Silent Side. Unlike the three motivational groups that have been discussed, the Expectation Motive deals with the future, not the present. It assists people in adapting to the future and what is to come. No matter how pessimistic a person appears to be, the Expectation Motive (hope) works within him/her to adapt to the unknown. Risks are taken every day because of the Expectation Motive. Without risk, life would fail to be a challenge.

An extreme example of the Expectation Motive is the "Cinderella Syndrome," which has been described in many magazines and professional journals as it relates to women. At issue is the belief that a young, handsome, and sensitive man will come charging into a woman's life and rescue her from boredom and unhappiness. Some of the books written by Danielle Steel, a popular women's author, rely upon the Cinderella Syndrome consistently, as do other women's books. This theme has an inherent appeal because it speaks directly to the motivation that is already there: the Expectation Motive, or the belief that someone will come to the rescue. Perhaps the Cinderella Syndrome leaves the woman with an unrealistic view of the world, especially of the future.

This is just one example of how women use the Expectation Motive, and much of the fiction and drama that is read or devoured by women consistently relies upon this theme. But the Expectation Motive can also serve people in a very positive and realistic way.

In a paper that is currently being reviewed (Maddock & Fulton, 1995a), we have observed the male counterpart to the Cinderella Syndrome in many factory workers that we have supervised and managed. In what we call the 90/10/10/90 Reversal Theory, we have posited that as many as 90 out of 100 workers have poor work habits because they believe, unconsciously, that either they will inherit money, be "discovered," or win the lottery. As a result, they beleve it really is not necessary for them to dedicate themselves to their work, whatever that work might be. For these individuals, working in mundane or otherwise unglamorous jobs is just temporary until one of these events occur. They are certain that the magical event will occur; the only uncertainty is when it will occur. We conclude that such a miraculous "discovery," inheritance, or winning the lottery will occur, at best, to only 10 out of the 100 "lower performers," instead of 90 out of 100—hence, the 90/10/10/90 Reversal Theory.

The Expectation Motive is integral in the utilization of professional services, where the consumer has no knowledge of what to expect but places his/her life in the hands of a physician, attorney, dentist, or other professional. In doing this, the consumer has learned to expect results. And if the results that were expected are not forthcoming, they often learn to live with the outcome. But in professional (medical, legal) settings the consumer needs more than just results. They need trust, confidence, and all of the other emotions typically associated with the Expectation Motive. Because of the naivete with which the consumer approaches the utilization of professional services, most if not all professional groups have licensing laws for the protection of the consumer. Chapter 21 deals with the selling, marketing, and advertising of professional services, and is based almost entirely upon the Expectation Motive.

The Expectation Motive is also critical in consumer activities involving gambling, where outcomes are uncertain. In the case of gambling and wagering, the consumer has to believe that he/she has a unique quality, trait, or attribute that allows him/her to beat the odds, despite all the people who have not beaten the odds (chapter 14). In this case, the Expectation Motive is referred to as "luck."

Expectation is a strong, powerful, and motivating force in human behavior that assists individuals in dealing with the future.

Play

The fifth major motivational group involves play. MacLean (1990) states that activities involving play are unique to mammals, along with nursing and audiovocal communication between parent and offspring. He also notes that the purpose of play is not clear, and that it appears spontaneously without any particular outcome or consequence. He hypothesizes that it may have had the original purpose of relieving the tension that results from crowding in the nest. In humans, play may be a form of conscious or "awake dreaming," that is, working out the impact of the day's events on the psyche, by way of controlled diversion. In our previous discussion of spiritual survival, this is how we characterized a child's image of spooks, etc.—as a controlled diversion of the impact of death on the child's psyche.

Play that is engaged in by children may or may not be purposeful or with intention. McMillan (1982) spent many hours observing children in play and conceived of self-paced play activities that led to the development of many self-directed play activities that are seen today, and for which he is credited with developing. McMillan observed that small children, given almost any kind of a configuration of iron pipe, PVC, castaway cardboard, etc., could, with the use of their imagination, entertain themselves. A child may take a carton that contained a new television set and play all day in a make-believe house, after cutting windows and doors in the box.

Similarly, the child may jump upon a configuration of iron bars and convert it into a police car or fire engine and play for hours. As a result of these observations, McMillan developed the pit full of rubber balls and many other self-directed children's play activities, in which children may play for hours in an activity that has no stated outcome, such as winning or demonstrating any kind of superiority.

On the other hand, adult play is almost always purposeful, goal directed, and contained. An example can be seen in how most adult games evolve into complex and differentiated businesses with athletes/businessmen becoming involved in many facets of the activity, outside of the game. We have already examined in this chapter how many adult games are territorial in nature, such as the Olympics. This explains why the competition is often so fierce and the stakes are so high. But beyond this, many games that are intended to be in the realm of territorial motivation often move into the area of spiritual motivation. When this happens, ordinary sporting activities move from being competitive to being bloodthirsty, and sports fans at this level are characterized by passion and fanaticism that appears to go well beyond the suggestion that "it's only a game."

In our culture, play at the adult level is competitive, aggressive, and very ambitious. In many cases, play has become big business, and undoubtedly (when combined with television) is one of the biggest businesses of our time. In our treatment of motives, most play will be discussed in terms of either territorial survival (competition) or spiritual survival, or perhaps, when viewed strictly at the level of exercise, in terms of physical survival. The exception will be when dealing with the play of children, which appears to have no stated purpose but is simply an end in and of itself. Also, there are certain adult activities, such as dancing or listening to music, that would appropriately be categorized as play, since they have no stated purpose or outcome, such as winning.

THE CONSUMER MOTIVATION HIERARCHY

As in any needs hierarchy or needs structure, there is an order or arrangement, in which there are needs or motives that are dominant and powerful and other needs and motives that are less dominant and less powerful. The structure of the motivation hierarchy that is discussed here is seen in figure 4-7 with the most dominant or powerful motives at the bottom of the pyramid, and the weaker motives at the top.

The consumer motivation hierarchy is based upon the proposition that spiritual survival, or the avoidance of spiritual death, is the most powerful, motivating, dominant, and driving force in human behavior. As such, it takes direct priority over the OR: Person Motive and the Physical Survival Motive. Similarly, these motives take priority over the Adaptation Motive, etc. However, the motivational structure will differ between products and between groups of people. The "typical" hierarchy is based on generic lifestyle research that we have carried out, which is described in chapter 12. Furthermore, in the product research that we have done, the order of motives lies generally in this order: spiritual survival, orientation to person, physical survival, and adaptation are stronger and more motivating, whereas the other Orientation Motives, sexual survival, etc., are not as influential (when they are present).

These motivational categories are not invariant, as developmental stages might be. In developmental psychology, as in Freud's or Piaget's approach to human development, stages are invariant. The child must go through one stage before passing on to the other. While motivational stages are not invariant, some motives appear stronger than others. The pyramid shows how they might line up, if all were present, in the use of a particular product or service.

This theory of consumer behavior is derived from research. The research is both qualitative and quantitative. As shown in chapters 7 and 8, this motivational hierarchy was developed out of theory and practice. In reality, the hierarchy has been tested both qualitatively and quantitatively. As a result, we have been able to construct a questionnaire that measures not only consumers' rational answers to questions, but also their emotions. As individual motives are quantified in attitude

Figure 4-7
Typical Motivational Hierarchy

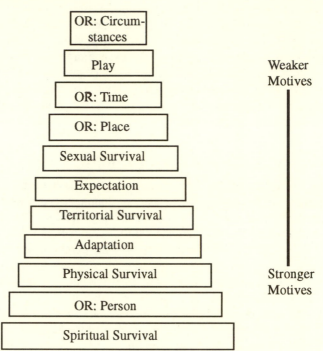

surveys or questionnaire formats and the data is collected, each motive and emotion can be verified through factor analysis and other statistical techniques. The whole process of quantifying consumer emotion and motivation is now available. This allows for prediction and for more accurate descriptions of consumer behavior. It will certainly simplify and improve the writing of marketing plans and many other activities in advertising, sales, and research.

MOTIVES, ELEMENTS, EMOTIONS AND BEHAVIORS

In table 4-3, the eleven basic consumer motives are seen in hierarchical order, as well as the various elements that are required to sustain each motive. From these elements (or the lack of them) emotions arise, and from these emotions, behavior. Not all of the behaviors or emotions are listed—just examples for the purpose of illustration.

The table shows that an analysis of the involvement of the unconscious goes well beyond the descriptive phase of consumer behavior and reaches into the whys and wherefores of why consumers do what they do. For the marketer, this information is critical; for the advertiser, it is essential. Understanding human motives

Table 4-3
Motives, Elements, Emotions, and Benefits in Consumer Behavior

MOTIVES	ELEMENTS	EMOTIONS	BENEFITS
OR: Person	Who	Self-esteem	Renewal
		Self-confidence	Acceptance
		Self-image	Confidence
OR: Place	Where	Escape	Solutions
		Freedom	Perspective
		Away from	Renewal
		problems	Relief
OR: Time	When	Escape	Relief
		Involvement	Nostalgia
		Simplicity	
OR: Circum-	Pace (of life)	Relief from	Stability
stances	Convenience	pressure	Regain perspec-
		Change, renewal	tive
		Affirmation	Forget hassles
Expectation	"Memory of the	Trust	Confidence
	future"	Hope	Commitment
		Faith, belief	
Territorial	Assets, greed	Security	Achievement
Survival	Career		Status & power
	Income		Control
	Competition		
	"Nesting"		
Sexual	Gender	Masculinity,	Identity
Survival	Inhibition	femininity	Safety
	Impulse	Control	Enjoyment
		Expression,	
		pleasure	
Physical	Food, air, water,	Health &	Security
Survival	health, taste	wellness	Protection
	Shelter	Security	Strength
		Safety (from	Well-being
		disease)	
Spiritual	Family values	Love	Perfection
Survival	Inner peace	Passion	Achievement
	Meaningful death	Guilt	Acceptance
	Witness signifi-	Acceptance	Uniqueness
	cance		Permanence
	Lawful order		
	Wholeness		
	Sense of calling		
	Membership		
	Renewal &		
	release		
	Human love		
	Sacrifice		
Adaptation	Imitation	Security	Status, achieve-
		Confidence	ment
Play	Impulse	Fun, laughter	Tension relief
			Self-expression

and emotions is the key to effective and ongoing marketing. Just as a policeman or detective needs to learn the motive to solve the crime, the marketer needs the motive to lead the consumer to the purchase. The marketer must market to the mind!

MOTIVATION, SURVIVAL, EVOLUTION AND THE UNCONSCIOUS MIND

The whole notion of the unconscious and the first attempt at "dual information processing" was introduced by Freud (Jones, 1955). For Freud, there was a conscious and an unconscious mind. The concept of the unconscious was used to explain irrational behavior; the conscious to explain rational, logical, and ordered behavior. Freud felt that the only way that rational thinking could occur was to make the unconscious conscious.

There were, however, several critical problems with Freud's theory. One was that it was very difficult to subject his observations to scientific research. Another was that it was difficult to apply. A third problem, as Epstein (1994) has pointed out, was that Freud's theory had a critical weakness in that it made very little sense from an evolutionary perspective. This is because it was essentially a maladaptive system, producing thought processes that were disordered, psychotic, delusional, and related only to primary process (infantile thinking). As Epstein has noted:

Operating under the direction of primary process alone, individuals would starve to death amidst wish-fulfillment hallucinations of unlimited gratification. That they do not, Freud attributed to the secondary process. This ad hoc solution leaves unexplained the questions of how the maladaptive system evolved in the first place, and how non-human animals are able to adapt to their environments at all without a secondary process (which is intimately tied to language). This raises an interesting question as to how a theory of the unconscious with such a critical flaw could have endured for so long. (p. 709)

In contrast, the approach to motivation that is presented here is totally survival based. The major motivational systems that are outlined in this chapter are totally involved in survival: spiritual, physical, territorial, and sexual, as well as in general orientation to person, place, time, and circumstances. In this sense, then, what is being presented when consumer behavior is analyzed is an adaptive system rather than a maladaptive one. One which is consistent with the principles of evolutionary development, as well as with what we see when we observe human behavior. It is consistent with the Freudian unconscious, and it also addresses the three critical weaknesses in Freud's theory: (1) it allows empirical investigation and research; (2) it is easily and readily applied to everyday behavior; and (3) it is completely survival-based.

MONEY

Is money a motivator? Whenever there is a discussion about motivation, the question of money is approached.

Money is not, and has never been, a *primary* motivator. Behavioral psychologists would not disagree with this. They would say that money is a reinforcer, and that some reinforcers are secondary motivators. But within the Silent Side, which looks at the causes and reasons for human behavior, money is a secondary, not a primary motivator. Money only gets us what we really want.

If the Adaptation Motive says that it is important to have a Lexus to keep up with the neighbors, then money will buy the Lexus and keep the Adaptation Motive from becoming frustrated. If the OR: Person Motive says that it is important that one change his/her appearance through plastic surgery, and the Expectation Motive tells us that we can trust Dr. Wintercorn not to ravage our face and our appearance, then money will help us to make that change, since health insurance will not pay for it. The point is that money is a secondary, not primary, motivator. It is a factor, not a motivator, in marketing. Moreover, if it does not exist for the specific consumer, it cannot be fabricated by the marketer.

CONCLUSION

We have surveyed the primary consumer motivations that cause people to act. First, the consumer makes an unconscious decision as to what he/she wants, then he/she somehow finds the money to do it. This second part—how he/she finds the money—may be more of a mystery than the unraveling of the motivational processes in the unconscious mind.

Marketing to the mind examines the motivational, causal processes that reside in the unconscious, irrational, silent side of the consumer. External reinforcers like money are valid considerations, but they are of secondary, not primary, importance. As stated, they cannot be created by the marketer. However, the unconscious is where the creative director and creative marketer come face to face with the real causes of behavior: the motives.

The unconscious mind is simple. It is not complex. In research carried out with over 5,000 consumers and 200 product categories, the five motivational groups that have been presented in this chapter explained why consumers do what they do, and what they can be expected to do in the future. We include nine chapters that show how it works in certain selected product and service categories. The astute and interested reader can interpolate how these motives work in many more examples that are not included here.

REFERENCES

Anastasi, A. (1961). *Differential psychology: Individual and group differences in behavior* (3rd ed.). New York: Macmillan.

68   Marketing to the Mind

Bakan, D. (1966). *The duality of human existence*. Chicago: Rand McNally.

Bandura, A. (1977). *Social learning theory*. Englewood Cliffs, NJ: Prentice-Hall.

Beer, M. (1966). *Leadership, employee needs and motivation*. (Monograph 129). Columbus: Ohio State University, Bureau of Business Research, College of Commerce.

Bennett, W. (1993). *The book of virtues: A treasury of great moral stories*. New York: Simon and Schuster.

Born, P. (1994, May 20). Calvin Klein hatches a "spiritual" escape fragrance. *Women's Wear Daily, 167* (98), 6.

Catching the big one. (1995, July 18). *NBC Dateline*.

Coty obscures a ghost myst (1995, June 16). *Women's Wear Daily*, 169, (116), 7.

Elliott, S. (1991, December 15). Has Madison Avenue gone too far? (Sexually explicit ads). *New York Times*, p. F1, sec. 3, col. 2.

Epstein, S. (1994). Integration of the cognitive and the psychodynamic unconscious. *American Psychologist, 49*, 8, 709–24.

Eysenck, H. (1970). *The Structure of Human Personality* (3rd ed.). London: Methuen.

Fenz, W. D., & Epstein, S. (1969). Gradients of physiological arousal in parachutists as a function of an approaching jump. *Psychosomatic Medicine, 29*, 33–51.

Fleischman, P. (1990). *The healing spirit*. New York: Paragon House.

Gould, S. J. (1994, September). Sexuality and ethics in advertising: A research agenda and policy guideline perspective. *Journal of Advertising Research*, 23 (3), 73-81.

Hansen, F. (1994). *Effect of sponsoring: an experimental study*. Unpublished research paper, Copenhagen: Copenhagen Business School, Marketing Institute.

Jamison, K. R. (1995, February). Manic depressive illness and creativity. *Scientific American, 272*, (2), 62–67.

Jones, E. (1955). *The life and work of Sigmund Freud* (Vol. 2). New York: Basic Books.

Kubie, L. (1961). *The neurotic distortion of the creative process* (© 1958). New York: Noonday Press.

Kubler-Ross, E. (1983). *On children and death*. New York: Macmillan.

Kuriansky, J. (1995, Spring). Sex simmers, still sells. *Advertising Age, 66*, 49.

Landy, F. J. (1989). *Psychology and work behavior*. Pacific Grove, CA: Brooks-Cole.

LaTour, M., & Henthorne, T. (1994, September). Ethical judgments of sexual appeals in print advertising. *Journal of Advertising Research*, 23 (3), 8.

Lippert, B. (1995, May 22). The babes are back (new commercials for Diet Coke). *Adweek* (Eastern ed.), *36*, (21), 46.

MacLean, N. A. (1992). *A river runs through it*. Chicago: University Chicago Press.

MacLean, P. D. (1990). *The triune brain in evolution: Role in paleocerebral functions*. New York: Plenum Press.

Maddi, S. (1994, November-December). Psychology of thrill seeking. *Psychology Today*, 52–53, 83–84.

Maddock, R. C., & Fulton, R. L. (1995a). Has Santa Claus really sabotaged the work force? Unpublished paper.

Maddock, R. C., & Fulton, R. L. (1995b). *The silent side of communication*. Des Moines: American Media, Incorporated.

Maddock, R. C., & Kenny, C. (1973). Impression formation as a function of age, race and sex. *Journal of Social Psychology*, 89, 223–43.

Maddock, R. C., & Sexton, R. O. (1980). Guilt, immortality and spiritual survival (Vol. 1, no. 1, pp. 5–30). Memphis, TN: *Medical Hypnoanalysis*.

Marshall, C. (1994, October 28). How much mileage is there left in auto sexuality? *Campaign*, p. 18.

Maslow, A. H. (1970). *Motivation and personality* (2nd ed.). New York: Harper and Row.

McClelland, D. (1975). *Power: The inner experience*. New York: Irving.

McKinnon, M. E. (1984, December). Guidelines for understanding nonverbal behavior. *Polygraph, 13* (4), 314–20.

McMillan, E. (1982, November 19). *Self directed play in children*. Paper presented at the annual convention of the International Association of Amusement Parks, Piers and Attractions, Kansas City, MO.

Morris, D. (1967). *The naked ape: A zoologists study of the human animal*. New York: McGraw Hill.

Packard, V. O. (1957). *The hidden persuaders*. New York: D. McKay Co.

Packard, V. O. (1959). *The status seekers*. New York: D. McKay Co.

Prakash, V. (1992, May-June). Sex roles and advertising preferences. *Journal of Advertising Research*, 43–51.

Rikard, L. (1994, November 7). Spirituality, hope on horizon as solace sought (advertising themes will contain spirituality to reach consumers' states of mind). *Advertising Age*, 65 (47), 21.

Rothman, M. (1989). Myths about science . . . and beliefs in the paranormal. *The Skeptical Inquirer*, 14 (1), 25–34.

Soper, B., Milford, G. E., & Rosenthal, G. (1995, September). Belief when evidence does not support the theory. *Psychology and Marketing*, 415–22.

Taylor, M. A. (1988). *The neuropsychiatric mental status examination* (© 1981). New York: PMA Publishing.

5

Absurdities

HOW TO PRODUCE MEMORABLE AND MOTIVATIONAL ADVERTISING AND MARKETING CAMPAIGNS

In the 1970s, Ally and Gargano produced a series of television spots for a new, start-up air express company named Federal Express (Federal Express, 1993). The ads were so successful that they brought immediate attention to this new company, which eventually went on to become the generic term for overnight shipments: "Just FedEx it."

The spots that were created are of interest because they are memorable and motivating. They were humorous, and some people would say that it was because of humor that they caught the attention of the viewer and turned him/her into a user. But we know from experience that humorous spots are not always motivating. They may entertain people, but research in recall has shown that, in some cases, they can be too entertaining, to the point that the product is in danger of becoming obscured.

Hopkins (1966) in fact suggested that advertising should never set out to entertain people. Ogilvy and Raphaelson (1982) issued a similar caveat, in which they said that copywriters should avoid the temptation to amuse and entertain their audiences. Despite these warnings, over the years there has been a strong interest in the use of humor in advertising and a number of articles have been written that look at the use of humor in different kinds of media. The results, to date, are inconclusive. For example, Sternthal and Craig (1973) indicated that humor would interfere with advertising comprehension, and in a study of research executives in U.S. ad agencies, 64 percent of those surveyed agreed (Madden & Weinberger, 1984). Conversely, in a study of 1,000 television commercials, Stewart and Furse

(1986) found that humor would increase the comprehension of an ad.

In recent research carried out by Weinberger et al. (1995), the authors of this study look at the use of humor in different products, based on a product typology similar to the ones derived by Percy and Rossiter (1992). These studies examine typologies that underlie differences in consumer products and usually place them in a grid, such as high-involvement vs. low-involvement products x informational (negative-drive reduction) vs. transformational (positive-drive reduction). In this case the grid is a 2 x 2 matrix, called the Product Color Matrix (PCM), which was developed to draw together many of the concepts from behavioral research that underlie the typologies of products.

Weinberger et al. examine the effects of humor in these different product categories on both a Recall Index and an Execution Recall. Their conclusion is that in two of the four product categories, humor appears to have no positive or negative effect. In one category, "yellow goods," which consists of snack foods, beer, alcohol, and tobacco, humor is justified by Starch scores in magazine research. In two categories, "white" and "red goods," the effects of humor are mixed. In one category there is a positive impact on attention, but a negative impact upon the association of the advertisement and the brand. The authors conclude:

While humor may make ads funnier and more enjoyable, it is clear that it is by no means a guarantee for more effective ads. This research sheds considerable light upon the issue of the usage and impact of humor when compared across different media and product groupings. While there are patterns in the use of humor across media, the impact is by no means uniform. Of course, much more needs to be done to examine other objectives beyond attention and comprehension that might be the goal of a humor based campaign. Again, no golden rules are provided here but perhaps a clearer map to finding some of the truffles in the oak forest.

It might be added that MacLean (1990) in an examination of the neural substrates of motivation and emotion, noted that attempts to localize the origin of play and laughter (and crying) in the brain, particularly in the prefrontal lobes, have not been decisive. MacLean adopts Koestler's (1964) definition of the origin of humor as "perceiving a situation or event in two habitually incompatible associative contexts." In our own paradigm, the two incompatible contexts would be sexual survival and spiritual survival, and in fact most jokes usually include these two "incompatible" spheres within a single context. However, since the neural substrates of laughter have not been identified or precisely distinguished, this only intensifies the confusion regarding the role of humor in advertising.

Research that has been carried out by us on the unconscious, which goes beyond attention and recall, adds some light to the subject of memorable advertising. The use of humor and comedy is seductive and alluring, but humor in itself may not be the key. Instead, the key to understanding these ads may be in two very important psychological methods.

Let us return to the examples of the Federal Express video spots. An analysis of all the Federal Express spots, ranging from 1971 to 1992, indicates that each spot fell within either one of two psychological categories: (1) absurdities; or (2) personalizations.

Creativity is usually defined as the combination of two divergent ideas melding into one. This is where humor comes from. A simple example of visual creativity would be the award-winning (local) television spot that showed a close-up of ice cream being scooped out of a half-gallon container in a background setting of classical music. There was no voice-over or audio, simply the classical music. A visual and the music were brought together, neither of which had ever been associated with the other. Many awards were captured for this spot. This is what is called "unique" or creative.

An absurdity is a variation of what we have defined as creativity. An absurdity is where a visual, in print or on television, departs *very slightly* from ordinary, everyday reality. Remember, the right brain "thinks" in pictures and then encodes what it sees into long-term memory.

A personalization is a message—verbal, visual, or both—with which a person identifies and takes very personally. A very simple example of a personalization would be a greeting card with a personal message. Personalizations are much stronger and more motivating than absurdities, since absurdities only promote recall and are not meant to inspire motivation. Personalizations, which are much more motivating and persuasive than absurdities, are for the most part based upon the motives that were introduced in chapter 4. Personalizations are covered in detail in chapter 6.

Advertising and marketing are memorable if they consist of either absurdities or personalizations. Hence, our discussion of absurdities will examine the second dimension of advertising and marketing–memory and recall (chapter 2). Although absurdities are memorable, they are not necessarily motivational or persuasive or associated with one of the motivational levels.

CUTTING THROUGH THE VISUAL AND VERBAL CLUTTER

The average family unit has access to 36 television channels and receives over 2.1 magazines in the home each month. This causes visual clutter. To make the marketing message unique and memorable, it must stand out from the noise.

The role of clutter, like the role of humor, is equivocal. For example, Brown and Rothschild (1993) conducted experiments that looked at the impact of clutter on recognition, aided recall, and unaided recall. Their results suggest that clutter may not inhibit recall. On the other hand, Kent (1995) examined a number of different causes of competitive clutter and found that, for the most part, they consisted of variables that were not under the advertiser's control. However, Kent concluded that clutter presented further opportunities for creative execution, research effectiveness, targeting, and planning to increase the effectiveness of advertising in competitive situations. The use of absurdities (and personalizations) may do just that.

There are two rules regarding absurdities:

1. An absurdity is a *slight* departure from reality, with the emphasis on slight. This means that the message cannot be totally or almost totally obscured in a surrealistic, abstract production that obscures reality.
2. An absurdity must be product related from a rational or logical point of view.

In the following examples from Federal Express, a new concept, overnight delivery, is being presented. The concept is one that is now taken for granted. The idea was that Federal Express could pick up your package and have it wherever you wanted it to be on the next business day. Some of the absurdities that were presented, along with their corresponding rational messages, are seen in table 5-1.

Table 5-1
Absurdities

Message	Visual Absurdity	Rational Message
Did you know that FedEx comes to your office and picks up your package?	Truck driving through office suite and executive handing driver a package	Convenience
Did you know that in order to get Federal Express, all you have to do is pick up the phone?	Man picks up a complete telephone booth off of the street	Convenience
Calling Federal Express is so simple, even a chairman of the board can do it.	Elderly chairman of board tries to call Federal Express, but forgets part of who he is calling and requires secretarial assistance.	Simplification
There is a paper explosion.	Flood of paper coming down the hall	Simplification
In this fast-moving, high pressure, get-it-done yesterday world, aren't you glad there's a company that can keep up with it?	Fast-talking man	Simplification Job security
Calling Federal Express is so simple you can do it in your sleep.	Sleeping man picks up entire phone and puts to ear	Simplicity Convenience

   The Energizer Rabbit represents an absurdity since the rabbit appears in settings where it would be most unlikely to see him. But the rational message is always attached to the voice-over: "Just keeps going and going and going ..." The message is durability. The GMC pickup, which is thrown off a bridge, is an absurdity, since that is something that is not ordinarily seen in everyday life. But the rational message comes through: durability and toughness, which in focus groups is what truck buyers *say* that they want. Some additional absurdities that will help to illustrate this concept are presented in table 5-2.

   In each case, there is a rational message that is attached to the absurdity.

   One campaign that has been observed consisted of absurdities with no rational message attached. The campaign was for Cruisers, Inc., a boat builder of small yachts of 26 to 36 feet. The yachts were seen sitting on top of buildings, in the Mohave Desert, on an interstate highway, and in other unusual and absurd locations. The problem was that the boats were removed from the water—too much of an absurdity for the prospective buyer. It approached the surrealistic. One thing a boat buyer wants is to be near the water. Although the results of this campaign are not known, the company's approach to selling boats has changed.

   An excellent example of a print ad that made use of absurdities in 1984 was an ad for Onan, a manufacturer of small gas and diesel generators for use in motor homes and yachts. It pictured a man relaxing in a deck chair on a homemade raft, with his feet propped up. There was no wind, but there was a makeshift sail at-

Table 5-2
Additional Absurdities

Message	Visual Absurdity	Rational Message
Animal talking about his pet food	Animal talking	Taste
Cheer has amazing capacity to get clothes clean	Actor washing soiled fabric in glass beaker	Cleansing Power
Dodge builds tough trucks	Dodge pickup being dropped from sky onto platform	Durability Toughness
Don't just ask for a Lite	Customer orders a Lite and bartender gives him a lamp	Brand identity
Campbell's soup melts away the cold	Snowman eating Campbell's soup and melting while he eats it	Soup is seasonal food

Figure 5-1
Onan Absurdity

(Used with permission of Onan Corporation)

tached to the raft. The sail derived its wind from a very large fan, the type that may be used in an office or attic. The fan in turn derived its power from the Onan generator. The rational message, which could be stated without words, was the portable power is available anywhere in the form of an Onan generator and it is quiet and convenient.

From time to time ads are produced that encapsulate the best of both absurdities and personalizations. The Michelin baby in the tire is representative of this growing and powerful category in advertising. Not only is a baby riding in a tire an absurdity, but it is a personalization simply because everyone personalizes babies. This is a given and is almost automatic in advertising. The insertion of a baby or puppy into an ad will get the audience's attention. This is because people personalize, and it is in this particular spot that these two powerful mnemonic methods—absurdities and personalizations—come together.

Another example of personalizations and absurdities coming together is a print ad for Compaq Computers, where the screen and the CPU are detached from the keyboard. A woman is sitting on a couch with the computer strung out beside her. The caption is "its attitude is . . . so detached." In this case personal characteristics are being assigned to an inanimate object, assisting and aiding the reader in personalizing and thus recalling the ad.

Not only is there visual clutter in television commercials, but magazines are also visually cluttered. This is why the marketer needs something unique to make the product stand out. Since television programming is, for the most part, reality based, advertising that is also reality based will just blend in with the programming. Hence, the need for absurdities.

Some products cannot make extensive use of absurdities. These are usually products that are associated with spiritual or physical survival, such as diamonds, professional services, health-care products and services, and products that people take more seriously in their lives.

WHY ABSURDITIES WILL GUARANTEE MEMORABLE ADVERTISING

Anyone who has lived through a highly emotional experience will undoubtedly recall that experience, vividly, for the rest of his/her life. This is why experiences such as rape, incest, surgical procedures, deaths, or even embarrassing moments are easily recalled and never forgotten. They reside in long-term memory but are easily and readily recalled into recent, conscious memory. Similarly, experiences that impact the entire nation and have an emotional effect upon the individual are easily recalled into conscious memory. For example, most people (old enough to remember) can recall, vividly, where they were, who they were with, and what they were doing:

- the day that Martin Luther King was assassinated
- the day that John F. Kennedy was assassinated
- the day that Richard Nixon resigned the presidency
- the day that Ronald Reagan was shot

Events such as these, and others that are more personal in nature, have a permanent and lasting impact. The reason for this is the way the brain—particularly the limbic system—derives information and generates emotion in the interest of self-preservation, survival, and preservation of the species. According to MacLean (1990), nowhere is this function seen more clearly than in epileptic seizures that result from a scarring of the limbic cortex:

Clinical findings provide the best evidence that the limbic system is involved in emotional behavior and, indeed, the only evidence that it underlies the subjective experience of emotion. Scarring of the limbic cortex from whatever cause may result in epileptic storms in which the mind lights up with vivid emotional feelings that, in one case or another, involve affects ranging from intense fear to ecstasy. As will be discussed, these affects not only play a basic role in guiding behavior, but are also essential for a sense of personal identity and reality that have far-reaching implications for ontology and epistemology. A consideration of underlying neural mechanisms leads to the question as to whether or not we, as intellectual beings, are forever faced with a delusional impasse. (pp. 247-48)

An absurdity, such as the Onan generator print ad that was described earlier and shown above, or any of the Federal Express advertisements that we have classified as absurdities, creates an immediate aberration that is outside the realm of ordinary, day-to-day experience. This aberration or absurdity is immediately noticed by the brain. This is the function of the limbic system, which sends out an alert when encountering new or unusual material. A signal is sent out, a signal that tells the organism to take immediate notice, since this is something different and unusual. This behavior is seen in most mammals, as when the dog immediately raises his ears into an alert position at the sound of an unusual or novel auditory stimulus.

Therefore, when the limbic system sends out this signal to the rest of the brain, the emotion causes the person who is now on an alert status to take immediate notice, just as the dog who raises his ears does. If the aberration is totally absurd and judged to be harmless, then it is dismissed and the person no longer remains on an alert status. He/she ignores it. However, if the absurdity is somehow product related—as in the Onan generator print ad—then the mechanisms of the right side of the brain are immediately motivated to resolve the absurdity and make sense out of it. This is an example of how the right brain and the limbic structures work together: first, the alert; and second, the resolution. When encountering an absurdity, the limbic system sends out the alert, guaranteeing that the ad will be noticed. In advertising, one of two things may occur.

In the case of the Onan absurdity, it was shown to a colleague, who had no interest in or knowledge of recreational generators. He was not into boating or camping. He demonstrated immediate interest and attention (alert), but the right brain was unable to resolve what he saw. The result was confusion. He attempted to explain it on the basis of "Onanism" and one or two other inappropriate explanations. The danger in using absurdities is that if they cannot be resolved by the right hemisphere, they may create confusion and even hostility. The right brain must be capable of effecting the resolution, and this is why the absurdity must be product related.

However—and this is the second occurrence—the Onan ad was run in a magazine called *Motor Boating and Sailing*. One might assume that the readers of this magazine were intimately familiar with the Onan, a leading brand of recreational generators. Hence, the absurdity would be easily resolved by the readers of this particular publication.

The reason that absurdities work, then, is because they will trigger emotion when the limbic structures put the brain on alert to something unusual or something different, an aberration or irregularity. This emotion will then either be resolved (in the case of product identification with the absurdity) or it will be dismissed (in the case of disorganization and confusion).

USING DISCRETION AND GOOD JUDGMENT WITH THE USE OF ABSURDITIES

An absurdity is used to overcome clutter, to stand out in an overcrowded marketplace and improve recall. But this can be overdone.

With the recent proliferation of PC programs for morphs, wipes, fades, etc., it has become easier to create absurdities, to the point where a large number of advertising spots could appear on the scene as they are written and produced. But just using these programs is not enough. The absurdity needs to be tied to a reality-based message. It needs to be reality based itself, and not a total departure from what is seen in everyday reality. Remember the importance of the Orientation Motive, which allows the person to see things clearly and as they really are. This is usually referred to as "reality testing." The absurdity is useful because it improves recall and is retained in long-term memory. But even more effective and powerful is the personalization, a spot that can be taken personally and with which the consumer can identify with his/her own real-life situation. It is very likely that the personalization will never be forgotten, which explains the 50-year ad recall that was discussed in chapter 1.

REFERENCES

Brown, T. J., & Rothschild, M. L. (1993). Reassessing the impact of television advertising clutter. *Journal of Consumer Research, 20* (1), 138–47.

Childers, T., & Jass, J. (1995, June 14). *Relational violations on the processing of print advertisements*. Paper presented at Association for Consumer Research-European Conference, Copenhagen, Denmark.

Federal Express, 1971-1992 (Advertising video) (1993). Memphis, TN: Federal Express Corporation.

Hopkins, C. (1966). *Scientific advertising*. Chicago: Advertising Publications, Inc. (1923; reprint).

Kent, R. J. (1995). Competitive clutter in network television advertising: Current levels and advertiser responses. *Journal of Advertising Research*, 49–57.

Koestler, A. (1964). *The act of creation*. New York: Macmillan Co.

MacLean, P. D. (1990). *The triune brain in evolution: Role of paleocerebral functions*. New York: Plenum Press.

Madden, T. J., & Weinberger, M. G. (1984). Humor in advertising: A practitioner view. *Journal of Advertising Research*, *24* (4), 23–29.

Ogilvy, D., & Raphaelson, J. (1982). Research on advertising techniques that work and don't work. *Harvard Business Review*, *60* (4), 14–16.

Percy, L., & Rossiter, J. R. (1992). A model of brand awareness and brand attitude advertising strategies. In *Psychology and Marketing* (Vol. 9, no. 4). New York: John Wiley & Sons.

Sternthal, B., & Craig, S. (1973). Humor in advertising. *Journal of Marketing*, 37 (4), 12–18.

Stewart, D. M., and Furse, D. H. (1986). *Effective television advertising*. Lexington, MA: D. C. Heath and Co.

Weinberger, M., Spotts, H., Campbell, L., & Parsons, A. (1995). The use and effect of humor in different advertising media. *Journal of Advertising Research*, *24*, 44–55.

6

Personalizations

WHEN CONSUMERS TAKE THINGS PERSONALLY

In chapter 4, a personalization was exemplified by a greeting card. This brief definition describes the way a consumer reacts to an ad when it is personalized. It speaks directly to his/her situation. This is not unlike the man who goes to church for the first time in years, listens to the sermon, and on the way out says, "Preacher, I believe that today you were talking directly to me."

A personalization is a more powerful form of advertising than an absurdity, because it speaks directly to one or more of the 11 motivational levels that are present in all humans and that were described in chapter 4. The ways to design a personalized ad or marketing campaign is to speak directly to one or more of these motivations, and then tie this personalization to a rational message regarding a specific product or service. Some examples are shown in table 6-1.

A personalization is a powerful mnemonic and a motivator because it is aimed directly at one of the Silent Side motivational levels introduced and discussed in chapter 4. This is why people take it personally, why it is remembered, and why it works so well.

An article appearing in *USA Today* on October 27, 1992, was entitled "Amex goes back to Ogilvy." Although there may be many reasons why this split occurred, the text of the article implies that the major problem with the new agency, Chiat/Day/Mojo, was the creation of absurdities after Amex had already been using personalizations. Amex chose to go back to its old agency, Ogilvy & Mather, which had used personalizations. Personalizations are always more effective than absurdities. Chiat had developed an absurdity, a large, green credit card popping up on a golf course or on the tail of the Concorde. Ogilvy & Mather had developed

Table 6-1
Personalizations

Product	Spot	Personalization	Motivational Level
Federal Express	Annual board meeting	Fear of failure	Territorial Survival
	"Everyone did a good job except Collier who didn't get the package there."	Security Fear of being singled out	
	"If the package does not get here by tomorrow, I'm out of business." Uses Dingbat Air Express and bldg. goes out of business.	Fear of failure Security	Spiritual Survival Territorial Survival
Quaker Oats	"It's the right thing to do."	Family values	Spiritual Survival
Taster's Choice (Series)	Neighbor goes next door to borrow coffee, gets love	Love	Spiritual Survival
DeBeers	"A diamond is forever"	Permanence	Spiritual Survival
Huggies	Babies dancing around in diapers	Love (babies)	Spiritual Survival
Avis	"We try harder."	Second best	Territorial Survival
Cadillac	Achieving a higher standard	Perfection	Spiritual Survival
Dupont stain-master carpet	Child spills everything all over the carpet	Disruption of the home (nesting)	Territorial Survival
Michelin tires	"What's riding on your tires?"	Family values Safety	Spiritual Survival Physical Survival

Table 6-1
Personalizations (cont'd.)

Product	Spot	Personalization	Motivational Level
American Express	Couple dining in a fine upscale French restaurant	Change of place Change of circumstances	OR: Place OR: Circumstances
L'Oréal (feminine)	"It costs more, but I'm worth it."	Gender	Sexual Survival
Diabetes clinic	"Give diabetes an inch and it will take a foot."	Injury Fear of loss of limb	Physical Survival

personalizations, featuring well-known executives in "portraits" (magazine ads) and "Do you know me?" (TV spots), illustrating the Adaptation Motive. Amex chose to go back to these more effective personalizations and move away from the absurdities that were used for less than one year.

A testimonial is a form of personalization, and is aimed primarily at the Adaptation Motive. The spokesperson says, "I do it, and I am somebody, so why don't you do it too?" The consumer personalizes it, because he/she wants to be like the spokesperson. The reason that personalizations are more effective than absurdities is because they are aimed directly at the consumer motives described in chapter 4 and at the emotion that arises from those motives, as seen in table 6-1. Anything associated with emotion will always be remembered.

WHAT DO PEOPLE PERSONALIZE?

What do people personalize from a psychological point of view? The list could be quite long, but the following are some suggestions. First are the things that people personalize from a *negative* perspective:

The fear of being discovered
The fear of being singled out for criticism
The fear of looking stupid
The fear of loss of control
The fear of loss of orientation
The fear of losing or loss
The fear of being wrong
The fear of getting fired (insecurity)
Loss of security (home, income, work)
Fear of attack
Loss of love
Fear of unpleasant situations

Fear of conflict
Worry
Anxiety
Fear of losing power
Being put on hold
Being treated discourteously
Being belittled
Fear of damage (life, limb, personal property)
Fear of illness
Loss of potency (sexual-men)
Loss of control (sexual-women)
Fear of being obnoxious
Fear of authority
Separation
Fear of gaining weight
Shame
Anger

People also personalize from a *positive* perspective:

Love
Security
Babies
Animals, especially puppies and kittens
Food
Power
Potency
Acceptance
Special recognition (positive)
Marriage and weddings
Cures (for disease)
Sacrifice
Disaster assistance
Achievement
Autonomy
Reunion

Of course these lists are not all inclusive, but they do give the reader some indication of the kinds of things that people personalize.

PUTTING THE FORMULA TO WORK

A formula is evolving for effective, memorable, and motivating advertising and marketing. The formula makes use of mnemonics, rationalizations, and emotions to create an effective campaign. In order to demonstrate it further, a few hypothetical spots, designed around the primary concepts of motivation and emo-

Table 6-2
Sample Marketing Strategies Created with Personalizations

Product	Scene	Motivational Level
Makeup/cosmetics	A woman on a desert island or in a distant land	OR: Person OR: Place
Restaurant	A man and woman in an upscale restaurant being waited on by a very attentive staff	OR: Person Spiritual Survival
Insurance	An insurance company assisting people who have just been through a natural disaster	Physical Survival
Telephone and communications co.	A telephone/communications company provides some of its executives to assist displaced executives in getting new jobs	Territorial Survival OR: Person Physical Survival
Health/home gym equipment	A weak, ineffective man becomes strong and muscular and ends up with a beautiful girlfriend	Sexual Survival (gender)

tion, are sketched out as examples in table 6-2.

A PRESIDENT USES PERSONALIZATIONS TO GET ELECTED

On Monday, November 3, 1992, Bill Clinton, governor of Arkansas, carved his way into the annals of U.S. history by being elected president. Although there were many factors involved in his election, a key factor was the highly personalized autobiography, which concentrated on his childhood in the tiny town of Hope, Arkansas, shown on the night before his election. With the assistance of experienced Hollywood producers and choreographers, a documentary was produced. Watching the documentary allowed the viewer to personalize:

The early death of his father
The struggle of his mother in making a living for the family

Growing up without a father
Small-town boy becomes president (American Dream)
Family values
Displacement (from mother while she was getting education)
Patriotism

The whole documentary was directed at an emotional (spiritual) rather than political or intellectual level. There was not one point at which the documentary asked for a vote. It simply immersed its audience in emotion and motivation, mostly at the spiritual level.

This classic documentary was positioned in such a way that campaign rhetoric and logic was ignored. It focused on Clinton: the boy, the man, and his lifelong dream of serving his country. It was a one-hour presentation that tapped into about every personal emotion and motive of those who were watching.

RESULTS

Three-dimensional advertising and marketing goes well beyond the singular rationalizations of a left brain approach. In the left brain approach, nothing really stands out as unique. Banks can talk about convenience; beer, about taste; casinos, about luck; automobiles, about comfort, stability, and economy; food chains, about price; politicians, about no taxes and more benefits. But three-dimensional advertising will find the unique position for every single product and service, because the search is initiated at the emotional level of the consumer.

The benefits of focusing upon consumer motivation through personalizations assist not only the marketer but the consumer as well. This approach to advertising will do all of these things, and more:

- Shape consumer attitudes about the product or service
- Develop alternative positioning strategies
- Uncover user wants, needs, motivations
- Compare motivations of heavy users, light users, and nonusers
- Rank attributes
- Uncover motivation to use the product or service in different types of users
- Develop ad copy
- Develop an overall marketing plan
- Uncover perception in users, light users, and nonusers
- Establish brand loyalty and recognition
- Increase response to advertising
- Analyze emotions and motivations so that the advertising and marketing attempts may target them
- Establish advertising and marketing strategies
- Develop employee hiring and training strategies
- Create interior and exterior decor
- Integrate the emotional, the rational, and the mnemonic (recall)

- Improve ambience
- Change design
- Analyze product and service resistance

CONCLUSION

Advertising that allows people to personalize what they have seen will be the most powerful advertising of all. For this reason, the hierarchy of motives that is presented in chapter 4 is considered the base or foundation for effective advertising through personalization. This is because what motivates people is also what they personalize. As Krugman (1994) stated in his article, consumer psychology is the study of what people like and what they do not like. So we begin with what people personalize, and then go from there.

Most marketers know that you cannot hit a home run every time. In fact, many marketers believe that you are lucky if you hit a home run one time in your career. Could this be because most advertising is more often a trial-and-error approach than scientific methodology? The motivational hierarchy presented in chapter 4 moves away from trial and error and guesswork and closer to precision, by concentrating on what people personalize. The marketer should focus on what the consumer likes and dislikes.

REFERENCES

Krugman, H. E. (1994). Pavlov's dog and the future of consumer psychology. *Journal of Advertising Research, 34* (6), 67–71.

Moore, M. T. (1992, October 27). Amex goes back to Ogilvy. *USA Today*, p. 5.

7

Motives and Emotions, Features and Benefits

HOW MOTIVES, FEATURES, AND BENEFITS INTERACT

Almost everyone is familiar with the feature and benefit aspects of products and services. The problem is that many advertisers expound on the features of their products and overlook the benefits to the consumer, who is the person that is going to make the final decision. This is a natural tendency, primarily because the benefits are often difficult to define.

Since benefits are directly tied to motives, the Silent Side of advertising and marketing clearly defines the need to address benefits to the consumer so that these may be incorporated into an overall marketing plan. When this happens, new features can become part of the product and product advertising. Also, advertising and sales may focus on what is really important to the consumer, as opposed to what is important to the marketer.

The results of qualitative studies demonstrate the direct relationship that exists between motives and benefits. The motives that were described in chapter 4 are common to all consumers, regardless of the product category. These motives were uncovered during 15 years of qualitative and quantitative research. Not all products contain all of the motives that were described in chapter 4. Conversely, we have never investigated a product where at least two of the motives were not present; and we have never found a motive outside of the 11 that have been covered. On the other hand, the benefits are product specific. There will always be a specific set of benefits that is tied to each product or service, and it will vary depending upon the product or service. Furthermore, it will be tied directly to a product feature, which is to be expected. When this happens, the marketer may focus on consumer benefits and motives rather than product features.

THE ROLE OF MOTIVES, EMOTIONS, AND BENEFITS
IN THE LARGE APPLIANCE MARKET

The first example comes from interviews regarding consumer attitudes toward purchasing large appliances. These purchases consisted primarily of refrigerators, but included consumers who had purchased ranges, stoves, dishwashers, and laundry appliances. Fifty consumers were interviewed in (1) in-depth motivational interviews; (2) focus groups; and (3) quantitative surveys of emotional demographics. Subjects for this study consisted of both men and women who had recently purchased a home (within one year) and were shopping for or had purchased kitchen or laundry appliances. All the data were analyzed together and separately, and a few of the results are presented here.

Spiritual Survival

When consumers (primarily women) said that they wanted a lot of space inside the refrigerator, it became obvious that they were buying not only with the immediate family in mind but with reference to potential gatherings of family and friends. In many cases the buyers were "empty nesters," whose husbands could not understand the need for a very large box, since the family had all moved out and there were only the two of them left at home. These family gatherings may only occur once or twice a year, but because of the spiritual nature of such an occurrence (family, love, being together, holiday celebrations, etc.) they held a position of primary importance. When a woman shopped for a large kitchen appliance, this was the highest priority for her: the opportunity to prepare food for large family gatherings and to serve it fresh and cold (or hot). The motive is spiritual survival, and the element is family values. Motivational elements are closely aligned to consumer benefits in all products.

Physical Survival

It is not surprising that most of the data from these studies came from the motive of physical survival. Since kitchen appliances involve the storage and preparation of food, physical survival should be rather obvious. As the reader can see in table 7-1, the benefits that are directly connected with the Physical Survival Motive involve cleanliness, sanitation, freshness, security, and safety. Keeping food at a temperature and at a level of freshness that is fit to eat involves security and safety. Product features such as lights, thermometers, heavy-duty compressors, freshness devices, and other important product attributes can be designed to appeal to the Physical Survival Motive and consumer benefits.

Table 7-1
Motives and Elements, Features and Benefits Expressed by Consumers in a Large Appliance Study: Refrigerators

MOTIVES	FEATURES	ELEMENTS	BENEFITS
OR: CIRCUM-STANCES	• Fits in space • Frost free-easy maintenance • Price	Practical Pace (of life) Affordable	Basic require-ment Time saver Cost
OR: TIME	• Savings, sales, discounts	Urgency/timing	Save money
SPIRITUAL SURVIVAL	• Overall interior space for family dinners, parties, get togethers • Accommodations for children, special shelves, bottle warmers • Thrill of plan-ning, looking, going to stores (husband & wife)	Family values	Family togeth-erness Family needs
PHYSICAL SURVIVAL	• Clean, clear crisper trays • Sprayer in vegetable compartment • Visual checks for freshness • Easy access (men)—no hunt-ing for food • Thermometer • Light in freezer • Light when freezer is on	Food Hunger/food Health	Safety, security Freshness Quick in/quick out Security & safety
TERRITORIAL SURVIVAL	• Controls simp-le and part of decor. "The more controls the more can go wrong."	Organization & control Design & decor Control of the home	Simplicity & appearance Organization

Table 7-1
Motives and Elements, Features and Benefits Expressed by Consumers in a Large Appliance Study: Refrigerators (cont'd.)

MOTIVES	FEATURES	ELEMENTS	BENEFITS
TERRITORIAL SURVIVAL (cont'd.)	• Exterior appearance • Specialized drawers & compartments		
ADAPTATION MOTIVE	• *Consumer Reports* • Sought after brands/high-dollar appliances that everyone wants • Testimonials of credible people	Do like others Status & achievement Follow the leader	Resolve uncertainty & fear of unknown Being a leader Achieve status

Territorial Survival

After talking with women about appliances, it is clear that they know exactly what they want. This is because the home is their territory and the kitchen is the command center. Despite the changes that have occurred in recent years where many women work and men stay home, this scenario still holds for most families. This is why women tend to have more to say than men in the purchase of kitchen appliances.

The command center must be organized. Benefits related to territorial survival involve organization of the home, which in turn may include lots of space, harmonious colors, storage capacity, and overall arrangement and structure. The benefits as they relate to territorial survival in this product category include organization and, in particular, control. Women feel, and rightly so, that the more organization there is the more control they have over their home.

The Adaptation Motive

The Adaptation Motive refers to buying products that other people have bought or recommended. One common source for the Adaptation Motive is *Consumer Reports*, particularly within the appliance product category. Young, first-time home buyers and purchasers of appliances, particularly men, rely heavily upon this source. This is because men do not share the same motives as women when it comes to the purchase of a refrigerator, so they turn to other sources. They know that they are

Table 7-2
Motives and Elements, Features and Benefits Expressed by Consumers in a Large Appliance Study: Ranges and Stoves

MOTIVES	FEATURES	ELEMENTS	BENEFITS
SPIRITUAL SURVIVAL (Love, family values, etc.)	• Large-size ovens for family get togethers and parties • Make stove/ oven with many more features & options—pre- pare more meals for family (oven used to be in center where family gathered)	Family values	Family togeth- erness
PHYSICAL SURVIVAL (Food, air, water, & safety)	• Controls up and away from children	Safety	Avoid injury
TERRITORIAL SURVIVAL (Organization & control in the home)	• Add more features to the oven/range such as toaster ovens, convection, etc., to increase space in kitchen • More options in color choices	Control & organization Kitchen decor	Increase con- trol & capabilities Organization of home
OR: CIRCUM- STANCES	• Self-cleaning & timers • Energy guide	Pace & convenience Smart buyer	Make life simpler Cost of opera- tion
OR: TIME	• Appliance on sale	Budget minded	Initial cost
ADAPTATION MOTIVE (Doing what others do)	• Brand names "high dollar stoves and ranges"	Status	Safety Achievement

not knowledgeable. The use of *Consumer Reports* adds to their belief that they are making this large purchase in a rational and logical manner. The Adaptation Motive also includes word-of-mouth recommendations from friends, testimonials in advertising by credible persons, and the belief that this is a popular brand. The benefits related to adaptation include status, achievement, pride, power, and authority: "I made a good decision." Usually the decision that was made was to follow someone else's lead.

Not all motives are involved in purchasing large appliances. In this study, only four motives were uncovered: spiritual, physical, territorial survival, and adaptation.

THE ROLE OF EMOTIONS AND MOTIVES
IN BEER DRINKING

Studies that have been carried out on beer drinking, particularly with heavy beer drinkers, indicate that it is an emotional activity and as such is associated with a variety of motivations. This observation is intuitive or arises from common sense. For example, one often quoted marketing statistic is that "10 percent of all the beer drinkers drink 90 percent of all of the beer."

A number of studies indicate that the brand of beer that a person drinks is heavily dependent upon the group that he drinks with. In order to become a "member" or to "belong" to that group, he needs to drink a particular brand of beer. Although commitment to this brand is a necessary prerequisite for group membership, it is not sufficient. There are other factors, primarily socioeconomic, psychographic, and demographic, that will also be factored into the group's decision to admit a new member and include him in all their functions.

Silk-screened T-shirts that advertised a particular brand of beer were particularly popular in the mid eighties, when a nationwide controversy ensued following the introduction of Spuds McKenzie, a "Party Animal," by Anheuser-Busch. The controversy occurred in the schools, and centered around whether students should be allowed to wear shirts that advertised beer to school. Like any controversy, publicity brought brand recognition. In most schools the T-shirts were banned, but the controversy increased brand recognition, awareness, and demand, particularly among younger beer drinkers.

The primary motive for the onset of moderate-to-heavy beer drinking is the Adaptation Motive. Conversely, the continuation of beer drinking is dependent on two other motives: physical survival (addiction) and/or OR: Person. This is not to say that adaptation does not continue to be a viable motivation throughout a person's beer-drinking career. It does, but it is often secondary or tertiary to OR: Person and physical survival.

A summary of motives, features, and benefits associated with moderate-to-heavy beer drinking is shown in table 7-3.

Table 7-3
Motives and Elements, Features and Benefits Expressed by Consumers in Research on Beer Drinking

MOTIVES	FEATURES	ELEMENTS	BENEFITS
RATIONAL, LOGICAL	• Cool, cold, refreshing • Taste	Thirst Taste	Relief on hot day (+)* Reason for drinking (+)
OR: PERSON (Temporary re-orientation in identity; escape)	• Brand image and position (of brand)	Self-esteem Self-image	Temporarily become new person; person I want to be (+)
TERRITORIAL SURVIVAL (Claiming one's rightful territory)	• Beer-drinking commercials emphasize establishing ones-self in a rightful place • Rugged individualism • Accomplishments	Competition	Ownership (+) American Dream (+) Belonging (+) Ability to dominate, control (+) Feel like "somebody" Identity–who I am (+)
PHYSICAL SURVIVAL (Whatever is necessary for physical survival)	• Not a feature (not advertised) (This could be a reason why actors cannot drink beer on television)	Thirst Physiological requirements	Satisfies addiction & craving (-)
OR: CIRCUM-STANCES (Temporary escape from stress, pressure, realities of everyday life)	• Escape • Relief	Pace	Temporary relief (+) Lack of commitment Escape, alleviation, cure, assuagement (+)
OR: TIME (Temporary loss of accountability to time)	• Removal from time • Positioned in former time	Pressure of time, deadlines, accountability	Escape from liability, accountability, reliability (+)

Table 7-3,
Motives and Elements, Features and Benefits Expressed by Consumers in Research on Beer Drinking (cont'd.)

MOTIVES	FEATURES	ELEMENTS	BENEFITS
ADAPTATION (Being part of an identifiable group)	• Being a part of a group • Belonging, conforming • Membership • Acceptance • Special group • Companionship	Follow leader Be like others Values Belonging (+)	Acceptance Personal identity (+) Establish and maintain belief system Establish oneself (+) Increase self-esteem (+) Self-image (+)
SEXUAL SURVIVAL (Gender, inhibition or impulse)	• Heavy, dark ingredients • Volume consumed • Brand image	Gender Impulse	Masculinity (+) Allows beer drinker to assume special powers (+) Strength, authority, masculinity (+)
OR: PLACE	• Place where beer is consumed	Where	Identity, escape (+)

*Designates positive and negative benefits

The problem of addiction is related to physical survival. For the heavy beer drinker, either physical or psychological reasons lead him to feel compelled to continue once he begins to drink. Research is now underway in the etiology of addiction, and recent findings point to the importance of physiological or genetic causes over psychological causes. But the jury is still out. In the meantime, for the heavy beer drinker's family, his employer, and others, addiction is a strongly negative benefit. But it needs to be included in this analysis since it is one of the "benefit's components" of beer drinking, albeit a negative one.

Territorial survival, sexual survival (gender and impulse), and adaptation are three motives that are very strong in heavy beer drinkers. Their beer and the identification of "their brand" is extremely important. Wearing T-shirts and having memorabilia with their brand on it serves the same purpose as souvenirs from a theme park: they extend and prolong the experience that is associated with beer drinking when, for whatever reason, the beer is not available.

The "experience" relates to the Orientation Motives (person, place, time, and circumstances), which aside from addiction are the primary motivations associated with this activity. These relate to the beer drinker's personal experiences when he drinks, which in turn motivate him. Some brands have emphasized the place where the beer is brewed or produced, but in our research this did not appear to have a very important effect. This is because the activity itself is personalized, which means that it makes little if any difference to the beer drinker where the beer is brewed.

Heavy beer drinking is strongly appealing to men and is much more infrequent in women, hence, the "sexist" references in this section where the only personal pronoun used is "his." This is because of the influence of the sexual survival or "macho" motive (gender), which also plays a very strong role in heavy beer drinking.

DUCK HUNTING

Duck hunting is another emotionally charged activity that for at least a small group of sportsmen, has shifted from the territorial to the spiritual realm. This is another way of saying that it has taken on life-size proportions, that it dominates their lives and is something that they live for all year long.

The whole activity of hunting was the original Territorial Survival Motive, as described by Morris (1967) in his book, *The Naked Ape*. Predating the agricultural and industrial ages, the thing that made a man a man was his ability to hunt. In primitive societies, a man's entire self-worth and value were judged by his ability to hunt, fish, and bring home food. Nowhere is this more clearly depicted than in Michener's book *Alaska* (1988), where the author describes what happened to men who were poor hunters or who interfered with others' ability to hunt and fish.

The remnants of the Territorial Survival Motive still exist today: in careers, in business, and in the home. It is seen every day in terms of the emotions that are associated with competition. But nowhere is the strength of this motive more clearly seen than in hunting, where a man still has the opportunity to "prove himself." This is the basic explanation for "fish stories"—the size of the one that "got away." It stems from the past, when hunting and fishing were a life and death endeavor, not just a pastime.

SUMMARY AND CONCLUSION

Duck hunting and beer drinking are unusually strong emotional activities with definitive benefits, corresponding product features, and concurrent motivations. They are recreational activities. Both are gender-related (sexual) activities in that they both appeal either to male or female, with some crossover, but very little

Table 7-4
Motives and Elements, Features and Benefits Expressed by Duck Hunters

MOTIVES	FEATURES	ELEMENTS	BENEFITS
SPIRITUAL SURVIVAL (Right/wrong, membership, inner peace, etc.)	• Isolated, quiet, & tranquil surroundings	Inner peace	Find inner peace (+)*
TERRITORIAL SURVIVAL	• Accuracy (of ammunition) • Bag limit	Competition	Feel portentous, prominent, competitive (+)
OR: PERSON (Temporary reorientation & identity)	• Primitive living • Back to basics • Unique activity • Special kind of person	Identity Independence Mastery over nature Confirms character (+)	Increase in self-assurance, self-sufficiency, & self-identity Self-esteem (+) Confirms identity as a special kind of a man (a provider) (+)
OR: TIME (Temporary escape from pressures of time)	• Escape from time • Total concentration	Deadlines Urgency Removal from time	Mastery over time (+) Relief from pressure (+) Lack of awareness of passing time (+)
OR: PLACE (Temporary escape to a different kind of place)	• Primitive living • Away from home • Challenging conditions	Mastery over nature Novelty & challenge	Escape from the ordinary Proof of independence & self-sufficiency (+) Ability, strength, fortitude, durability, endurance (+)

Table 7-4
Motives and Elements, Features and Benefits Expressed by Duck Hunters (cont'd.)

MOTIVES	FEATURES	ELEMENTS	BENEFITS
SEXUAL **SURVIVAL** (Gender, impulse, inhibition)	• Masculine activity (with strong roots in tradition, gene- tics, & history) • Difficult con- ditions	Gender	Proof of endur- ance, grit, ingenuity, forbearance, & strength (+) Stamina & strength (+)
ADAPTATION ("One of the boys")	• Elite group • "Men only"	Membership	Membership, belonging, fraternity (+) Stamina & strength (+)

*Designates positive and negative benefits

(<1%). Both of them are what most people would consider highly emotional activities.

   Because these activities are so highly emotional they are used here to illustrate
the principles of marketing to the mind. At a later point in the book (chapter 22)
other activities will be analyzed that are usually not considered to be emotional:
banking, printing and office services, and overnight delivery services. At that
point it will be shown that there is emotional activity in *all* consumer activities,
and that the marketer who captures the emotion is on the leading edge of his/her
profession.

REFERENCES

Michener, J. A. (1988). *Alaska: A novel*. New York: Random House.
Morris, D. (1967). *The naked ape: A zoologist's study of the human animal*. New York:
   McGraw Hill.

8

Right Brain Motivational Research

MOTIVATION AND THE MIND

The motivational theories that have been presented here have evolved in work done with consumers. Over 5,000 consumers have been interviewed in over 200 product categories in research settings. The manner in which this research was carried out—using visualization exercises to access the unconscious—is described in this section.

Traditional, academic marketing approaches have not always been that helpful to marketers and advertisers when it comes to uncovering emotional approaches to consumer decision making. This is because the dominant approaches to motivation today rely heavily upon rational and logical thought processes. If the marketer relies upon the traditional marketing approaches for guidance, he/she will not go far beyond customary explanations that consumers routinely give about price, taste, cleanliness, convenience, values, etc.

Marketing to the mind deals in primary, not secondary, motivation, so that the concerns that are addressed are more relevant and pertinent to the questions, "What motivates consumers?" "What initiates action?" Marketing to the mind addresses the question of why consumers do what they do and it explains behavior. Traditional marketing research addresses the question of what consumers do and it describes what they do. Marketing to the mind is explanatory whereas the traditional approach is descriptive. But instead of working against each other, they complement one another and work together, which will be seen in this chapter.

RESEARCHING THE UNCONSCIOUS MIND

Ever since Freud introduced the unconscious in 1915, there have been very few attempts to define it more specifically and scientifically. Instead, the major thrust in psychology has been on learning and learning theory. Many psychologists reject the notion of an unconscious and instead carry out research on behavior (external), which is more observable and measurable. The unconscious, in which there is a lot of information on motivation and emotion, is often overlooked. This is a major oversight and gap for many professionals, especially for professionals who work with emotions and with motivation such as creative directors, school teachers, police officers, attorneys, marketers, and sales persons.

The unconscious mind does not lend itself to research, since the constructs and concepts have not been well defined. What is presented here is the research method that led to the definition of motivation in consumer behavior that was described in chapter 4. Using visualization methods, much unconscious data is uncovered and thus can be used in a motivational context.

The definitions of motivation have already been dealt with in detail in chapter 4, with applications outlined in chapters 5 and 6. It is now important to measure these constructs and subject them to further methods of investigation. This procedure then transcends very quickly into the area of quantitative measurement, which in turn yields a new area within market research: emotional demographics, or *motigraphics*.

The research methods that were used in these Silent Side investigations involved two separate phases:

1.   In-depth "visualization" interviews, that gather motivational information that is related to product motives, emotions, features, and benefits.
2.   Broad-based quantitative studies using large samples, in which motivational information is included in traditional market research so that the emotional demographics can be analyzed. This phase uses large samples for purposes of generalization to the entire universe.

BACKGROUND: VISUALIZATION IN MARKETING AND ADVERTISING RESEARCH

McLuhan (1951) in his book *The Mechanical Bride* states that the press and advertisers have used visualization to paralyze the mind. As a result, he claims that visualization can be used to energize the mind.

Although we do not believe that advertising paralyzes the mind, we do believe that visualization will energize it. Advertising is, primarily, a visual medium. If anything, advertising can awaken the mind, if done right. But as David Ogilvy warned, "You can't save souls in an empty church" (Ogilvy & Raphaelson, 1982).

There are very few published sources on the use of visualization in consumer research and decision making (Maddock & Fulton, 1995; Rossiter & Percy, 1983).

Rossiter and Percy suggest that measures in research for visually based theory are almost nonexistent, and much more needs to be done. However, visualization has been used very widely in other fields, primarily as an energizer. Adams (1980) discusses the use of visualization in diagramming and plotting various courses of action. Some chess masters visualize their games in their heads, and examples of those who play up to 50 games simultaneously while blindfolded are well known. Successful coaches speak of getting players to visualize plays rather than trying to memorize them. In recent years, some have even used visualization to improve their golf game, since golf, like chess, is a game of concentration (Van Kampen, 1992).

Lewin (1968) gives us an appreciation of the importance of the ability to visualize. He says that the facility of "thinking in pictures" begins very early in life. In fact, in Piagetian research, it originated in the sixth to the eight month, when an infant could "make an interesting sight last." For Piaget, this "object constancy" was the very origin of thinking: the internal representation in the mind of an external object that had disappeared (Piaget, 1971). And for Freud (1953b) "even in those whose memory is not normally of a visual type, the earliest recollections of childhood retain far into life the quality of sensory vividness." Freud also was struck by the ultraclarity (*Uberdeutlichkeit*) of the mental pictures and the sense of reality that they inspired, and said, "they might have been described as hallucinations if a belief in their actual presence had been added to their clearness" (1953a).

THE ROLE OF VISUALIZATION IN CONSUMER RESEARCH

Rossiter and Percy (1980) found that subjects who were presented with a large picture of an advertised product were more persuaded than were subjects who were presented a smaller picture. From their research they have constructed a visually based theory in which advertising serves a reinforcing function. These investigators suggest that a very basic component of consumer decision making is visualization. In this scenario, a consumer generates visual imagery from what he/she has seen in advertising, which is retrieved from short-term memory. The example that they use is that the consumer may see a rugged individualist smoking Camel cigarettes and say (to himself), "Camels are for rugged individuals." This strategy has worked well for Marlboro, where much of the advertising consists of only the single graphic of the Marlboro Man, and no copy other than the surgeon general's warning. Rossiter and Percy conclude that in consumer decision making, "an individual acts not on an abstraction or a concept but rather on some short-term memory representation of the abstraction or concept" (1983, p. 119).

PROCEDURE

To access the right side of the brain, consumers who are interviewed are asked to use their visual mind (versus their thinking mind) throughout the entire interview. These respondents are recruited by field services in accordance with demographic requirements, as in any field study. They are reimbursed for their time, and appointments are made. Alternates ("floaters") are also recruited in case of no-shows.

The interviewers were all trained in in-depth interviewing, especially with reference to the motivational theory that has been outlined in *Marketing to the Mind*. Interviewers were all college graduates, most with master's degrees in psychology, marketing, or a closely related field. These degree requirements are consistent with the need for the interviewer to be able to conceptualize at a fairly high level, to draw together divergent thoughts, and to define underlying areas of motivation. Interviewers also must have a fairly high tolerance for ambiguity, since they know that they will not be given all the answers but instead will be looking for the answers. This is always true when charting a new course.

The interviews are approximately one-hour long. As an introduction, the respondent (consumer) is brought into a room and seated in a reclining chair. If two-way observation or video tapes are to be used, their consent is obtained. They are then asked if they have a photographic memory. Most of them know what is meant by a photographic memory, but usually indicate that they feel that they do not have one. At this point the interviewer explains that, in fact, everyone has a photographic memory but he/she just does not use it on a regular basis. The interviewer then goes on to explain that when a person closes his/her eyes and "pictures" something that happened to him/her, or a place where he/she had been, it is different than "remembering." When asked if they have ever done that, almost all of them nod in the affirmative. The interviewer then explains that this is what is meant by a photographic memory.

The interviewer then takes the respondent through a brief exercise where the subject is asked to close his/her eyes and picture the living room in his/her home, "as if really there." This is a very simple, familiar exercise that introduces the subject to the procedure. Also, since he/she is visualizing a very comfortable and familiar surrounding (den or living room), he/she becomes relaxed and almost immediately drops any defenses. The subject is then asked to "go into some of the other rooms" (of his/her home) to facilitate the exercise. After a few more minutes of description, with the interviewer emphasizing "tell me what you see," the subject is asked to open his/her eyes again. At this point the subject is debriefed and asked how it felt and if he/she was comfortable with the procedure. Subjects almost always answer in the affirmative, and then they are ready to continue with the procedure.

THE IN-DEPTH INTERVIEW IN CONSUMER RESEARCH

The interview procedure that was just described is generally referred to as an in-depth interview or a one-on-one. The major difference in this method from the methods that have been used in traditional market research is visualization. This method is typically used in police interviews, where witnesses are led to recall an accident scene, a license plate number, or to help detectives recover valuable evidence through visualization. In fact, some of our experiences include being called to police stations to help recover evidence from a witness, or even to be present to help substantiate a confession. A crime witness may see a license number in an accident, but be unable to recall the last three numbers on the plate. In most cases when the witness was taken back to the accident scene (in his/her mind) and asked to visualize it, he/she was able to reconstruct what was needed to recover evidence.

Visualization is a right brain exercise. Instead of asking participants to remember, they are simply asked to use their photographic memory, as in visualization. They are generally capable of bringing back an amazing number of details that otherwise would have been overlooked or obscured. In addition, the emotions involved in the purchase decision often come to the surface, as the following examples illustrate:

"When I'm in the casino I feel like a new person. I have a burst of energy. It's just like me all alone, and the slots. I get with one machine and stay with it. It's like there's no one else there—just me and that machine. There's no night and no day, no dinner and no breakfast. It's just me and that machine."

"When I'm standing looking at all those detergents I get confused and frustrated. The prices are all different, but so are the sizes. The colors are all different. I feel just baffled. I need to take this blindfold to the store and just play Blind Man's Bluff. I'd do just as well." (overstimulation)

RECRUITING AND SAMPLES

Initial recruitment selects subjects with reference to demographic considerations, such as age, sex, users, nonusers, etc. The motivational structure of the Silent Side is differentiated and specific enough to flush out differences between these groups. Also, reimbursement varies in accordance with the level of subjects who are being recruited. Physicians, investment bankers, and hospital administrators are at the high end of the compensation scale ($100); fast food users, visitors to Graceland (Elvis Presley's home), and users of various products and services are at the other end ($25–$35).

Because there are only 11 basic motives in the unconscious (2 groups x 4 + 3 = 11), large sample sizes are unnecessary. On the other hand, traditional market research requires large sample sizes because of individual differences. Many subjects have to be recruited to overcome the distribution of traits throughout the population and to account for individual differences. When interviewing on the right side of the brain, motives seem to "float to the surface" of the interview. Consumers talk and visualize in terms of product features, product benefits, and elements, which are quickly and easily translated into motives. Therefore, the in-depth interviewer needs to use a form that includes all the motives and provides a space for features and benefits to be noted. A suggested blank form appears in figure 8-1, but it is better to summarize the content of these interviews in terms of software that is available. This computerized method of "sorting motives" is superior to the form in figure 8-1, and will be discussed at a later point in this chapter.

ANALYSIS OF IN-DEPTH INFORMATION

As consumers talk and "visualize" with their eyes closed, they begin to see what it is like to have a shopping experience for a particular product. They begin to relive the emotions that they have as they go through the experience: energy, expectation, disappointment, confusion and frustration, excitement, enthusiasm, thrill, agitation, annoyance, etc. The in-depth interview is where all these emotions flow to the surface—emotions that are typically overlooked in traditional market research.

In-depth interviews can be carried out on small numbers of respondents, since this phase of the study is for the purpose of hypothesis generating (Percy, 1982). All of the motivational information that is needed can be derived from just a few interviews. When the project enters the second phase, motigraphics, these motives will be confirmed quantitatively. But unlike focus groups, the power of this motivational approach often leads to a plethora of creative recommendations. In addition, the in-depth interviews follow a systematic and purposeful plan or structure, which make them much different, qualitatively, from focus groups and other one-on-one procedures (Percy, 1982).

To summarize, the purpose of the in-depth portion of any project is to get consumers to visualize. When visualization occurs, under the right conditions, the interviewer is, to a large degree, addressing the right side rather than the left side of the brain. Although the respondent is still "thinking," feeling and emotion also occur. A new dimension is added to market research and that dimension is motivation and emotion. This is the third dimension of advertising, sales, and marketing. This is marketing to the mind!

RIGHT BRAIN INTERVIEWING IN MARKET RESEARCH

The mechanics of the "right brain" interview are as follows:

- Visualization
- Relaxation
- Repetition

Figure 8-1
In-depth Interviewer's Format (Condensed)

IN-DEPTH INTERVIEWING FORM

Date : _____

Client:_____Subject:_____

Respondent:_____

MOTIVES	ELEMENTS	BENEFITS (+)	BENEFITS (-)
SPIRITUAL SURVIVAL			
PHYSICAL SURVIVAL			
OR: PERSON			
OR: TIME			
OR: PLACE			
OR: CIRCUM-STANCES			
SEXUAL SURVIVAL			
TERRITORIAL SURVIVAL			
RATIONAL			
EXPECTATION			
ADAPTATION			
PLAY			

Visualization has already been described. When the respondent is asked to visualize what he/she sees, he/she totally concentrates. Furthermore, remote memories are brought into focus. The subject is relaxed with no extraneous or competing stimuli. There is no food, no drink, and nothing to pull his/her attention away from the issue, which is usually the product or service that is being investigated.

In addition, subjects are relaxed. They learn about their photographic memory and how to use it. Often, when researching a theme park or museum or other pleasant experience that they have had, the pleasant experience is re-created. This is because the interviewer continually reminds them that, in their mind's eye, they are really there. We have actually experienced cases where respondents refused to take the honorarium, because they felt so good at the conclusion of the interview. Several said that they should have paid us for the experience!

The third aspect of the right brain interview is repetition. In these types of interviews, there is considerable repetition. The problem with traditional research and focus groups is that the question is only asked one time. For example,

Q: Why don't you read the daily newspaper?

A: I don't have time.

In actual research conducted by several major newspapers, this answer was given over and over again: "I don't have time." It did not occur to the researchers to go beyond this, and so they never received the real answer to the question of why people did not read the paper.

In a deposition an attorney would pursue such a question to discover other facts. An example of how this is done in this type of interviewing follows:

Q: What is it about the newspaper that you don't have time for?

A: I'm always in a hurry and a rush in the morning.

Q: Do you have time for other things, like breakfast, etc.?

A: Yes, but it takes awhile to read the paper.

Q: What about the paper takes so long?

A: Well, you start out on page 1 and all you really want to read is the stuff that's happening on the national scene. But then to finish the story you have to go to page B-1 or someplace, and the next thing you know you're either lost or reading something else.

This suggests that there may be a formatting problem with the paper. Many people read the paper on trains, planes, or buses, and it becomes unwieldy. Perhaps a tabloid format would be better. This suggests a motivational problem: a problem in OR: Circumstances. Part of this motivation relates to pace (of life), and part of it may be related to convenience (or lack thereof).

This methodology pursues the question to the next level. For example, respondents often say that the reason they bank at Last National is because it is convenient. Researchers hear this explanation over and over again, and will often cut the sample size because of the repetition. They do not see any reason to go any further. Now, look at this approach:

Q: Why do you bank at Last National?

A: Because it's more convenient.

Q: What about Last National makes it more convenient?

A: It's on the parkway.

Q: Aren't there other banks on the parkway?

A: Well, yes, there are three others there. But at Last National they treat you very special.

Q: How do they treat you special?

Now we are about to get into several motivations. The respondent may be addressing OR: Time, where lines are nonexistent and the personnel are very efficient. Or he/she may be addressing OR: Person, where bank staff take time with him/her and recognize his/her banking needs even before he/she does. In other words, they are not abrupt with him/her. In accordance with OR: Circumstances, they simply make it more convenient for him/her to do his/her banking and simplify the task. There is much more to it than location. In the sample interview above, the interviewer has gone one step beyond the obvious and often repeated rationalization, "it's more convenient." And he/she is about to move into a third level with the question, "How do they treat you special?"

In summary, the success of the interview revolves around visualization, relaxation, and repetition. Relaxation, the second step, takes place automatically when the respondent is shown how to visualize and begins to do it. It also is increased during the interview as the interviewer continually reminds the respondent that he/she is relaxed, and is becoming more relaxed as the interview progresses.

THE STRUCTURE OF THE INTERVIEW: ORIENTATION TO TIME

For each project, the interviews will be structured as in a focus group, with a moderator's guide. The guide will specify the dimensions of the project, and designate the particular questions that are to be asked. A major difference is that the respondent is totally concentrated on the product, or service. In doing this, the interviewer removes orientation to time. Therefore, respondents are not bound by the constraints of time. The interviewer may want to take the respondent back in time to the first time he/she had experience with the product. For example, in researching baked goods, a respondent may go back to his/her fourth birthday party, when his/her mother was baking a cake. Feelings will be elicited, and important motivations (and elements of motivations) will arise during this interview. The interviewer will continually encourage this, by telling the respondent "you can feel it," or "you are really there." Taking someone "back" in time may involve the visualization of a clock or a calendar, in which the hands on the clock go back or the pages on the calendar are torn off. There are many different methods that may be used, all of which rely upon visualization.

From a subject's first experience with the product we may move up to the second time, and then perhaps to the last time. In a banking project, the interviewer started with the very first experience in a bank (usually with a parent when very young); then the first time after being married; and then the last time that he/she changed banks. At each step of the way, the decisions made by the consumer were analyzed in terms of the 11 motivations that were introduced in chapter 4. It is important—very important—to understand that there are no motives outside of these 11, other than the rational ones that we already know about. How these motives are analyzed within the interview will be discussed later.

MORE EXAMPLES: ANALYZING CONSUMER DECISION MAKING

In an interview on paper products, the consumer is asked to go back, "in his/her mind's eye" to the supermarket. The respondent is then placed in front of the shelf full of various paper products and asked to "pretend" or imagine that he/she is really there. Some subjects go so far into the process that they will talk in the present tense. It then becomes quite obvious that the interviewer is getting valid and reliable information. There are, of course, some respondents who have difficulty with visualization, but they are rare. This is because visualization is the first format for thinking, and everyone has experience with it. No one is a newcomer to this exercise!

The purpose of standing in front of a shelf with all of the various paper products is to analyze the mental exercises that consumers go through at the point of the purchase. It is at this point—and at many others—that it is vitally important to have a capable interviewer, or much of what happens at this phase of the interview could easily become a "fishing trip" for the interviewer and a waste of time for the subject. Interviewers must be thoroughly trained, and have an understanding of resistance, which is discussed below.

One of the major reasons for assessing emotions is to get around the problem that all market researchers and their clients have encountered: "How do I stop getting respondents to tell me what they think I want to hear, and tell me the truth?" When researchers gather information that is what the respondents think they want to hear they often make product changes that do not work. When emotional information is gathered, then the client is making his/her decisions on the basis of a very firm and resolute footing.

ANALYSIS OF RESISTANCE

Freud (1953c) discussed the importance of resistance in psychotherapy, and implored physicians and future analysts to pay particular attention to resistance: "I will merely indicate briefly that this concept of resistance has acquired the highest importance for us in understanding the origin of an illness as well as the mechanism of its cure" (p. 109).

The same words could be applied to the analysis of marketing, advertising, and our applications to the challenges or problems that a business might be having. Indeed, the principle use of this type of visualization research is to analyze resistance. The analysis of resistance comes in many kinds of requests, and some examples follow:

• Since all banks (casinos, supermarkets, etc.) are similar, what can I do to make mine stand out?
• Why do people drive by my restaurant to go to others, whose menus are not as extensive?
• How do I reinstill consumer confidence and trust (health insurer)?
• Why am I losing market share in two markets while gaining in three others?
• How can I recover customers who are taking their business to a newer, larger store?
• How can I break through the resistance to fat-free food items?

Freud (1953c) goes on to say, in his analysis of patients:

Although we have instructed the patient to follow the rule of communicating all thoughts that occur to him, he seems unable to do so. He soon begins to hold back first one thought and then another. He gives various reasons to account for this: either the thought was quite unimportant, or it was irrelevant or it was totally meaningless. . . . We recognize in this behavior of the patient's a manifestation of the "resistance" present in him, which we are never free from during the whole duration of treatment. (p. 109)

Consumers do the same thing. They resist. This is why it is necessary to use special techniques, such as we have introduced in this chapter, to access the Silent Side or right side of the brain.

Freud goes on to say that it is in the analysis of the resistance that patients give their therapist that the real meanings are uncovered. Another way of saying this is that when you find out what they are resisting, you find out what is really meaningful to them. Still another way of looking at this problem is in the old and familiar aphorism, "It's what she's *not* saying."

From our experience, and backed by research, it is safe to say that consumers often resist what is most meaningful to them. No doubt, it is most definitely meaningful to the client, or the marketer. This resistance—or overcoming it—makes all the difference as to whether or not new customers become old customers and old customers bring in new ones.

COMPUTER-AIDED INTERVIEW ASSISTANCE

One-on-one qualitative interviews that emphasize visualization generate hypotheses for emotional demographics (motigraphics), which can then be used in a variety of ways. But despite the use of visualization, relaxation, and repetition, the information that comes out of these interviews would be useless if it could not be categorized and classified. It is the motivational matrix in chapter 4 that allows us to do this.

One problem with qualitative research, as Percy (1982) has noted, is that it follows no systematic or purposeful plan. Consumers may spend two to three hours in a focus group, and the information may not only be disorganized, but much of it may be lost, since there is no overall scheme for classification.

Although this visual interviewing is qualitative, the responses can be categorized and classified. Significant work has been carried out by Piaget (1971), Kohlberg (1969), McClelland et al. (1953), and others where qualitative data has yielded quantitative results. There are many examples from psychology, particularly where quantified data is classified, that it can then be scored and entered into a regression analysis or analysis of variance. The first step in this process is classification. The problem with focus group data is that usually it is not classified or categorized and so it can never be organized and quantified.

The interviewer in this process carries out four very important procedures in the move toward classified data. First, he/she gets the respondent to relax. It takes trained and competent interviewers to do this. Some people are just naturally more adept at getting others to feel relaxed and not pressured. Second, the interviewer has the respondent visualize. Since visualization is a natural process, this is a relatively simple procedure to introduce people to and to teach them to do. Third, the interviewer is repetitious. This, too, requires some experience and training. And fourth, the interviewer classifies the information that is recovered from the respondent.

Classification is involved, but not as complex as it may seem. That is because respondents, when talking about the unconscious impact of products and services, will talk in one of the 11 motivational categories that have been described in chapter 4. Also, the actual mechanical classification of these statements is aided by a computer program. The suggested program, Three by Five (1994), is written by MacToolkit for the Apple MacIntosh computer, and is distributed by many software catalog houses. The IBM/PC Compatible version should be available sometime in the future from the same company. This program allows the interviewer to manufacture 3 x 5 cards electronically, and then put them into electronic stacks or piles for subsequent analysis. These "cards" can then be printed out in a list, with each statement on each card being in the "pile" that is most appropriate. For example, statements about love, family values, patriotism, and perfectionism would be placed in a pile marked "spiritual survival." Since all the motives consist of abstractions, neither the consumer nor the interviewer will relate to them. Instead, the interviewer attends to the "elements," which will determine into which "pile" statements are to be sorted. The experienced interviewer can do this on a laptop computer while he/she is interviewing the respondent. When it is done in this way, there is no loss of data or reliance upon someone's remote memory.

In Three by Five, a stationary pad can be constructed that consists of the 11 major motivational categories. The pad will always be available as a generic format for each new project, and from that point on all the interviewer needs to do is sort the statements into the appropriate piles. A report at the end of the project will

Table 8-1
Classification of Elements into Motivational Categories

Spiritual Survival	Physical Survival	Territorial Survival	Sexual Survival
Family values	Food	Competition	Gender
Inner peace	Air	Assets	Impulse
Meaningful death	Water	Domestic (home	Inhibition
Witness signifi-	Shelter	issues)	
cance	Health	Income	
Lawful order (per-		Greed	
fcctionism)		Career	
Wholeness		Nesting	
Sense of calling			
Membership			
Renewal & release			
Human love			
Sacrifice			
OR: Person	**OR: Place**	**OR: Time**	**OR: Circum-** stances
Self-who	Where	When	Pace (of life)
		Timing	Convenience
		Urgency	
Adaptation	**Expectation**	**Play**	
Testimonials	Future		
Follow the leader	Trust, faith		

automatically place each statement into the appropriate motivational category. The report is flexible, and changes can be made. Since there will be too many statements to include in the quantitative part of the interview, many of these may be "culled" at this point but an appropriate number will be kept for quantitative analysis.

SAMPLE SIZES IN VISUALIZATION RESEARCH

In many cases the interviews are very tedious and repetitious for the interviewer. Obviously this is because, after the tenth or 11th interview, the material begins to become redundant. This should be encouraging, for it is a signal that, at the level of the unconscious, people are basically alike. There are not that many differences between people at the unconscious level. Hence, there is no profit or gain in conducting 20 or 30 in-depth interviews that use the visualization method.

The small sample size may be difficult for many clients to accept. Clients are used to large sample sizes in traditional market research. Traditional market research, like any kind of research, is keyed to looking at attitudes, attributes, and abilities, not at motivation. Attitudes, attributes, and abilities are, for the most part, normally distributed throughout the population, and they are subject to tremendous variation due to individual differences. Motivations, on the other hand, are not normally distributed in the same way that hands, legs, arms, and feet are distributed, with everybody getting two of each. However, as we will show, the in-depth process is only a part of the total research methodology, which includes the very best of both qualitative and quantitative aspects of market research.

RECRUITING AND STRATIFICATION

When a product or an issue is being examined and there are believed to be motivational differences, then the samples should be segmented. For example, there are substantial motivational differences between men and women with certain products such as shoes. In a study to determine how a decision is made on the purchase of a television set, both men and women should be interviewed. Such a study might include six to eight respondents in each group. This will yield a large enough sample of motivational statements that may be used in the follow-up study of motigraphics. In addition, a sample of 16 to 20 respondents will yield a large number of practical, useful recommendations based on the unconscious motivations that have been uncovered up to this point. In many marketing cases, major strategy decisions can be made on the basis of Silent Side interviews alone. They will in turn be used for follow-up action.

THE CONTENT AND STRUCTURE OF IN-DEPTH
INTERVIEWING

The first part of the interview, cited above, has been described: the subject learned about visualization and was introduced to his/her own photographic memory. Most of the subjects did not know that they had a photographic memory. Following this initial exercise, the subject begins the actual visualization exercise as it relates to the product. At this point, the subject is asked to close his/her eyes again and the interviewer suggests that he/she becomes very relaxed. Once the interviewer is assured that he/she is relaxed, the subject is asked to imagine the picture of a calendar, or perhaps a clock. He/she is then asked to watch the clock moving backward, to a specific point in time, and then a scene is suggested.

In the course of going back, the subject is asked to return to a specific time, usually to the first time that he/she had become familiar with the product, used it, or when it was introduced to him/her. This time could vary from a few months to many years ago. Nonusers, or those who have had no experience with the product or service, are asked to imagine what it was like. A variation may be to ask them to go back to the first time that they heard about the product or used a competitor's product.

From this point on, various other scenes can be brought up by the interviewer as the subject is gently guided back to other experiences with the product. The more relaxed the subject becomes, the more information is accumulated. This is a rule of thumb; yet it is based on experience. Therefore, interviewers are trained to repetitiously suggest to the respondent that he/she is relaxed throughout the interview.

As described above, quantitative studies, focus groups, and "shopping studies" can be carried out within this framework. One study in particular yielded results that attested to the importance of an Orientation Motive; in this case, OR: Circumstances.

Two wine labels were being compared at the final stages of readying a new wine product for the retail market. One set of labels, figure 8-2, was created and executed by an advertising agency. The second set of labels, figure 8-3, was executed by the client's in-house creative staff. Prior to the introduction of the product at the retail level, identical products were labeled with both sets of labels and a customer perception or "shopping study" was conducted.

A "wine store" was set up and customers were given a stated amount of money to spend in the store. The test labels were placed alongside various national name brands such as Paul Masson, Taylor, Gallo, etc. Customers were told to choose whatever wine appealed to them, and if they ran out of money they were told that they would be given an additional amount.

In an exit interview, the "customers" were asked to describe what they saw, what appealed to them most, and what appealed to them least. They described the different brands that they saw, but surprisingly they did not even mention the Altima wine in figure 8-2 until they were pushed by the interviewers into a response. The Altima wine (in figure 8-2) was by far the most unpopular in the selection, and not one bottle was purchased. Instead, they overwhelmingly preferred the plain and simple letters displayed on the labels executed by the client's in-house creative

Figure 8-2
Wine Labels (Agency)

Figure 8-3
Wine Labels (In-house)

staff (figure 8-3).

Consumers gave their own interpretation as to why the wine in figure 8-2 was not appealing to them. It was based upon the label. Their explanation was "there was some other crazy wine in there, and it just went like this." At this point, they waved their arms through the air in a nonverbal attempt to dramatize the long, curly, wavy serifs that characterized the letters. They were repelled by the artist's attempt to draw their attention to the label. The answer to the respondents dislike lies in the vital issue of OR: Circumstances. It was stated in chapter 4 that consumers do many of the things they do because they want to be temporarily disoriented from the day-to-day routine that characterizes their lives. Conversely, consumers do not want to become disoriented at a time when they are attempting to make a decision, such as when they are at a point of purchase. They especially do not want to be disoriented when they are making an important "buy" decision, such as the purchase of wine. Wavy, outstretched, and exaggerated serifs on letters have the effect of disorienting the consumer and causing confusion. In chapter 16 this confounding effect will be discussed in more detail when it is shown that a primary reason for theme park visitation is personal disorientation to circumstances, time, etc. But a completely different motivational set is operating with parents who take their children to a theme park. This is because they have responsibility for their children at the theme park, versus thrill seekers who have no responsibility and whose only purpose in going is to look for disorientating experiences (OR: Person).

PRODUCTS AND SERVICES RESEARCHED

A list of some of the products and services that have been researched follows:

Automobiles (new)	Automobiles (used)	Automotive after market
Women's shoes	Real estate	Fine china
Casino gambling	Horse races	Political (Congressman)
Political (governor's race)	Highway taxes	Psychiatric inpatient care
Outpatient speciality services	Theme park	Beer
Soft drinks	Dog track	Cosmetics
Fragrance	Video games	Amusement parks
Computers	Airlines	Schools
Universities	Name changes	Talk radio
Price resistance	TV news	Newspaper
Political (gambling)	Political (issues)	Breakfast
Rice	Potatoes	Canned milk
Shortening	Ice cream	Electric utility
Public utility	Nuclear power	Baked goods
Neighborhood restaurants	Tires	Women's fashions

Although not a complete list, it gives the reader an idea of the diversity of products to which in-depth motivational research, as described here, can be applied.

A few of the client questions that were answered with the visualization methodology were:

• How can I get a stronger demographic into my facility? (race track)

- How can I defeat an antigambling statute? (municipality)
- How can I get elected to the U.S. Congress? (politician)
- How do I run an effective political campaign? (governor)
- How can I instill brand loyalty? (casino, bank)
- What do I do to recapture market share with a mature and unexciting product? (canned milk)
- What can I do to get people to read my newspaper? (vs. the competition)
- Should a pizza restaurant go into the breakfast business? (fast food pizza)
- How can a fast-food restaurant be unique in today's market?
- What can a banking institution do to obtain a unique position in today's market?
- How does a health insurer regain people's trust? (health insurance)
- How does a public utility move from "bad guy" to "good guy" in the face of rising utility rates? (public utility)

All these questions and more can be answered. In each case, results point toward positioning, repositioning, establishment of the brand, implications for employee training, implications for interior and exterior decor, ad copy, marketing plans, and more!

Traditional market research takes a reactive approach. A hotel leaves a brief questionnaire in the guest's room, asking the guest to take a few minutes to fill it out. Most will ignore it, unless something has happened that has made them unhappy or dissatisfied. Then they will fill it out. This is reactive. When the marketer studies consumer motivation through visualization and right brain research, he/she will find out what motivates the consumer before marketing to him/her (pro-active) and will increase the probability that the sale will be made.

HOW THREE-DIMENSIONAL RESEARCH INPUTS TO ADVERTISING, MARKETING, AND OTHER AREAS

Whether the reader is marketing products or services, the application of this research can yield valuable information for operations. For example, consumers often tell about the attitudes that they have encountered in employees who are the only representatives of the institution they have ever seen. The front-line teller may be the only representative of the bank that is ever seen by the public. When this is the case, the methodology that has been described has broad implications for employee training and customer service, not just marketing. This is often true when consumers "feel that there is something wrong, or different" but they cannot really express what it is.

Other implications for marketing, advertising copy, strategies, positioning, decor, and design are limitless, because a whole new data set is being introduced. This data set consists of the perceptions of users and consumers that arise from the Silent Side rather than from the conscious, rational side.

Figure 8-4
How In-depth Motivational Research Inputs to Other Areas

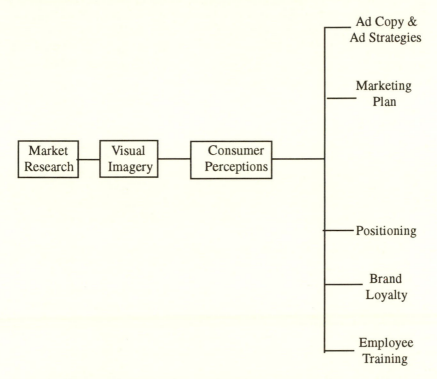

CONCLUSION

The market research methodology that has been presented here has been successful in establishing and validating the 11 motivational categories that were presented in chapter 4. These are the four Orientation Motives (OR: Person, OR: Place, OR: Time, and OR: Circumstances); the four Survival Motives (Spiritual Survival, Physical Survival, Sexual Survival, and Territorial Survival); the Adaptation Motive; the Expectation Motive; and Play. Psychology has been equivocal when it comes to the establishment of a comprehensive theory of motivation, other than motivation through behavior modification or learning theory. For example, in criminal trials it is not unusual for two behavioral scientists to examine the same accused person with the same tests and instruments and come out with two widely divergent opinions on the subject's mental status and motivation to commit the crime. This is because of the failure to agree upon certain basic and simple elements of human motivation, such as the Orientation Motives, and upon the root or basic causes of human behavior.

We have introduced the motivational elements, we have elaborated upon them, and we have outlined the methodology in which these motivational elements are used as classifiers. At this point, specific marketing applications will be presented for a number of different consumer activities, products, and services. In this way it will be seen and clearly understood how the methodology has been used in a unique and challenging way to open up new directions in marketing and advertising and to break through consumer resistance.

REFERENCES

Adams, L. J. (1980). *Conceptual blockbusting: A guide to better ideas* (2nd ed.). New York: Norton.
Freud, S. (1952). The Unconscious. In *Britannica Great Books* (Cecil M. Baines, Trans.). Chicago: Encyclopedia Britannica, Inc.
Freud, S. (1953a). Constructions in analysis. In *Standard edition of complete psychological works of Sigmund Freud*. London: Hogarth Press and the Institute of Psychoanalysis. (Original work published in 1937)
Freud, S. (1953b). The interpretation of dreams. In *Standard edition of complete psychological works of Sigmund Freud*. London: Hogarth Press and the Institute of Psychoanalysis. (Original work published 1900)
Freud, S. (1953c). Psychoanalysis and legal evidence. In *Standard edition of complete psychological works of Sigmund Freud*. London: Hogarth Press and the Institute of Psychoanalysis. (Original work published 1906)
Kohlberg, L. (1969). Stage and sequence: The cognitive-developmental approach to socialization. In D. A. Goslin (Ed.), *Handbook of socialization theory and research*. Chicago: Rand-McNally.
Lewin, B. D. (1968). *The image and the past*. New York: International Universities Press, Inc.
Ogilvy, D., & Raphaelson, J. (1982). Research on advertising techniques that work—and don't work. *Harvard Business Review*, 14–16.
Maddock, R., & Fulton, R. (1995, June). Unconscious components of consumer behavior. Copenhagen, Denmark: Association for Consumer Research.
McClelland, D. C., Atkinson, J. W., Clark, R. A., & Lowell, E. L. (1953). *The achievement motive*. New York: Appleton.
McLuhan, M. (1951). *The mechanical bride. Folklore of industrial man*. New York: Vanguard.
Percy, L. (1982). Using qualitative focus groups in generating hypotheses for subsequent quantitative validation and strategy development. *Proceedings of theAssociation for Consumer Research, 9*, 57–60.
Piaget, J. (1971). Mental imagery in the child: *A study of the development of imaginal representation*. New York: Basic Books.
Rossiter, J., & Percy, L. (1980). Attitude change through visual imagery in advertising. *Journal of Advertising, 9*, 10–16.
Rossiter, J., & Percy, L. (1983). Visual communication in advertising. In R. Harris (Ed.), *Information processing research in advertising*. Hillsdale, NJ: Lawrence Ehrlbaum Associates.

Three by Five [Apple Computer software]. (1994). Santa Monica, CA: MacToolkit.
Van Kampen, K. (1992). *Visual golf*. New York: Simon & Shuster.

9

Updating Focus Group Techniques for Investigating Consumer Motivation

Richard Maddock and Larry Percy

BACKGROUND: THE DECADE OF THE BRAIN

During the last decade, significant advances in the neurological and behavioral sciences have come about because of developments in electrophysiological recording, neurochemical techniques and the ability to look closely at the neurophysiological substrates of normal and disordered behavior in human beings. Cacioppo and Berntson (1992) suggest a multilevel integrative analysis of behavior, where neuroscientists can look at both micro and macro levels. They further suggest that the overall advantage of looking at both levels might not only allow us to look at multiple causation of phenomena, but also to look at the interaction effects between these levels, or the relational effects. Their overall point is that "reductionism," especially within the last ten years, has allowed us to understand some very complex social and psychological phenomena. However, they also argue that reductionism alone is not the answer, but that scientific breakthroughs come at many different levels of explanation.

Perhaps the most productive work to be carried out in the last ten years has been in the areas of emotion and of the unconscious mind. Prior to this decade, both of these subjects were constructs that had been introduced by Freud, but upon which there had been very little empirical research or data collection. MacLean (1990) has summarized much of this work, beginning with the work of Papez (1937) on the functions of the limbic system. To summarize Papez's findings in his own words:

It is proposed that the hypothalamus, the anterior thalamic nuclei, the gyrus cinguili, the hippocampus and their interconnections constitute a harmonious mechanism which may elaborate the functions of central emotion, as well as participate in emotional expression.

The other new area of interest is the subconscious. Epstein (1994) presents evidence from his own as well as a number of other investigations which show that there are two cognitive systems, automatic/intuitive and rational, that run side-by-side in a parallel fashion and yet operate on two entirely different sets of rules. One is holistic, the other is rational. The first is intuitive, and the second is logical. He cites experiences from everyday life, such as religion, which have no logical basis and yet have permeated every known society that has ever existed. He also cites extensive research that has been done.

In an even more recent summary, Azar (1996) outlines the empirical work that is being done on the subconscious by Bargh and Chaiken, Greenwald, Garcia and others. These researchers, generally using familiar words as stimuli, have found that the subconscious will often react with specific behaviors, stereotypes or prejudices that are not part of an individual's conscious awareness. For example, Bennett (1985) showed that patients under anesthesia were told that during a postoperative interview they should pull at their ears. During the interview that followed, nine of the 11 subjects did pull at their ears, although they did not remember having heard any instructions to do so. Similarly, Libet (1985) found that when a weak electrical pulse was delivered to the skin, about a half second of brain activity is required for the patient to become more conscious of the stimulus; indicating that the impulse is received first by the unconscious and then delivered to the conscious mind.

The purpose of this brief overview of the current state of psychology is to show that there are reasons that the *zeitgiest* went through some enormous changes in the last decade. In addition, within the last ten years there has been a recognition that the overly simplistic paradigms of Skinner and Pavlov virtually ignored cognitive processes, and there has been a gradual move back to a study of the "mind." Within the last decade there has been considerable change in the way that psychologists look at behavior and its causes. We see this as an advance in the science.

One way of dealing with this new look at behavior in marketing and communications is through a better understanding of motivation and its role in consumer choice behavior. We have already seen in chapter 3 where Rossiter and Percy (1987) identified eight motives (following the work of Fennell, 1979) energizing all human behavior, including product usage and purchase behavior. In their theory, they suggest that motives play a key role in the establishment of brand attitudes, because these attitudes are anchored to a purchase motivation (Rossiter, Percy, and Donovan, 1991).

These researchers look at motives within the context of a homeostatic or equilibrium concept in which there are two fundamental motivating mechanisms: one positive and one negative. With the onset of a positive stimulus (walking past a bakery and smelling fresh-baked cookies), the consumer is motivated to seek that stimulus (buy the fresh-baked cookies) until satisfaction sets in and they return to equilibrium (eat cookies until full). With the onset of a negative stimulus (a headache), the consumer is motivated to reduce or remove that stimulus (take an aspirin).

The importance of this idea of motivation is that it is critically related to consumer attitudes toward product categories and brands. Consumer attitudes "energize" behavior because they are the link between the category or brand and motive. It is the attitudes held about the cookies or aspirin (from examples above) that enable the consumer to satisfy the motivation or drive and return to equilibrium. As a result, for effective marketing, Rossiter and Percy (1987) would argue that it is essential to understand the nature of the motivations operating in a product category, and to be able to classify them.

We are in total agreement with this, but the question is how does the marketer uncover *actual* motivation? As of now, the best answer is probably qualitative research, which interestingly enough in social psychology literature is often referred to as "motivation research." While in-depth interviews are sometimes used, perhaps the most common methodology is the focus group.

The origin of the focus group could be traced to the work of Lewin and his students (Lewin, Lippitt, and White, 1939), where these investigators compared autocratically managed, democratic, and laissez-faire groups, finding that the democratic group was far superior to the other two in terms of producing results in an assigned task. But these investigators did much more than this. According to Strong (1995) they initiated the study and the science of group dynamics; they undertook in-depth investigations into the area of leadership; they described the forces that influence group members; and they described the "glue" that holds people together in a task-oriented group. As Strong has stated:

Lewin probed and elaborated on dynamic processes between people, processes that account for people's actions and in turn are created and channeled by the actions. It was this perspective and its concepts that early writers transported from social psychology to counseling psychology. These writers believed that because counseling is a process that goes on between counselor and client, counseling can best be understood in terms of the concepts of the dynamic processes that exist between people. (p. 687)

We would certainly agree with this. In fact, it is the only real reason for conducting focus groups. But the purpose of Strong's article is to show that social psychology in 1995 is no longer a source of ideas, studies and references about dynamic processes between people, since the mainstream of American psychology has moved away from the interpersonal (between people) and focussed almost entirely upon the intrapersonal, or the dynamics within people. And Strong is very unhappy about this, because he believes that the work of Lewin and his students was a valuable contribution to the science of counseling and to psychology as a whole, and indeed it was.

PROBLEMS WITH FOCUS GROUPS TODAY

The whole field of marketing research has also opened its doors to new technologies. Electronic responding, interactive television, interactive networks, remote control cameras and digital transmission will boost the amount of focus group research done over the next decade. All of these new methods have grasped the attention and the admiration of those who are constantly trying to update their research methodologies (Heather, 1994). However, the mainstay of most of these new technologies is the basic, qualitative focus group. Unlike psychology, marketing has not moved away from the basic group as its manner of doing marketing, and this continues to create problems. For in many ways, focus groups do not work.

It is estimated that the industry conducts about 100,000 focus groups a year, and it is expected to reach 200,000 by the year 2000 (Greenbaum, 1993). But do focus groups really solve problems, or do they create them?

Percy (1982) has indicated that qualitative research in general, and focus groups in particular, follow no systematic or purposeful plan. Instead, they are used as an inexpensive and easily interpreted means of gathering information about a question where answers are forthcoming quickly and readily. He further states that the problem caused by the use of focus groups is that they should be used only for hypotheses-generation; instead, they are used as an end in and of themselves.

Ferguson (1995) has indicated that focus groups may indeed be "unfocused," which is based on the fact that too many marketers use them as a "cure all." He said that the problem with the use of focus groups is that they are considered a "quick and dirty" way to get some information; and more often than not it's too quick and too dirty: in the wrong place, at the wrong time, with the wrong people and an inadequate moderator. As Percy has stated, they are not a substitute for doing real research and making big decisions.

Boldt (1993) did focus group research to get reader feedback on the editorial page of the *Philadelphia Inquirer*. The bottom line in this research, as he states it, is that "a focus group is like Alice's Restaurant: you can get anything that you want."

One of the most extensive reviews of the failure of focus groups is presented by Martin (1995). He believes that the "obsession" with focus groups has gone too far. He uses a number of examples. Perhaps the most salient is Chrysler's use of focus groups to introduce the concept of the new minivan in the eighties. Consumers turned thumbs down on the concept, but Chrysler turned thumbs down on the consumers and instead, went ahead with the development. The minivan then went on to become the success story of the eighties. Added to the list that never would have made it if the companies had listened to the focus groups are: Federal Express, CNN, the cellular telephone, VCRs and fax machines.

Our own experience with focus groups has been similar, especially within the medical context. In the late seventies, we ran a number of focus groups to see if consumer-patients would consider medical treatment closer to their home, rather than going downtown to the "medical center." They turned thumbs down on it, using the rationalization that they would always go to the medical center because the university was there and "because everyone knows that the best doctors are there." By 1982 this situation had completely reversed itself, and by 1990 the major downtown hospitals relied primarily upon Medicaid patients, and also served to take the "overflow" from suburbia.

THE IMPORTANCE OF THE MODERATOR TO SUCCESSFUL FOCUS GROUPS

When properly conceived and used, focus groups can be an effective method of uncovering consumer preferences, and the causes of consumer behavior. To be useful, it is essential that one sample across all potential target audience groups, and then conduct at least three groups with each to ensure a "tie-breaker." Nothing is more frustrating than conducting two focus groups, one seemingly contradicting the other. It is also essential that the output of the groups be organized, classified, and arranged in such a manner that it may be easily interpreted and understood. But the single most important key to the validity of the focus groups is the moderator.

The moderator of a focus group must be trained and qualified in dealing with both the intrapersonal and the interpersonal dynamics of the groups. As Rossiter and Percy (1987) have pointed out, the results of any focus group are largely dependent upon the psychological and marketing understanding of the moderator, because the research results are so heavily based upon their interpretation of what was discussed. This also means that the moderator must be the one to listen to and analyze the tapes of the focus groups. Only the moderator knows why a particular question was asked or a particular line of inquiry pursued.

Directed Focus Groups

There are two labels that are traditionally used to describe the leader of a focus group: a group moderator and a group facilitator.

It is our understanding that the moderator conducts the group along the lines of the democratic task group, defined by Lewin et al. (1939). This is usually in a non-directive, free-floating style in which participants are encouraged to respond but not necessarily made to respond by being "put on the spot." An analogy to this type of a focus group is the individual or group therapy that is conducted by a "Rogerian" non-directive therapist.

On the other hand, we understand that the group facilitator conducts the group along the lines of the more autocratic task group, again defined by Lewin (1939).

In this context, he/she takes a much more active, dynamic role. Although auto-cratic leadership was traditionally defined to be less productive, it should be re-membered that Lewin and his students were looking at task groups, and a focus group is usually not a task group. So it would be incorrect to apply his findings to focus groups. A focus group is only asked to come up with ideas, opinions, and points-of-view so that the group dynamics governing the focus group would be quite different than the dynamics of the task group.

We use the analogy of going fishing, with or without a GPF, or a fish finder. Although some people say that the GPF takes the sport out of ocean fishing, no one can deny that it certainly adds to the excitement of the sport. A facilitated group may not be humanistic and democratic, but it certainly is more productive and more exciting! The reason for this is that the facilitator is trained in what to look for, and where to go. Just as a cardiovascular surgeon knows what he/she is looking for when he/she opens a chest, the group facilitator knows what to look for in terms of elements, motives, and rational reasons for purchase. He/she guides and steers the group, while a transcriptionist sorts the statements into various cat-egories on the electronic computer program that was designed for this purpose and discussed in chapter 8.

Such highly directed, controlled and regulated focus groups are not without precedent. For example, Hoeffel (1994) describes the analysis of tape recorded voices using a computer program that uses an artificial intelligence linguistics program to assign values to customers' statements. IBM used this program to sort customer preferences on the AS/400 computer. This program distills customer comments into a prioritized list of issues, and the respondents agree with the pri-oritized list when they see it.

Similar, but less automated, is an approach described by McGregor and Morrison (1995) where focus groups gathered to comment on and edit news tapes about the Gulf War. Their conclusion was that the groups that did editing proved superior in nearly every way to ordinary focus groups.

Finally, Agar and MacDonald (1995) have analyzed focus group transcripts using a simplified version of techniques used in conversational analysis, and by interpreting the utterances as indexes as more comprehensive "folk models" that were derived from other data. In these cases, the focus groups provided a much richer and deeper understanding than what was provided by the simple "stand alone" group.

Talk Show Format for Directed Focus Groups

In our experience, the more effective format for the focus group is the talk show format, where the facilitator actually "runs the show" in terms of the agenda. This requires that the facilitator take the time to familiarize himself/herself with the product that is being examined, and that he/she know the motivational systems that are expected to emerge. In fact, the facilitator is expected to facilitate the emergence of these motives. They are then classified by a transcriptionist, who is also familiar with the system. However, this is not a difficult conceptual task, since it consists of a simple sorting of consumers' statements on an electronic "sorter."

Amateur and armchair psychologists have long recognized the dichotomy that exists between the "extraverted" and the "introverted" personality. This is one of the best known classification systems in psychology, regardless of the person's orientation. In focus groups, people tend to sort themselves into these two categories. In the talk show format, those who want their opinion to be heard may be seated in the front (on a platform, if available) so that they may be seen and heard. They take the position of the talk show "guests." The more introverted individuals are seated in the audience, but their participation is potentiated by the facilitator, who moves around the room with a microphone, taking a very active stance and encouraging total participation from everyone. As anyone knows who has been in a focus group, there are some who are more active than others. The facilitator evens this out; so that in a sense, the talk show focus group is more democratic than the ordinary focus group, even though, in Lewin's structure, it would be described as more autocratic.

There are some secondary benefits to the talk show format. One important benefit is that clients and representatives from the agency are usually watching. Viewing a focus group where everyone tries to talk at once, in which there is no particular structure, and which is, in general, non-directive, can be very tedious. Viewing a talk show can not only be informative, but it can be entertaining, and often is.

UNCOVERING MOTIVATIONS THROUGH FOCUS GROUPS

While directed focus groups, especially in a talk show format, help, the use of focus groups to uncover motivations is a real challenge and one requiring a strong understanding of motivation on the part of those conducting a focus group. Without a solid background in the psychology involved, it may be impossible to penetrate the barriers to identifying the motivations associated with the behavior under study. Rossiter and Percy (1987) have described a number of these barriers:

- Subjects may not follow what the interviewer is looking for
- They may not know what their motivations are
- They may not be able to remember them if they do know
- They may not be able to talk about them if they do remember
- The interviewer may not probe deep enough to gain the understanding necessary to classify the motivations

One way to help overcome these barriers is for the focus group facilitator to work within a clean classification system for motives.

As we have noted in chapter 10, it is not unusual in social psychology to have scoring systems that are based upon the classification of qualitative data that is obtained from individuals or groups. Examples of these systems are seen in the work of Kelly (1955) in his work with groups, and Kohlberg (1984) in his work with individuals. In each case the qualitative output is stored in categories, which in turn are scored for quantitative analysis.

The system developed by us in over 15 years of research, is a motivation classification system that takes the output from consumers and sorts it in terms of the motivational and emotional categories that interest the consumer in a product or service (Maddock, 1995). It is based upon the motivational hierarchy that was presented in chapter 4. These categories were derived from visualization research that was carried out in individual, one-on-one interviews that we believe tapped motivational structures of the limbic system and the right hemisphere, and have also been applied in focus groups. The reason that the information that emerges from focus groups can be structured in terms of the unconscious motivations is that people actually do talk in these terms, if you listen to them.

These motives can be applied to unstructured discussions that are held in focus groups, as long as the groups are conducted in an orderly fashion and only one person talks at a time. We will discuss the conduct of these groups (format) below. But in order to apply these motives and this motivational structure to the content, a few ground rules must be applied.

1. Not all of these motives apply to each product. In fact, the only product that we have found so far that includes all motives is the automobile.
2. Although the motives are presented in a pyramid (figure 4-7) from the strongest (Spiritual Survival) to the weakest (OR: Circumstances), they are not meant to be invariant. They will vary from product to product.
3. Motives cannot be dealt with directly, because they are abstractions and are easily open to misinterpretation. Consider what happened in 1995 when Calvin Klein tried to deal directly with the Sexual Motive in selling jeans.
4. In order to deal with motives, the researcher must deal with the elements that arise from the motives but are closely tied to them.

When the elements that are listed in table 4-3 are used for the purpose of sorting, all statements made by respondents can be classified into their respective motive category. This refers, however, only to statements that are of an affective, emotional nature (right hemisphere).

On the other hand, Rossiter and Percy (1987) have developed a theory of motivation that consists of eight purchase motives that tend to be associated with more left brain, rational reasons for purchasing.

CONCLUSION

Changes in technology over the past decade, emphasis upon neurological research, and a realization that reductionistic strategies don't work, have contributed in making significant changes in the science of psychology, as well as significant changes in the way that we look at our world. Emphasis upon the microcosmic structures that underlie the functions of the brain and maladaptive psychological phenomena are now being studied as neurophysiological phenomena. This has resulted in enormous progress in psychopharmacology, including the introduction of such antidepressants as Prozac and Paxil, which are totally unrelated to the old class of tricyclic antidepressants.

As Cacioppo and Bernston (1992) point out, it was technical developments such as this that led to the declaration by Congress that the nineties was the "decade of the brain." Although some would believe that this microlevel approach is reductionistic, Cacioppo and Bernston have pointed toward the opportunity of a multilevel integrative approach. Unlike Strong (1995), who denounces psychology's preoccupation with the minute and the intrapersonal, the authors see this as progress toward a more integrated approach, with the study of motivations at its heart.

Focus groups, although used extensively in market research, generally yield either very little information or, more importantly, information that turns out to be either equivocal or confusing. The solution that is recommended is a change in content and in format. Content can be organized and classified through a simple sort, so that ideas and concepts generated in focus groups will be related directly to motivations that are associated with product features and benefits. This involves a sorting procedure where a trained observer (or facilitator) classifies the motives that are expressed in the focus group into the appropriate rational and emotional classifications. The rational categories have been described by Rossiter and Percy (1987) and the emotional categories by Maddock (1995).

Format changes can be brought about by shifting to the talk show format, which is a more autocratic or authoritative design, but one which is more effective in generating the discussion, opinions, ideas, and concepts needed to fully understand the appropriate customer motivations. This format involves a focus group leader who is more involved in "directing" the group, in achieving the client's stated goals, and in generating responses from the group. It was noted that the talk show format is not only more productive, but it is more entertaining to the client. However, this approach requires a more competent and experienced leader to provide this direction.

It is also our position that, in terms of cost, this approach is less expensive than the traditional approach. This is because much more information is forthcoming from the group, and the client is able to get specific answers to his/her questions or concerns, as opposed to the more general and global responses that arise from a focus group.

REFERENCES

Agar, M., & MacDonald, J. (1995). Focus groups in ethnography. *Human Organization*, 54, 178 (9).

Azar, B. (1996). Influences from the mind's inner layers. American Psychological Association *Monitor*, 27, 2, 1(2).

Bennett, H. L. (1985). Behavioral Anaesthesia, *Advances*, 2, 11–21.

Boldt, D. (1993). Focus group follies. Bulletin of the American Society of Newspaper Editors, 4–9.

Cacioppo, J. T., & Berntson, G. G. (1992). Social psychological contributions to the decade of the brain. *American Psychologist, 47*, 8, 1019–28.

Epstein, S. (1994). Integration of the cognitive and the psychodynamic unconscious. *American Psychologist, 49*, 8, 709–24.

Fennell, G. (1979). Motivation research revisited. *Journal of Advertising Research*, 15, (June) 23–28.

Ferguson, R. (1995). Focus groups may proved unfocused marketing direction. *Advertising Age, 66*, 24, 26(1).

Greenbaum, T. L. (1991). Outside moderators maximize focus group results. *Public Relations Journal*, 47, 9, 31(2).

Greenbaum, T. L. (1993). *The handbook for focus group research*. New York: Lexington Books.

Heather, R. P. (1994). Future focus groups. *American Demographics*, 16, 1, 6(1).

Hoeffel, J. (1994). The secret life of focus groups; computer analysis of taped interviews can reveal what customers are really saying in ways that go beyond words. *American Demographics, 16*, 12, 17(3).

Kelly, G. A. (1955). *Psychology of personal constructs*. New York: Norton.

Kohlberg, L. (1984). *Psychology of moral development: the nature and validity of moral stages*. San Francisco: Harper and Row.

Lewin, K., Lippitt, R., & White, R. K. (1939). Patterns of aggressive behavior in experimentally created "social climates." *Journal of Social Psychology, 10*, 271–99.

Libet, B. (1985). Unconscious cerebral initiative and the role of conscious will in voluntary action. *Behavioral and Brain Sciences*, 8, 529–66.

MacLean, P. D. (1990). *The triune brain in evolution: Role in paleocerebral functions*. New York: Plenum.

Maddock, R. (1995). A theoretical and empirical substructure of consumer motivation and behavior. In F. Hansen (Ed.). European Advances in Consumer Research, Copenhagen: *European Association for Consumer Research, II*, 29–37.

Martin, J. (1995). Ignore your customer. *Fortune, 131*, 8, 121 (4).

McGregor, B., & Morrison, D. E. (1995). From focus groups to editing groups: a new method of reception analysis. *Media, Culture and Society, 17*, 1, 141 (10).

Papez, J. W. (1937). A proposed mechanism of emotion. *Archives Neurology and Psychiatry*, 38, 725–43.

Percy, L. (1982). The use of qualitative focus groups in generating hypotheses for subsequent quantitative validation and strategy development. In A. A. Mitchell (Ed.). *Advances in Consumer Research, IX*, 57–61.

Rossiter, J., & Percy, L. (1987). *Advertising and Promotions Management*, New York: McGraw-Hill.

Rossiter, J., Percy, L., & Donovan, R. (1991). The place of motivation in Rossiter and Percy's theory of action for advertising. *Proceedings of the Society for Consumer Psychology*, 59–62.

Strong, S. R. (1995). From social psychology: What? *The Counseling Psychologist, 23*, 4, 686–90.

10

From Qualitative to Quantitative

In chapter 7 we said that benefits are tied directly to motives, and we looked at some examples of how many different motives can be operating for different individuals engaged in the same behavior. This leads to a very real practical problem, because it does not make good sense to try and address every possible motive that might be involved in product usage or brand purchase. We must isolate the most relevant motives that maximize our potential.

The way we go about this is by qualifying the extent to which the various motives uncovered in the qualitative interviews are relevant in the target market. We do this in two steps: a prequantitative phase where all the motives and implied benefits are uncovered in the qualitative study among a small sample of our target market; and then a truly projectable quantitative study of our target market where only the relevant motives and benefits are examined.

THE ROLE OF RELEVANT MOTIVES AND ATTITUDES

The need for this two-step qualitative-to-quantitative study lies in the nature of the relationship of benefits, derived from underlying motivations, and also in the attitudes toward a product, service, or brand. Attitudes toward brands, products, or services (in fact, attitudes toward anything) are a function of what might be thought of as "logic" and "emotion." As we have seen, most marketers and advertisers only seem to pay the most attention to the beliefs or logical components of attitude. But assessing the correct motivation (the unconscious mind), which is part of the emotional component, is essential to a proper understanding of why people behave as they do.

It is motive that drives all behavior, and the emotional component of someone's attitude is energized by a previous motivation. The key here, however, is relevant motivation. From deep within, a motive activates a drive state that is expressed as a "feeling" or "emotion." We have seen how important it is to uncover these feelings, and this is the job of right brain visual interviews. These interviews, in theory, uncover all the motivations that potentially influence the behavior we are studying. For marketing and advertising, however, we need to isolate the most relevant motives, and we use various quantitative techniques to do so.

How do we go about this? We must remember that in terms of consumer behavior, both beliefs and feelings are operating to form attitudes that influence buying decisions, or other behaviors of interest. This means that, depending upon what motivations are operating at a particular time, it would be possible for consumers to hold several attitudes toward a brand (or anything else). The qualitative studies uncover all the possible motivations, and then the quantitative studies determine which ones operate when, and how often.

As Rossiter and Percy have pointed out, advertising does not create brand attitudes by dealing directly with underlying motivations; for as we have seen, more often than not people are not conscious of their real motives. Rather, they have a sense of the "feeling" that the motivation stimulates. To be effective, advertising must come up with benefits that connect the brand with the motivation. It must be consistent with the attitudes people hold because these attitudes are derived from their understanding of how all their beliefs and feelings about the brand combine into the "buy" signal.

There is an important linkage here that the prequantitative step is designed to uncover. People believe certain things about a product, brand, or service, and associate product benefits with those beliefs. For example, you may believe that orange juice has Vitamin C, and that Vitamin C is good for you. Why would someone want that benefit? In other words, what motivation is likely to be associated with the benefit "good for you"? Most likely, it would be physical survival.

While this is a rather obvious example, this is the sort of linkage that the visualization interviews uncover. But an equally credible linkage might be as follows: you believe orange juice has Vitamin C, and your friends all drink it because they feel it is good for them. Same attitude, and same basic benefit, but the motivation could now be adaptation. You drink orange juice because you know your friends think it is "good for you." Different motivations for different people may be underlying the same basic benefits, and this is what gets sorted out in a prequantitative study.

The other side of this is that we need to clearly ascertain that the many possible motives uncovered in the visualization interviews are the relevant motives for the largest segment of our target market. This means uncovering the most desirable benefits, and relating them, in the correct purchase or usage environment, with the most frequently operating motives. This linkage is vital. Unless we know what the underlying motivation is, we cannot know what consumer or product benefits will be most likely to contribute to a positive brand attitude. Again, as Rossiter and Percy make clear, benefits are only the surface means used in advertising to connect the brand to why the buyer should want it (the motivator). The marketer must know what the motivation is before any benefit can be used to influence attitude. Without linking the benefits to proper motivation, advertising is not likely to work.

HOW THE PREQUANTITATIVE STEP WORKS

Coming out of the qualitative work we have a good sense of the set of motives operating in our market that are likely to effect behavior. We also have a rather intensive set of possible benefits associated with these motivators. What we do not have are "findings." We have a collection of remembered events from which we are able to infer motivation. Now we must select those motives that are truly relevant.

Using a small-scale sample of our target market (from 30 to 100), a very rigorous "exploratory" quantitative study is undertaken. We look at all the scenarios associated with the motives uncovered in the visualization interviews. This is almost always a large number. Using various clusters or factor-analysis techniques, we reduce these scenarios to smaller, more manageable groups. From this analysis we have a set of "feelings" and beliefs from which motivations are inferred.

For example, in a study of golfing behavior, the following reflects some of the beliefs and their corresponding motives that were uncovered:

Belief	Motivation
Health concerns	Physical Survival
Perfection in the game, inner peace	Spiritual Survival
Loss of time & escape through concentration	Orientation to Time
Competitive for the sake of competition	Territorial Survival
Because peers do it	Adaptation
Feel better, improve self-image and self-esteem as golf score improves	Orientation to Person

As you can see, this is a logical grouping of beliefs and a measurable influence of the motivations likely to be associated with them. But the actual visualization interviews can create as many as 100 or more belief scenarios, too many for inclusion in the projectable quantitative study. The prequantitative step helps develop a meaningful, workable set of motives to be measured in the final study. These beliefs are measured in the second step—the projectable study—to identify the truly relevant motivations for devising an effective advertising strategy.

Much more is measured at this stage. While identifying the appropriate motivation—benefit link is the most crucial part—we also need to look at all the factors that underlie the consumer decision process. For example, how do all these beliefs relate to overall evaluations of brands, products, or services? Here we can use attribute modeling to help us understand the full scope of the attitude structure operating when choices are made. Another important factor is how people view the competitive environment. Are different attributes associated with different alternatives in the marketplace? If so, does this lead to different beliefs or does the belief structure remain the same? In other words, brands may be seen as having different attributes, but those attributes are believed to offer the same benefits, or different attributes may imply different benefits.

Remember this link: attributes—benefits (beliefs)—motivations. We must explore the full range of possibilities in this prequantitative step to ensure that we include only those things in the fixed study that are going to be truly helpful. Think of the prequantitative step as a funnel where the vast amount of preknowledge we have about our product or service and the information gathered in the visualization interviews are reduced to a manageable and meaningful set of variables that will define behavior in our market. Now we are ready for the actual quantitative study.

CONDUCTING THE QUANTITATIVE STUDY

We are finally ready to qualify our hypothesis. In this final step, a projectable sample of our target market is interviewed. In many ways this study is similar to other traditional market research studies. We measure attitudes and behavior, all those things we found to be important in the prequantitative study. But there is a major difference: we can also measure the emotional demographics, or what we refer to as motigraphics.

To each person in the study, along with his/her demographics, we will also add a new dependent variable: relevant motivations associated with the behavior under study. This means we are able to segment according to motivation, optimizing the benefit positioning for our product or service.

Returning to our golf example, from the set of beliefs and implied motives that we developed in the prequantitative step, we used statements such as those that follow to help identify the sizes of the various emotional segments we were dealing with:

- When golfing, I completely lose track of time (OR: Time).
- On the golf course, I feel like I am a part of nature (spiritual survival).
- When I'm on the golf course, I feel like I am in complete command (territorial survival).
- I feel like a totally different person when I am golfing, as opposed to the way that I feel when I'm at work (or with my family) (OR: Person).
- It is important that I get gradually better and better at this game, with practice (expectation).
- Golf is for fun and enjoyment, and winning isn't that important to me (play).
- I enjoy the game, but also play because it is expected of me where I work (adaptation).
- When I'm on the golf course, I am totally concentrated on perfecting my game (spiritual survival).

Respondents were asked to rank their agreement with these statements on a scale from one to seven. Another way to rank them would be to compare them with each other (which statement is most true of you, or least true, etc.). Another way to present these statements is in a true/false format. Although the format may vary, the purpose of the research is to answer some of the following questions about motivation:

- What percentage of golfers play just because it is expected of them?
- What percentage of golfers are really serious about the game?
- What are the messages that golfers really want to hear?
- Do players who are differently motivated want different products?
- Do they read different magazines? Which ones?
- What television programs do they watch?
- What differences might we expect in wearing apparel?
- What motivational messages will be most forceful in advertising?
- What brands of equipment do they prefer, and why?
- What books are they likely to read?
- How does motigraphics co-vary with demographics and with psychographics?

Answers to questions such as these gave the client direction in advertising, merchandising, location selection, and purchasing. Some of the findings were:

- Golfers who are motivated primarily by spiritual survival spend significantly more money than other golfers.
- Golfers who are motivated by territorial survival and adaptation also spend significant amounts when compared to all others except those who are motivated by spiritual survival.
- There are some strong relationships between psychographics and motigraphics.
- Golfers motivated by spiritual survival, territorial survival, and adaptation are more likely to read, and the magazines that they read most often were listed.
- There are differences between the groups in terms of motivation and the amount of time they spend playing golf.

What is important in a study such as this is the selection of motivational elements that arise out of the right brain visualization interviews, so that the motivations can be accurately and correctly assessed.

11

The Sensory Side of Advertising and Marketing

SENSORY AND EMPIRICAL SUBSTRATES OF MOTIVATION

The problem with the major motivations that have been introduced in chapter 4 are that they are considered to be *constructs*. A construct is an invented word to describe basically what cannot be seen. Since psychologists (and marketers) deal to a large extent with concepts that cannot be directly observed, they rely upon the notion of constructs. Examples of constructs from psychiatry and psychology are intelligence, personality, ego, and mental status. An example of a construct from the field of marketing is positioning.

Critics, particularly behavior-oriented psychologists, will say that constructs are not verifiable and therefore have only limited usefulness. However, in the absence of constructs we are left only with behavior, which in terms of an explanatory device leaves much to be desired. To make use of these motivational constructs that have been introduced—survival, orientation, etc.—we must give some support to their actual existence so that they may be used in the design and perfection of advertising and marketing.

It needs to be understood that constructs, such as the ones that we are concerned with, can never be proven. Scientists may verify hypotheses, but they never prove them. That the world is round, not flat, is a strongly verified hypothesis. So too is the evolution of species. There is little doubt about these phenomena. But the reason there is little doubt is because of the support that has been gathered over the years, not necessarily because of proof. The manifestation of evidence has been improved, but not proven.

Support for the motivational constructs that have been introduced in chapter 4 will be presented in two chapters: the present one, where we present sensory support, and in chapter 12 where we present empirical support. Sensory support arises from many experiments that have been conducted, over the last 100 years, on the brains of humans and animals and that uncovered, either accidentally or purposely, the brain centers of emotion and motivation. Empirical support for these motives is derived from our own research in which respondents were asked to fill out lifestyle questionnaires, and then the motives were verified with the method of factor analysis. Further support is presented in subsequent chapters, which describe the results of our extensive research with consumers.

THE NATURE/NURTURE CONTROVERSY

Psychologists, particularly behavior-oriented psychologists, have been strongly influenced by the philosophies of John Locke, who believed that the mind was a "blank slate" and that learning started at birth (or perhaps shortly before). For these psychologists, learning is the key to understanding the mind, as well as understanding motivation and emotion. But the work of Piaget, Kohlberg, and others, which was described in chapter 3, as well as the current findings in the area of biogenetics, leads most people to question if not doubt the "blank slate" approach to epistemology and knowledge. Although no "proof" has been offered, there certainly is a growing body of support for an "innate" factors theory. Nowhere is this difference seen more clearly than in the debates between Chomsky (1968) and Skinner (1987).

In American psychology, behaviorism has controlled research and knowledge at least since Watson's campaign in 1912, when he said that "behaviorists have reached the conclusion that they will drop from their scientific vocabulary all subjective terms such as sensation, perception, image, desire, purpose and even thinking and emotion as they were subjectively defined." As a result of this crusade, nurture won out over nature and many of these vital "cognitive" components of behavior were ignored. Experimental psychologists, as well as marketers and other academics, performed experiments in recall and recognition, since learning was believed to be the basis for all behavior. Particularly in the area of neuropsychology, almost all the research that was carried out was in the tradition of learning and learning theory. Investigators would create lesions in a section of the brain, and then observe the results of those lesions upon running a maze or engaging in a task that involved problem solving. The genetic or innate factors were virtually ignored. As a result, emotion and motivation, which advertisers consider the most significant ingredients in their work, were overlooked almost entirely. This is unfortunate, for as we stated in the introduction, creative people in particular were left without a "blueprint" or a methodology for designing effective and persuasive advertising. But other populations, such as students, teachers, patients, and managers, were also left without a road map, and when they completed basic classes in psychology it left them with a feeling of disappointment and a belief that they did not have the tools that they needed for problem solving—certainly not the ones they were looking for when they signed up for the course.

SENSORY SUPPORT

One very comprehensive and exhaustive resource on the subjective (emotional/ affective) origins of behavior is found in MacLean (1990). Hopefully this will be a harbinger. As he states in the opening pages of his book, "no measurements obtained by the hardware of the exact sciences are available for comprehension without undergoing the subjective transformation by the 'software' of the brain."

MacLean presents a discussion of the brain that specifically deals with the subjective self and its relations to the outer, external environment. In doing so he has relied upon extensive experimentation, his own and others, that has been carried out with the brain and nervous system. What makes his research and his interpretations of others' research so unique is that he has focused upon the origins of the subjective (emotions) rather than the objective (learning). As he has noted, philosophers and psychologists have studied the problem of epistemology, but in doing so have virtually ignored the brain.

THE TRIUNE BRAIN

MacLean (1990) has relied upon explanations that depend heavily upon the evolutionary development of the brain. In cross-section, he shows that it can clearly be seen that the human forebrain:

expands along the lines of three basic formations that anatomically and biochemically reflect an ancestral relationship, respectively, to reptiles, early mammals and late mammals. The three formations are labelled Reptilian (lower); Paleomammalian (limbic system) and Neomammalian (forebrain, cerebral cortex and cerebellum). (p. 9)

MacLean states that these three divisions are responsible for three different mentalities and, as such, give rise to emotions and emotional behaviors that can be traced back in time to ancestral sources. MacLean warns that these are not autonomous brains, but instead uses the term *Triune* from the Greek, which means operating independently but at the same time interlocked and functioning together.

An example of how one of the lower brains is involved in human behavior is in nonverbal behavior. Although animals cannot talk, no one would doubt that they communicate, nonverbally. However, a very large part of human communication is also nonverbal, but since talking is so prominent in communication the nonverbal part is often ignored. Usually the speaker supports his verbal message with nonverbal gestures and movements (Fulton & Maddock, 1995). This is an example of the Neomammalian (cortex) and Paleomammalian brain working in concert with one another. As MacLean has noted, the evolutionary study of neural architecture is a wholistic rather than a fragmented approach.

EMOTIONS AND THE BRAIN

In a study of human emotion, the forebrain will dominate most of the discussion. However, we have already presented evidence in chapter 10 to show that the limbic system of the mid brain, as well as the Reptilian or "R-complex" (lower brain) are intimately involved in the expression of emotion (LeDoux, 1994). Recent experimentation and research with neurotransmitters and with the structures of the limbic system have had very positive results, especially in the chemical treatment of depression and other emotional disorders. And surely animals have emotions. But as LeDoux has shown, although the limbic system, consisting of the amygdala, hippocampus, and hypothalamus, is instrumental in the expression of emotion, there is still much more involved. MacLean has stated that the limbic system has the function of "turning up and down the volume" or intensity of the emotions, whereas the forebrain handles the actual expression of emotion in the human animal and in many lower animals. As a result, this discussion as it relates to advertising and marketing will focus almost entirely on the role of the forebrain in mediating the emotions.

THE PREFRONTAL LOBOTOMY

Perhaps the most well known fictionalized account of the prefrontal lobotomy was presented in the book *One Flew Over the Cuckoo's Nest* (Kesey, 1962). In the book and in the subsequent screenplay, a sociopathic individual (played by Jack Nicholson) was accused of being a community nuisance and was taken to a state psychiatric hospital. Because of his charm and sociopathic personality, he commanded the respect of all the patients, organized them on field trips and boating expeditions, and, to the dismay of many of the staff, some of the patients began to show substantial improvement as a result of his leadership. However, since he was oppositional and virtually ignored all rules, he disturbed the routine of the hospital and eventually was given shock treatment. When that did not work, a prefrontal lobotomy was performed. As the writer and the screenplay try to imply, this surgical procedure changed everything, and he became a "different person," quiet, retiring, dull, unmotivated, and compliant with hospital routine and regulations. And more importantly, the patients who followed his lead went back to being "sick." He became one of them, and quietly settled into the routine of being "sick" with them.

In an actual (not fictitious) well known example, a prefrontal lobe injury incurred by a railroad worker named Phineas Gage was reported by Harlow in 1848. This 25-year-old man was tamping a charge of powder with a tamping iron that suddenly exploded and drove the tamping iron upward through his left cheek and

Figure 11-1
Skull of Phineas Gage

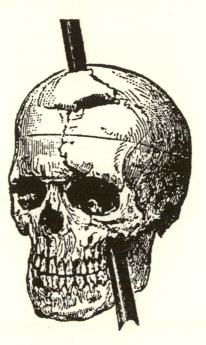

(Warren Museum, Harvard Medical School)

out the top of his skull. He was able to walk away from the accident and talk about what happened.

Recovery from the injury took about three months. After that time, he returned to work, but his co-workers noticed striking differences. Whereas Gage had been a steady and reliable worker, he became profane, undependable, fitful, and impatient. He would not take advice. He was rude to other people. But most importantly, he also became a "drifter." While he had been a steady and reliable worker prior to the accident, he now drifted aimlessly about, at one time going to South America and then back to California, where he died of seizures 12 years later.

The importance of Gage's prefrontal lobotomy is obvious. But for purposes of the Silent Side of motivation, it is especially important since it speaks directly to the four Orientation Motives: person, place, time, and, to a lesser extent, circumstances. Gage's co-workers described him as a different person. Indeed, this is how patients who have undergone this surgical procedure are described afterward by their relatives and friends.

In terms of orientation to place and time, Gage had been a responsible worker and remained on his job, in one place, for several years. But after the accident, he drifted from place to place. Although most people who undergo this procedure are aware of the need to work, they do not express any urgency (OR: Time) in finding employment. Most noticeable in Gage and others with prefrontal lobotomies is a lack of commitment to planning and organizing, as they seem to have no goals or direction but wander aimlessly about with little if any ambition or aspiration. This example suggests that the motives that we have described as the Orientation Motives are integral to functioning as we know it, and are destroyed, partially or wholly, when damage is sustained to the prefrontal lobes, particularly to the prefrontal granular cortex.

Since we have already compared the disorientation status in person, place, time, and circumstances in patients with Alzheimer's disease, it is appropriate to look at other experiments that have been conducted. MacLean (1990) reviews the 1876 work of Ferrier, who decerebrated the frog. Following this procedure, he noted that the frog would simply sit and stare, motionless: "It remained fixed and immovable. It had no physical or psychic suffering, desire or interest. Surrounded by food, it will die of starvation, unless fed artificially." Ferrier could well have been describing an Alzheimer's patient in the final stages of the disease, where all phases of the Orientation Motives have been completely lost, including OR: Person, the last of the Orientation Motives to be lost.

Also consistent with the symptoms of Alzheimer's are patients on whom incisions have been made on the prefrontal lobe on the upper and lower halves. These procedures, undertaken by Freeman and Watts in 1944 and described by MacLean (1990), involved incisions that were made on the prefrontal lobe. The patient appears quite unchanged following incisions on the first and second quadrants of the front lobe. However, after the third quadrant is sectioned, the patient's verbal responses are diminished to one-and two-word replies, and after the fourth quadrant, the patient becomes basically unresponsive, except to urgent questions. Also, these patients are expressionless, monosyllabic, and there is a complete loss of orientation.

THE EXPECTATION MOTIVE

There is considerable evidence that, as prefrontal damage is incurred by patients, the ability to deal with the future is also severely impaired. After all, the human animal is the only animal that has the capacity to chart and plan the future, or expectation. As MacLean has stated it:

The *psychological explanation* in question is based on the inferred special capacity of the granular frontal cortex to anticipate the nature of future experience on the basis of past and ongoing experience . . . Manifestations following frontal lobotomy indicate that the granular frontal cortex is implicated generally in functions related to an anticipation of, and preparation for, future experience in light of past and ongoing experience. (pp. 531–33)

It would follow that if the planning function was interrupted by prefrontal lesions, the Expectation Motive would be involved. According to MacLean, this motive involves "intuitive calculation" and has a close relationship to OR: Time. He states that these calculations involve both long-and short-term planning. An example of short term would be an outfielder calculating the angle and distance of a fly ball and catching it. The example he gives of long term is a South Sea Islander who walks to the shore, raises a wet finger to the wind, and then navigates a boat to a pinpoint island 50 miles away. (p. 551)

THE ADAPTATION MOTIVE

We have not attempted to localize the Adaptation Motive, simply because it is already well documented. As noted in chapter 4, the Adaptation Motive is seen in diagnostic ultrasound during the third trimester, as the infant moves his/her hands up to the face and continues to do so after birth for about six months. This is primarily a motor activity. After birth, adaptation is seen in ducks, which imprint upon their mother immediately after hatching, or upon the first moving object that they see if the mother is removed (Lorenz, 1935). Although imprinting does not occur in humans, neonates do establish a very strong bond or attachment upon their mothers, or to whomever serves as the primary caregiver.

According to MacLean (1990) the function of maternal communication may be assigned to the Paleomammalian brain. With the evolution of the limbic system, three types of behavior occurred that were not common to reptiles: (1) nursing in conjunction with maternal care; (2) audiovocal communication for maintaining mothers-offspring contact; and (3) play. So it might be that what we are referring to as the all-encompassing Adaptation Motive resides in the limbic system, since it is unique to mammals and is observed even before birth. But soon after birth this motive converts to the innate tendency to "follow the leader" (imitation) and remains that way throughout the rest of our lives. This is an abrupt transition, and the two behaviors do not seem to be that closely connected. Bandura (1977), who writes in the behaviorist tradition, would see this motive as a lifelong learning phenomenon and not an innate, emotional occurrence.

THE SURVIVAL MOTIVES (SPIRITUAL, PHYSICAL, TERRITORIAL, AND SEXUAL)

Since even the lowest of organisms are concerned with the day-to-day effort to survive, the Survival Motives must be considered basic to all species and therefore originating in the Reptilian brain. These include the functions of physical, sexual, and territorial survival, along with reproduction, mating rituals, and the continuing search for food, air, and water. At the level of the human animal, this may include spiritual survival, which by definition cannot be assigned as a motive to animals.

But according to MacLean (1990), experiments over the last 50 years suggest that these thymogenic functions also arise from the limbic system (Paleomammalian), which has three main divisions. The two older divisions are associated with the olfactory apparatus (much larger in animals than in man) and are closely associated with oral and genital functions having to do with procreation and self-preservation. MacLean notes:

An analysis of the phenomenon of limbic epilepsy provides a basis for a classification of three categories of affects that is particularly relevant to epistemic questions pertaining to ontology, including a sense of time and space. It is of special epistemic significance that the limbic cortex has the capacity to generate free floating, affective feelings conveying a sense of what is real, true and important. In regard to global functions, there is diverse evidence that the limbic system is essential for the interplay of interoceptive and exteroceptive systems required for a sense of personal identity and the memory of ongoing experiences. The phenomenology of psychomotor epilepsy indicates that the limbic system is implicated in dreaming and in certain psychotic manifestations. (p. 17)

Another indication that the limbic system may be involved with spiritual survival is in the transition to the three behaviors that MacLean noted above that were not common in reptiles. One of these behaviors involves parental responsibility to offspring, which is one of the crucial elements of spiritual survival and which we have labeled family values. MacLean also mentions that psychomotor epilepsy provides us with evidence that the limbic system is involved in "feelings of self-realization, as evident by such experiences during the aura as feelings of an enhanced sense of reality, an increased awareness or self-duplication." Such feelings could come about in a drug-induced state, or could occur naturally with the excitement and revival that occur during the state of what Fleischman calls "renewal and release."

In his conclusion, MacLean (1990) speaks directly to the phenomenon of spiritual survival in the "dichotomy that exists between the neocortical and limbic systems that may account for a dissociation in intellectual and emotional mentation":

Moreover (and this cannot be overemphasized) [emphasis his] the phenomenology of psychomotor epilepsy suggests that without a co-functioning limbic system, the neocortex lacks not only the requisite neural substrate for a sense of self, of reality, and the memory of ongoing experience [OR: Time and Expectation], but also a feeling of *conviction as to what is true or false* [emphasis ours]. (p. 578)

It appears that in these references, MacLean is dealing with some of the most complex and abstract of thoughts, similar to what we have called spiritual survival or what Maslow might refer to as self-actualization. Yet, he has an interesting conclusion:

This presents a problem of crucial epistemological significance because there is no evidence that the limbic structures of the temporal lobe are capable of comprehending speech, nor is there any basis for inferring a capacity to communicate in verbal terms. Hence, it would appear that the manufacture of belief in reality, importance, truth or falsity of what is conceived depends on a mentality incapable of verbal comprehension and communication. To revert [to] a previous comment, it is one thing to have a primitive, illiterate mind for judging the authenticity of food or of a mate, but where do we stand if we must depend on that same mind for belief in our ideas, concepts and theories? (p. 579)

There is a danger, however, of overemphasizing the emotion that arises from the Reptilian and Neomammalian brain. This emotion is known to be impulsive, vindictive, self-serving, and protective. It is not altruistic, benevolent, or generous. So it is quite obvious that the spiritual motives that allow us to live together— love, concern, cooperation, patriotism, and altruism—depend to a large extent upon the neocortex. Without the neocortex, there would never have been a country as we know it, where law and order abide and justice is meted out fairly and evenly. And in cases involving disaster, like hurricanes or other natural calamities, people act impulsively, without forethought or anticipation, expecting no reward or recognition for their often heroic acts. Believing such behavior could originate from the Reptilian brain (spiritual motivation) is therefore unrealistic.

EMOTION AND INTELLECT

We often encounter individuals who are dumbstruck by the dichotomy that exists between rational and reasonable behavior and the emotional, irrational behavior that will occur within the same individual. How could a college president make obscene telephone calls to female students? How could an international figure in psychiatry have sex with certain of his female patients, while they were under anesthesia? How could a respected and adulated spiritual leader spend his days off picking up prostitutes? How could a person who is well educated and from a respected family commit a heinous crime? The answer, according to MacLean, is that

our intellectual functions are mediated in the newest and most highly developed part of the brain, while our affective behavior continues to be dominated by a relatively crude and primitive system. This situation, I noted, provides a clue to understanding the difference between what we "feel" and what we "know." (p. 266)

REFERENCES

Bandura, A. (1977). *Social learning theory*. Englewood Cliffs, NJ: Prentice-Hall.

Chomksy, N. (1968). *Language and the mind*. New York: Harcourt-Brace.

Fulton, R., & Maddock, R. (1995). *The silent side of communication*. Des Moines, IA: American Media, Incorporated. (Book and video)

Kesey, K. (1962). *One flew over the cuckoo's nest*. New York: Viking Press.

LeDoux, J. E. (1994, June). Emotion, memory and the brain, part 1. *Scientific American*, 270, 6.

Lorenz, K. (1935). Der Kumpen in der Umwelt des Vogels. *Journal of Ornithology, 83*, 137–213, 289–413.

MacLean, P. D. (1990). *The triune brain in evolution: Role in paleocerebral functions.* New York: Plenum Press.

Skinner, B. F. (1987). Whatever happened to psychology as the science of behavior? *American Psychologist, 42*, 780–86.

Watson, J. B. (1924). *Behaviorism*. New York: The People's Institute Publishing Co.

12

The Empirical Side of Advertising and Marketing

FIGURES DO NOT LIE!

In order to lend support to the motivational structure that was introduced in chapter 4, quantitative research has been carried out with the purpose of verifying these motivational structures. These motives comprise and underlie the "structure" of consumer motivation and emotion, which, based on our hypothesis, is critical to advertising and marketing. The critical nature of these motives is based on the fact that they are the driving forces in the decisions to purchase, on a first time, a regular, or a reoccurring basis. Customer loyalty, motivation, and indeed, the viability of the product or service all rest upon the existence of these motives and their relative strength. So although the numbers do not "prove" the existence of the motives, they do add strong support.

METHODOLOGY

The methodology that was used in verifying the motives introduced in chapter 4 was factor analysis.

SUBJECTS

Approximately 200 respondents were asked to volunteer as participants in this project. The project had two phases, and 120 were involved in phase 1 and 80 in phase 2. Some were students in an evening extension division of a community college. As such, there was a broad sample of ages, ranging between 19 and 54.

The ratio of male to female was about 40:60, and the racial mix was consistent with the U.S. population, except that there were no Hispanics or Orientals. About 25 percent of the participants were taking classes in the college at night or on weekends, which provided an excellent mix of age, race, sex, etc. These students received extra course credit for their participation. The rest were volunteers who came from the surrounding community.

PROCEDURE

The procedure involved filling out a 200-item questionnaire that was designed to ask specific questions about lifestyle. The questions were related to the 11 motives that have been introduced in this book:

- Orientation to Circumstances
- Orientation to Time
- Orientation to Place
- Orientation to Person
- Play*
- Sexual Survival (Gender, Impulse, Inhibition)
- Territorial Survival
- Physical Survival
- Spiritual Survival
- Adaptation
- Expectation

*This motive, which refers primarily to the play of children, was not covered in this analysis.

The questions that were asked were in a bipolar semantic differential format. In other words, subjects who filled out the questionnaires were asked to make a choice on a scale between two extremes, as follows:

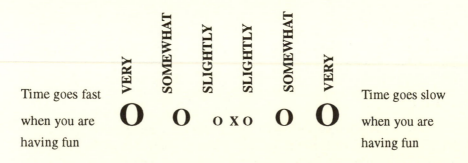

The undecided position was in the middle (X) and respondents were asked to avoid it as often as possible. This semantic differential (polarized method) of asking questions generally yields the best data for purposes of analysis. It is perfectly legitimate, and does not force a skew of the data, but it does provide data.

The data was subjected to factor analysis (varimax) with subsequent rotations to simple structure. Based on the responses, many questions were omitted since they did not load significantly on any of the factors that were yielded in the study. After omission, a "second round" or phase 2 was initiated, with respondents answering a new questionnaire. This new questionnaire consisted of all of the questions from phase 1 that loaded significantly on one or more factors plus new questions from phase 2 that were being tested. These new questions, which also dealt with lifestyle and various beliefs, were designed to bring out or "sharpen up" the original study, particularly to see if certain factors that were weak in phase 1 would appear stronger in phase 2.

RESULTS

The factors that arise from this study are amazingly close to some of those that were predicted, but are not exactly the same. The order of the factors as predicted in the pyramid is somewhat different. However, this order could easily change in the future, and is based on a number of issues that are not related to importance, such as the way the questions were asked. The factors are listed in order and the percentage of variance contributed by each factor to the total variance (70%) is noted next to the factor name. The items that define the factor, along with their respective loadings (correlations) are listed under each factor heading.

Factor 1:　　**OR: Person**　　　　　　　　　　**Percent of Total = 13%**

.74　I consider myself up to date
.73　I remain aware of all current fads
.70　I love to shop
.61　I like living in a big city (vs. living in a cabin in the woods)
.58　I like to wear whatever is in style
.53　I like a fast pace

Factor 2:　　**Spiritual Survival**　　　　　　**Percent of Total = 9.2%**

.83　Prayer is more important than sports
.80　Reading the Bible in schools should be allowed
.70　Families that pray together stay together
.57　We will be punished or rewarded for our actions in this life
.57　My family is more important to me than my work

Factor 3:   **Sexual Survival—Gender—Female**   <u>**Percent of Total = 6%**</u>

.80 I love getting flowers
.74 I like feeling feminine
.59 I like wearing lots of jewelry
.57 I have lots of different perfumes at home
.46 I like to be treated special

Factor 4:   **Adaptation Motive**   <u>**Percent of Total = 5.1%**</u>

.80 I want what everyone else has
.75 If the majority do it, it must be right
.56 I read articles about what others think

Factor 5:   **Sexual Survival—Impulse—Male**   <u>**Percent of Total = 4.5%**</u>

.86 I want a car with lots of power (vs. a safe car)
.82 I want a car that is fast and hot

Factor 6:   **Physical Survival**   <u>**Percent of Total = 4.0%**</u>

.78 I eat anything that tastes good
.70 The air I breathe is OK

Factor 7:   **Expectation**   <u>**Percent of Total = 3.8%**</u>

.88 You can't always trust a doctor
.70 I don't trust just anyone to operate on me
.63 I question my doctor
.45 You can't trust just anyone in this world

Factor 8:   **OR: Place and Optimism**   <u>**Percent of Total = 3.6%**</u>

.81 I think that the future looks good for me
.51 I like to get in the car and just drive
.74 I like a change of scenery
.38 There is much more to life than what we see before us

Factor 9:   **OR: Circumstances**   <u>**Percent of Total = 3.3%**</u>

.76 Drugs help me to gain perspective
.67 I like being a part of the "good old boy" network
.45 A drink at the end of the day helps me to forget

Factor 10:   **Expectation (2) (Pessimism)**   **Percent of Total = 2.9%**

.81 I have to look out for myself
.58 I always wear seat belts

Factor 11:   **Male—Sexual Survival—Gender**   **Percent of Total = 2.7%**

.78 My actions don't influence how I feel about myself
.43 I never read anything about glamour
.41 I don't like antiques
.37 I don't like to read romance novels

Factor 12:   **Territorial—Female**   **Percent of Total = 2.7%**

.81 I really feel appreciated by others for what I do
.58 A career is more important than anything else

Factor 13:   **OR: Time**   **Percent of Total = 2.5%**

.78 Marijuana should be legalized

Factor 14:   **OR: Place**   **Percent of Total = 2.3%**

.77 Getting away from it all relieves me
.67 I need to escape more than most people

Factor 15:   **Sexual Survival—Impulse—Female**   **Percent of Total = 2.1%**

.82 I would rather be sexy than intelligent
.41 I choose clothes that are sexy and seductive (rather than conservative)
.47 I would rather be with friends than family

Factor 16:   **Sexual Survival—Inhibition—Female** **Percent of Total = 2.0%**

.76 I am cold most of the time
.41 Love is worth more than money
.40 I enjoy going to museums (vs. night clubs)

Factor 18:   **OR: Person (2)**   **Percent of Total = 1.7%**

.72 A person's career makes that person what he/she is
.40 What you eat is what you are

Factor 19:   **Expectation (2)**   **Percent of Total = 1.7%**

.75   People should choose their own doctor

Factor 20:   **Sexual Survival—Impulse**   **Percent of Total = 1.6%**

.68   I like making quick decisions
.60   I never plan to slow down
.41   My family consumes me

Factor 17 is omitted since it dealt with a single item, gun control, that is not related to any of the motives.

The amount of variance contributed by these combined factors to the total is 70 percent. The remaining 30 percent is in a number of other factors that all contribute less than 1 percent and have very small loadings. Throughout the analysis, loadings of less than .40 were dropped because they were not statistically significant.

EMPIRICAL SUPPORT

Ten of the 11 motives described in chapter 4 received empirical support in our research. The eleventh motive, play, was not measured at the time that this research was done. This eleventh motive has received substantial support in research done on the brain and central nervous system, and is well documented by MacLean (1990) and by others who have observed and described children at play.

The "uncovering" of the 11 motives that were described in chapter 4 in the form of these factors does not "prove" the existence of these motivations in consumers. However, the factorial evidence offered lends strong support to the existence of these motives and the underlying emotions. More work needs to be done and, indeed, is being done as the questionnaires are refined, narrowed down, and made more specific. However, to date this represents one of the first attempts to do an empirical investigation on underlying consumer motives that are largely unconscious and unspoken.

REFERENCE

MacLean, P. D. (1990). *The triune brain in evolution: Role in paleocerebral functions.* New York: Plenum Press.

13

How Motivation is Used to Design Effective Advertising and Marketing Strategies

The research methods that were described in chapter 8 will find new and exciting "secrets" within the product which then may be used to design effective and creative marketing strategies. For this reason, creative directors grasp the Silent Side approach. Most of them feel that traditional market research has left them out of the picture, because it is descriptive, not explanatory. As they tell it, traditional research does not tell them what they really need to know to motivate people and to execute creative strategies. There are no similar complaints about marketing to the mind! For this reason, it is strongly recommended that the visualization research be carried out, at least in a qualitative phase. However, bear in mind that to be precise both phases need to be carried out, so that motigraphics can define the motives by segment.

This visual methodology is so effective that creative and persuasive strategies may be designed without the research, as long as the 11 motives are used as they are recommended here. In fact, the many creative directors who have done this have seen results that have worked for them. We have no doubt that some will continue to use the visualization research and the motivational hierarchy for every campaign that they undertake, rather than trying to reinvent the wheel each time.

Let us look first at how other well known marketers have designed their advertising around the 11 specific motives that we have uncovered, all of which have been found to reside within the unconscious mind.

Avis, with their Number Two campaign, is the standard when we try to understand the whole approach to positioning (Reis & Trout, 1981). But this is only half of the picture. Avis said, "We're number two," and in saying so, they positioned themselves against the leader in the rental car market, Hertz. We all know that. But Avis also said, "and we try harder." This is not a positioning statement. It is a motivational statement. It speaks directly to orientation to circumstances. What circumstances? Hasn't almost everyone had the experience of waiting in a long line at the airport, only to finally go out into a steaming-hot parking lot and find that he/she has the wrong key? After trudging back into the airport, and waiting in line again, he/she gets the right key, only to go back and find that the ashtray is full and there are newspapers and candy wrappers in the back seat. Those circumstances! But Avis said that they changed all that. By trying harder, they changed it. The next thing that happened was that the other car rental companies were positioning next to Avis, since they had to work harder too! "We're number two and we try harder." The first part is a positioning statement, the second part, a motivational statement.

One of the most memorable campaigns ever run was in 1982–83, when Coke used "Mean" Joe Greene of the Pittsburgh Steelers as a spokesperson. Memorable in this context refers to motivational. In this spot, Joe Greene, worn out from a game and on his way to the locker room, stops to talk with a small boy who offers him a Coke. The boy could not have been more than eight at the time. This commercial grabbed the hearts of all America. Why? Commercials that are this strong and persuasive are almost always targeted to the spiritual survival level. One may ask, "What's spiritual about it?" Remembering the elements of spirituality, it all fits together. One element—the one involved here—is affirming acceptance (Fleischman, 1990). Joe Greene, who was close to a deity for youngsters and sports fans, bends down to an eight year old, who offers him a Coke! And he takes it! All Americans who watch feel just what that boy felt: the power of affirming acceptance by a major player on the American sports scene. That is spiritual survival in motivation.

McDonald's, in the "early days," marketed to the level of physical survival. After all, it was selling food, so it all made sense. "Two all beef patties, special sauce, lettuce, cheese, pickles, onions on a sesame seed bun!" Why would something this simple catch on and have universal recall, especially with kids who were McDonald's customers? It caught on because it dealt with food, and food is one of the major elements of the Physical Survival Motive.

Later when McDonald's elevated its advertising to the next level of motivation, it changed over to "you deserve a break today." Recognize the motive? It is OR: Circumstances. From this it moved on to family values and spiritual survival, which was as high as it could go on the motivational hierarchy.

Wendy's, Burger King, and the others have stayed with food, which is the major element of what they sell, on the physical survival level. Perhaps not the strongest advertising, but it is safe. As Wendy's Dave Thomas says, "When you gotta have one, you gotta have one." The element is food, the motive is physical survival. But in addition, Wendy's uses Dave Thomas, the founder, and many people are aware that he does not even have a high school diploma! This adds another major motivation: expectation. "Perhaps I can make it big some day like he did, even though I do not have much going for me!"

One fast food franchise, Arby's, has stayed with "Go West. It's better out here." Recognize it? Neither do we. It may be working for them, but it also may be an example of advertising that is not motivational, since it does not say anything about either the product or the experience.

These brief examples illustrate effective, motivational advertising. The research that we are describing, and the subsequent motivational classification, is both a method and a format. It addresses the content and the structure of advertising. But more importantly, it addresses the content of advertising in terms of its compatibility with the mind! This is why we call it marketing to the mind!

RULES FOR DESIGNING ADVERTISING AND MARKETING STRATEGIES THAT ARE FULLY COMPATIBLE WITH THE MIND

With these considerations there are rules that should be followed if the marketer wants to design advertising that is compatible with the mind.

Motives Are Seldom Approached Directly

Motives, like spiritual survival, physical survival, etc., are abstractions. And consumers do not respond to abstractions. In research carried out by Paivio (1971, 1978) the general finding was that pictures are retained better than concrete words and concrete words are retained better than abstract words. In his experiments, these words were presented visually rather than in an auditory format.

In examples cited earlier in chapter 4, Coty and Calvin Klein have recently attempted to design motives into their advertising by talking about the spiritual side of women. This is believed to be a unique approach. However, for most people the word "spiritual" is an abstraction that means very little. If it does mean anything, it means "something about religion." But in advertising, spiritual has nothing to do with religion. It has to do with psychology. It is a psychological construct that is present in the mind, and effective advertising needs to address this construct. But not in terms of an abstraction.

Will the advertising proposed by Coty and Calvin Klein work? It may. But it would be stronger if they addressed the elements of spiritual survival, rather than addressing the motive itself. The research carried out by Paivio strongly supports this. Another problem with this approach is that spiritual survival may not be the strongest motivation involved in the use of cosmetics. In cosmetics, orientation to person is more influential and persuasive. This is based upon our experience with advertising-impact analyses. This issue is covered in more detail in the section in chapter 18 on cosmetics.

The design of effective motivational advertising, then, should be in the appeal to the elements of the motives rather than to the motives directly. Put another way, a beautiful sunset *just is*. Try and describe that beauty and the image is distorted by the detail of the description.

For example, in talking about food, most food marketers agree that close-up color pictures of the food product itself are a very effective way to market and advertise certain food products. It makes more sense to picture the food itself than to talk about physical survival. Why? Because physical survival, although easy to understand, is an abstraction. But anyone can relate to the picture of a hamburger or a cheeseburger with fries!

Look at what happens when sexual survival as a motive is approached directly. An example is Brooke Shields in Calvin Klein jeans. Many people were offended. In 1995 so many people were offended by the new round of Calvin Klein ads, which were seen as bordering on "kiddie porn," that the company was obliged to pull the ads and a federal investigation ensued. This is the real danger in appealing to sexual survival: sexual survival can be highly controversial and thus spiritual survival is assaulted and offended. Although it is difficult to find articles in journals and trade magazines on spiritual survival, it is easy to find articles on the use of sex in advertising. Interestingly, most of the articles are against it. To some it is even an ethical issue. This is an example of how directly dealing with a motivational category can backfire and cause marketers many problems that they had not anticipated. In fact, we might even go so far as to say that a direct approach to motivation could be dangerous, whereas the indirect approach (to the related elements) is always more effective and less likely to result in misinterpretation.

The elements described by Fleischman (1990) and used by us to score and define spiritual survival are concrete representations of that motivational category. Most people understand what it means to become renewed and refreshed, to have a meaningful death, or to be affirmed and accepted. These are scenarios. These are the finer points of motivation, the ones that make up the motives themselves. There are very few who cannot understand them. Similarly, there are three elements of sexual survival: impulse, inhibition, and gender. Very few are offended by any of these, except impulse. Even impulse, when treated correctly, can be dealt with in an effective way, and with minimal offense to the audience. In summary, motives should never be directly addressed, but indirectly through the elements of the motives and in scenarios that address these elements.

Motivational Advertising Should Be Layered

If there is already a rational appeal, then two layers of emotion are enough, or more than enough, to get through to the consumer. Beyond the two layers consumers begin to get confused and disoriented, which in turn leads to a fast exit or a turnoff.

There is enough clutter in the media. The creative director should refrain from using clutter within the ad itself. Usually one emotion and one rational issue are all that the consumer can handle. After all, the ad needs to prompt a purchase or response. It need not be a complex "novel."

Direct Penetration of the Unconscious with Personalizations

Advertising that is directed toward the motivational structures that have been described is advertising that people will personalize. A personalization leads to recall. People will recall whatever they can personalize. Ads that directly penetrate the unconscious are more lasting, even if they are not liked by the consumer. For example, "ring around the collar" was experienced by the consumer as an annoying and irritating advertisement. Nevertheless, it increased market share. Why? Ring around the collar is something that almost everyone has seen and experienced personally. Furthermore, this phenomenon is attached to strong emotion: embarrassment. Therefore, it is memorable. Personalizations must be product related, motivational, and emotional. When they meet these three criteria, recall is assured.

Positive and Negative Suggestions

Since there is no logic in the unconscious mind, it receives all suggestions as undirectional. The sign that reads "Wet Paint" invites everyone to touch it, and some to even sit in it. It is not that the unconscious is defiant. It is just that it processes negative suggestions as if they were positive. For example, consider Mr. Whipple telling shoppers, "Please don't squeeze the Charmin!" Telling shoppers *not* to pick up the Charmin was found to be an extremely successful way of getting them to do just the opposite: to pick it up and take it home!

Absurdities

Absurdities are mnemonics. Therefore, by definition they increase recall. Absurdities may not be as motivating as personalizations, but they are memorable. This is because the consumer pictures something that is unusual and outside the scope of everyday reality—but not so far outside the scope as to be outrageous!

This has already been discussed in chapter 5, where it was shown that an absurdity automatically puts the limbic system on alert. The limbic system is the brain's emotional center. Once the emotional center is alerted, the right hemisphere goes to work attempting to integrate the product with the emotion. If this cannot be done, then the absurdity will not work. An absurdity is outrageous when it lies completely outside the realm of the everyday reality that the consumer experiences.

Absurdities are often referred to in the academic marketing literature as *relational violations*. They have the advantage of being memorable, but are not necessarily motivating or personal. This is because they do not always deal with motives, elements of motives, or emotions. McDonald's slight absurdity "two all beef patties, special sauce," was memorable because it directly targeted an element of the Physical Survival Motive: food.

Resistance

When we are asked to apply the unconscious to business problems, most of the time these requests center around resistance:

- How do we get people to stop at our bank, instead of driving by to get to "their bank"?
- Why do people say that they don't eat junk food, when an analysis of their pantries and "garbage inventories" suggests differently?
- How can I get consumers to start using my product, instead of the old "tried and true"?
- How can I turn a day trip into a destination?

Freud (1959) said that the biggest problem that an analyst had to deal with in therapy was the resistance of the patient. And yet, he also presented this as the greatest opportunity. His point was that people resist what is most meaningful to them, and to get to the bottom of the issue, the therapist must deal with resistance. Freud's observation may not be analogous to marketing situations on a one-to-one basis. However, when analyzing customer resistance to a product or service, we have found that an understanding of consumer resistance often opens the door to new-found opportunities!

For example, in the wine study explained in chapter 8, we found that people resisted the artsy labels because to them the purchase of wine was a serious endeavor that required forethought and planning. Wine is not just another grocery product. This creates a new opportunity for merchandising, pricing, marketing, advertising, and positioning.

In a study of banks, we found that consumers avoided and resisted using a well-placed and well-situated bank in a shopping mall, because it was open to the mall and there was very little privacy. The customers who did use the bank cashed checks and money orders, but they did not apply for loans and mortgages, or start saving plans. Why? Because to customers, borrowing and saving represented a serious kind of banking, and the circumstances, which consisted of confusion and noise, were not conducive to such a serious endeavor (OR: Circumstances). The challenge was to present serious banking in a high traffic, informal setting. The customers were trying to tell the bank that they did not care for such an arrangement. Despite this, by dealing with customers' unconscious motives we were able to offer the bank a solution.

Because beer (for heavy beer drinkers) is so closely tied to orientation to person (personal identity) and sex (gender—male), heavy beer drinkers resist drinking light beer. Light beer is not consistent with the identity (OR: Person) that they are trying to establish when they drink beer. If they were concerned with physical survival, they might be more inclined to drink light beer. This is just one more fact that shows how other motives—Adaptation, OR: Person, and Sexual Survival (gender)—are more important when it comes to beer drinking than health and physical survival.

Projection and New Product Development

The Silent Side research method described in chapter 4 is one that is totally projective in nature. A projective methodology is one in which the subject or the respondent supplies all the data, as opposed to the researcher supplying the data. In most market research procedures, the researcher provides the structure and the respondent does what he/she does best: responds.

Since this method is projective rather than objective, it is ideal for the introduction and development of new products. In working to introduce a new food product, which had no precedent in the market and no competitors, we took consumers back to their first experience with this product, which consisted of the homemade version of what was to become the new food product. Then as we brought them forward into the present and then into the future, we incorporated all the old as well as the more recent elements of the product, and the consumers supplied all the data. As a result, a very successful product was brought to market, and the projective research that we carried out was applicable to all the facets of the product: development, taste, labeling, merchandising, ingredients, sales, and advertising. And although much of it came from the conscious side, much of it also came from the unconscious, ensuring that there would be no conflict within the consumer, who will also be the end user. He/she tasted the food, commented upon the ingredients, and in the end designed the label and the package.

In the same way, new rides for theme parks were developed, and new themes were added. Frequent visitors were taken through the entire sequence, often starting with the first time (in their life) that they had ever ridden the attraction, and then recalled similar events up to the present. Through each phase their emotional response was microscopically examined. This is projection. There is no way that thrill seekers can explain logically why they do what they do (mountain climbers, surfers, etc.) because these are not rational activities.

As a mountain climber in Jackson Hole, Wyoming, the one goal of the author was to ascend the Grand Teton: 13,766 feet above sea level and 6,200 feet above the valley floor. This became almost a spiritual effort. Although I worked as a ranger who went out on rescues and picked up dead bodies of young, inexperienced climbers as well as older, experienced ones, nothing could divert me from my goal. Finally after my second year with the National Park Service, I made it to the top. My goal had been reached. I was now ready to ascend many other peaks, and began making plans to go to Alaska.

One day, while sitting around the rescue station, I listened to experienced climbers, who had been to the top many times, as they talked about harder and more difficult routes to the top: Class 5 and 6 climbs. All of a sudden, it did not make sense any more. If someone had been to the top of the Grand Teton three or four times, why would he/she still want to find a harder, more difficult route to the top? I guess this feeling was intensified by the death that summer of the ranger who had taught me many climbing techniques in the National Park Service Mountain Rescue School, when he fell to his death from the top of a 1,200-foot glacier. This did not deter me; but after hearing people talk about a harder way to the top, all of a sudden the sport did not make sense to me any more. I guess I was never a committed thrill seeker! More importantly, I was unwilling to move the sport of mountain climbing up to the spiritual survival level in my life. I could not be that passionate or fanatic about climbing mountains. Some people are, however, and for them mountain climbing is a spiritual activity.

In an effort to design a new product, service, or logo we often go to consumers and users of the product. They often tell us what they think we want to hear. But in right brain visual interviewing, most of what the consumer thinks that we want to hear is bypassed. This is done by providing the respondent with a very personal, highly idiosyncratic projective experience with the product, or service. Usually it is a pleasant experience, and when it is, respondents become even more relaxed and more cooperative, giving out more information that is useful, informative, and directly applicable to the design of the new product.

Analysis of Advertising

As Percy and Rossiter (1983) suggest, there are many facets to visual advertising that have yet to be uncovered. And with clutter, the consumer may literally be bombarded with stimuli to the point where there is a cognitive overload. Percy and Rossiter suggest visual advertising formats, but admit that there is much more research to be done in this area.

Typically the way the consumer handles overload is to screen out many of the stimuli that just cannot be processed. Based on research quoted earlier (when suggestions were given to subjects in surgery, under anesthesia) the way the mind handles overload is to bypass the conscious mind and pour much of the excess into the unconscious. Silent Side research is an excellent way to determine what the potential buyer is seeing, hearing, and experiencing before the ad or the sale is finalized. Is it possible that he/she is hearing or seeing something that he/she does not want to hear or see, unconsciously? Could he/she be getting negative suggestions? The visualization technique is an excellent way to "flush out the unconscious" and to find out if the ad or the product is saying something that it should not be saying, or showing, to the unconscious.

INCORPORATING MOTIVES INTO CREATIVE
STRATEGIES: CASE HISTORIES

Athletics: Football Team

A local college football team suffered from poor attendance, and part of the attendance problem was due to a poor record. The community was appealed to in terms of "it's your team; come out and support it." It did not work. Obviously, this was an attempt to arouse guilt, and guilt is a negative motivator. What the public wanted to see was good football, and the last thing they wanted was to fill their spare time with a guilt trip.

At long last the school decided it needed to shore up its recruiting efforts. Silent Side research suggested that it should videotape some of this, and send it to local sports shows and TV stations. In this way, the fans and potential fans could feel like they were part of the rebuilding process. In addition, attempts to manufacture guilt trips were shelved and the whole endeavor was positioned alongside patriotism. Patriotic pep rallies, bands, and displays were held at half time and before the games. Many came just to participate in the patriotic festivities. In this way, spiritual survival was addressed indirectly through the element of family values, love, and patriotism. Attendance rose dramatically. Rallies before and during the game had the effect of bringing many of the people in the community together and went far beyond the original goal of getting local support for the football team.

Pest Control Services

A local exterminator had painted, as part of the logo, a large rodent on the side of the service trucks. Although customers thought that the rodent was "cute" (he was smiling, had a little T-shirt on, etc.), visualization research revealed that the same customers were embarrassed to have the truck in their driveways, because neighbors would think (or know) that they had rodents or bugs in their home. This never came out in the conscious, "loud side" research that was done. The customers considered the rodent to be an announcement to the whole neighborhood that their home was dirty or infested. Obviously, the rodent was a source of considerable resistance, and the removal of the artwork resulted in the removal of customer resistance and increased business. The motivation here is physical survival and the element of physical survival is good health and hygiene habits. A secondary motivation is adaptation (what will the neighbors think?).

Theme Park

A regional theme park was converted into a destination attraction by providing rides and other experiences that were fun and disorienting, and putting facilities for meals and overnight accommodations on the grounds or close to them. These major changes dealt with the following motivations: orientation to person; orientation to circumstances; and play.

Toilet Tissue

A major brand of toilet tissue had silk as part of its brand name so that the company could emphasize "silky softness." Visualization research uncovered the fact that consumers felt that silk would stop up their toilet. This resulted in a major name change, which effectively ended the resistance to the brand, and sales increased.

Exercise Equipment

A major manufacturer of home health and exercise equipment asked why people would say that they had exercised at home, when in-depth research indicated that they really did not exercise. In an era where the emphasis is on health, fitness, and well-being, it is easy to understand why they might say that they exercise, but why don't they actually do it?

Visualization research uncovered the fact that there was a spiritual-side block to exercise, healthy living, and overall healthy lifestyle. This block is referred to as *fatalism*, and it is associated with the spiritual survival element of lawful order. Many people believe, subconsciously, that when your number is called, your time is up, and there is nothing that you can do about it. Many people do not believe that life can be prolonged or that the "master plan" of the universe can be changed. The belief in fatalism is not necessarily theological. About half of the fatalists in this study supported their argument with genetics rather than theology.

Motigraphics, which followed the qualitative visualization research, indicated that indeed, the proportion of people who believed in fatalism was quite large (64%), and may have accounted for the people who did not exercise. The respondents would spontaneously offer various rationalizations like "my uncle sopped up grease off the plate every night, and lived until he was 88," or "my grandpappy chewed and smoked for 80 years, and lived until he was 95." For this subsample of the population, that was all the "proof" that they needed. "When your number is called . . ."

Advertising and marketing campaigns were devised to reverse this belief. They were not directed at the motive of spiritual survival, since motives are never addressed directly. Instead, campaigns targeted the spiritual elements of wholeness and membership and the adaptation element of testimonials. Well-known figures in the sports and entertainment world were employed to show how they had taken control of their lives (Adaptation Motive). Moreover, the spiritual element of membership was used to promote inclusion in a very unique and elitist group of people: the healthy ones.

Community Cultural Exhibit

A community had sponsored several major cultural exhibits in exchange with other nations. On exhibit in a large convention hall were many of the treasures of other cultures. Attendance in past years had been only fair, if not somewhat disappointing.

One particular event, which ran for about seven months, generated little interest in the focus groups that were conducted prior to the actual opening. It appeared that it would draw very few visitors. However, in Silent Side research done prior to the actual opening there was a tendency of the respondents to focus on the issue of death. This was because the exhibit itself focused on treasures taken from ancient tombs, graveyards, and pyramids.

As a result of these findings, the pre-exhibit advertising and marketing focused almost entirely on the spiritual element of meaningful death. By the time the exhibit closed, attendance had increased 10 percent over any previous exhibit. Since cultural exhibits are not entertaining, they appeal to a smaller segment of the overall population. Therefore, this increase was considered more than acceptable. Individuals who attended the exhibit were interviewed about their motivation to attend as they left the exhibit. They strongly indicated that it was the emphasis upon meaningful death that got their attention. This is another affirmation of unconscious consumer motivation.

Recreational Center

A community built a large recreational center with shops, stores, exhibits, and displays. There was even a small museum on the grounds. Unfortunately, after several years of operation, it was clear that it was not accepted by the community. One reason was because of location; the other may have been because it was not an entertainment facility.

The prospect of turning the property into a large entertainment facility or theme park would have been prohibitively expensive. As a result of Silent Side research and diagnostic interviews, a focus was placed on the spiritual survival motivational element of membership. Several different private clubs were set up. Some of these clubs provided entertainment of their own. The clubs, being private, required memberships, but there were eventually enough of them that they appealed to a wide variety of interests and incomes. In this way, citizens of the community had an opportunity to make use of the property and it was within reach of almost everyone. In addition, improvements and additions brought in tourists as well as local residents.

Security and Alarm Services

It was noted in chapter 4 that a service that provides security and alarm protection can remove itself from the overcrowded field of competitors who only address the motive of physical survival (the element of safety). Instead, the company may operate at the level of spiritual survival by appealing to the spiritual element of family values. This places the emphasis on love and concern for the safety of family members, and as a result removes the product and services away from the clutter of competition and confusion as to who is best or who is "different" in the security business.

Fast Food

A fast food restaurant in one of the Scandinavian countries was impressed with the success of McDonald's and wanted to "position" its facility in a similar fashion. It is noted in chapter 13 that the success of McDonald's lies in its marketing to physical survival (food, air, and water) and the realm of spiritual survival (family values). The Scandinavian restaurant had a family of ducks that made their way out of a nearby canal and waddled about 1 1/2 blocks to the restaurant, several times each day. Interestingly, they passed other restaurants in order to "patronize" this one. This appeared to be a "natural" way to capitalize on family values, by focusing upon the family of ducks. The restaurant could then utilize spiritual survival as a motivational approach. This became a keystone for print and video advertising, and was largely successful in moving the restaurant from the bland and crowded "food and beverage" image to the family values' area.

Catalog Sales

Many catalog sales merchants compete directly with department stores. In the area of fashion, especially women's fashions, a problem buying fashions through a catalog is directly related to a major motivation in purchasing: OR: Person (see chapter 17). Specifically, the buyer cannot see how she looks in the apparel. This is a major hurdle, since women's fashions are directly tied to the motive of OR: Person. In catalog shopping, this crucial and often determining element is missing.

To solve this problem and put catalog merchandisers on an equal footing with department stores, arrangements were made for the prospective buyer to send her photograph to the catalog merchandiser. The merchandiser then "dresses" the photograph of the customer in the fashions of her choice, sending it back on modem or floppy disc. Then the catalog shopper can easily see what kind of a person she will present when she wears that particular fashion or outfit. This methodology will become even easier to employ in the future, as more and more catalog merchandisers display their products on the Internet and other on-line interactive services.

Managed Health-care

In projects involving health-care, the critical motivational issues are expectation and, of course, physical survival. In chapter 21, the importance of the Expectation Motive is delineated.

An ambulance service was responsible for picking up heart attack victims from a rural retirement community and taking them to a local hospital about 30 miles away. However, many of these victims' families, who would accompany them in the ambulance, refused to stop at the local hospital and insisted on going another 30 miles to a neighboring medical center, where the victims would be treated by "their doctor." The ambulance attendants strongly advised against this, because in heart attack cases, time is critical. Not one heart attack victim heeded the attendants' advice. As a result, release forms had to be included in the ambulance to protect the company from liability. A number of patients were pronounced dead on arrival because of their insistence on going the extra 30 miles to "their doctor."

This illustration points to the importance of the Expectation Motive in health-care. Heart attack victims—and their families—are willing to challenge the odds (and they often lose) in order to be treated by their own doctor. In situations where managed-care companies and insurance companies feel that they have lost the trust of the public, we re-inspired the public and instilled trust, by adjusting the focus. That focus is on expectation and the future, or the hope that it brings.

Health-care Advertising and Focus Groups

A focus group watched a video that showed a man removing his artificial leg before going to bed. The video spot sounded a warning: "This could happen to you if . . ." Had the spot been approved by the focus group, it would have run in many regional spots across the country, at a time when medical advertising had only recently been approved by the FCC. One rather opinionated individual in the focus group felt that the warning was too severe; in his words, it was "gross, obscene, and uncaring." But the ad agency felt that it had a winner, and asked to carry out Silent Side interviews on the members of the focus group, individually rather than under the influence of one opinionated leader. In addition, several other individuals were interviewed who were not part of the original focus group.

Based on the appeal to the motive of physical survival, we determined that the ad was a winner. It spoke directly to the issue of physical survival. On the recommendation of the Silent Side staff, the ad was produced and won two Clio awards. In addition, the same ad has been running for 12 years, and has had an overwhelming impact. More importantly, it was able to motivate people to have a checkup before they did lose their leg, an appendage, or even their life!

Building Materials

A manufacturer of building materials used for finishing homes was convinced that his market consisted of contractors and do-it-yourselfers. But Silent Side interviews with women who were recent first-and second-time home buyers, as well as those who had recently remodeled, indicated that they were the primary decision makers for the product. This was because this product was involved in the finishing of the home. When motigraphic techniques were used as a follow up to the qualitative interviews, the initial observations were confirmed. As a result, a whole new marketing approach and a different distribution plan was formulated.

Fragrance

A major marketer of cosmetics relied upon Silent Side interviews to develop a new product. The new product would enter the highly competitive and already crowded fragrance market. Interviews allowed for visualization of the entire application process and regression to the first use of fragrance, memorable events, and even olfactory tests while blindfolded. Eventually, the whole product evolved, including packaging and labeling. Within three years the product was within the top 20 of over 300 fragrances that were on the market. This was considered a significant achievement, and the marketer confirmed that research into the unconscious mind was well worth the investment!

Remote Retirement Resort

Although people like to dream of retiring in a remote, uncrowded, and isolated spot, they often become more and more reluctant as they reach retirement age, because of medical problems. They do not feel that they will have access to medical services, and, more importantly, they do not want to leave their personal physicians and the medical facilities that they have used for most of their lives (expectation). This uncertainty produces doubt and ambivalence, making it difficult for the developer to sell property, and for potential retirees to fulfill their dreams of retirement.

Using motivational research, it was determined that physical survival had to be addressed. The conflict was between the two elements of spiritual survival (inner peace, renewal and release) and one element of physical survival (health and wellness). In past advertising and sales promotions, the issue of physical survival was not addressed. This was judged to be a mistake, in that the inner tension between the two dominant motives had created a powerful approach-avoidance conflict within potential customers.

The only way to address this conflict was to provide a 24-hour, seven-day a week helicopter medivac to a nearby medical center. This limited the risk in buying property, since it meant that excellent medical care was available in 30 minutes or less. Testimonials were used, as well as visuals that addressed the issue. This was done directly, rather than indirectly, or not at all. A beautiful, upscale, and very expensive resort that had captured the dreams of many retirees became a reality for many, once the issue of physical survival was addressed.

Supermarket

A supermarket was losing most of its customers to a very large, all-purpose general store that not only had groceries but also large and small appliances, fashions, cosmetics, hardware, paint, building materials, etc. Silent Side research uncovered part of the problem: Women preferred to do their grocery shopping at the general store because it gave them an "excuse" to look at new fashions. Men preferred it because they could browse through the hardware, automotive, and fashion sections of the store. The big challenge was women, since they tend to do most of the grocery shopping.

The supermarket, in an effort to get their customers back, knew this was an uphill battle. Short of selling fashions in the supermarket the store was at an impasse. An experiment was tried following the lead provided by visualization research. The supermarket already sold cosmetics, but they stopped short of offering a full-service cosmetics counter, such as may be found in large department stores. The experiment involved putting in a cosmetic services counter, where a cosmetologist was available, during the daytime hours, to assist women with their makeup and other cosmetics. From time to time visiting cosmetologists would also be available. Furthermore, the entire cosmetics area was "enclosed" with a tent-like covering, offering the feeling of privacy and intimacy. One by one, the customer flow did indeed pick up. However, only those who were drawn by this unique service seemed to come, and so plans are still being made for bringing other once loyal customers back.

Automotive

It is difficult to get respondents to talk about the "automobile of the future" since they have never seen it. And some people are reluctant to use their imaginations in describing the car of tomorrow. In automotive research, significant designs and features have been mapped out by allowing consumers and potential consumers to "describe what they see" in terms of the car of the future in Silent Side interviews. Since the Silent Side is a totally projective technique, respondents can literally "build a car" in their minds and then share it with the designer. Although people have different tastes, after a small number of interviews (10–20) the features that are described by them will begin to overlap and come together. Since they have never "seen" this car, they are free to add or take away anything they want to. This is projective. When this procedure is followed, the customer literally helps to design the car. Many new models and model updates go through this critical phase.

Public Utility

In a time when utility rates were literally "going through the ceiling," a privately owned statewide electric utility company was perceived as "oppressive." Consumers who often think in concrete terms, even in areas that they know nothing about, in this case could not see beyond the utility company. Their hostility was directed at the employees who read the meters, worked on the lines, or came to their homes when a repair was needed. Additional anger was directed toward the men and women who worked for the power company, who staffed the local community offices.

Right brain research found that this hostility was to the "boiling point." The customers felt like "victims" since they did not have a choice as to where to buy their power. On the other hand, the utility felt like it was in the middle, since it had no control over what it was charged by its supplier of electrical power. But it was difficult to get the consumer to understand the utility's position. Furthermore, it had gone well beyond that, with the consumer feeling overwhelming hostility and resistance toward the utility.

Based upon interviews and motigraphics, it was determined that the only way to salvage this situation was through an appeal to the Adaptation Motive. As a result, a well-known, local sports figure who had a statewide reputation as a hero was used as a spokesperson. This was a highly successful campaign that resulted in a considerable dimunition of hostility and resentment and a return to "business as usual." Once again, the Silent Side was used as a diagnostic procedure to uncover the resistance and to reverse the trend.

Cruise Line

The proliferation of cruise lines has created a problem with brand equity and commodity products. How do you tell one from the other? Bigger ships? Faster ships? More exotic ports? Better entertainment? Better service? Better food? What?

In setting aside a cruise line as a unique and atypical experience, consider the various possibilities as revealed in table 13-1.

ADVERTISEMENTS THAT APPEAL TO MOTIVATIONS

As a recap of how to appeal to motivation and emotion, look at well-known marketing campaigns that have followed this same design—appealing (intuitively) to the motivations and to the emotions.

Table 13-1
Motivations, Emotions, and Benefits of Going on a Cruise

Motivation	Element	Benefits
Spiritual Survival	Renewal and release	Become a new person, unwind, get charged up again
	Inner peace	Find new meaning, release the old, find new reality
	Membership	Meet new people and life takes on new meaning
	Family values	Bring kids along; separate activities for them, too
	Love	Couples find each other "Love Boat" format
Physical Survival	Health	Exercise, build stamina, healthy food, games, activity, competition
Play	Escape, release	Dancing, music, games, entertainment
Adaptation	Testimonials	If they do it, you can do it too
OR: Person	Self-esteem	Build self-confidence by meeting new people, thru relaxation, by getting a new perspective
OR: Place	The sea & exotic ports	The ship and its appointments, features, etc.
OR: Time	The endless sea	Make time stand still

Table 13-2
Advertisements That Appeal to Motivations and Emotions

Marketer	Image	Motivation	Element
Burger King	"Have it your way."	Expectation	
McDonald's	"You deserve a break today."	OR: Circumstances	Pace (of life)
Avis	"We try harder."	OR: Circumstances	Convenience
Prudential	"A piece of the Rock"	Physical Survival	Security
Northwest Airlines	"Some people just know how to fly."	Physical Survival	Security
Hallmark Cards	"When you care enough to send the very best"	Spiritual Survival	Human love
Disney	"Once upon a time is here."	Play OR: Time	Escape
Baptist Hospital	"A leader in world medicine"	Adaptation	
L'Oréal	"Expensive— but I'm worth it."	OR: Person	Self-image Self-esteem
Hertz	"We put you in the driver's seat."	OR: Person	Self-esteem

HOW MOTIVATIONAL RESEARCH PROVIDES OTHER ANSWERS

Since unconscious research deals with motivation, it answers questions outside of the realm of marketing and advertising. When addressing motivation, questions that are not easily answered become more clear. After all, any area dealing with human behavior involves motivation, and the Silent Side addresses the whole issue of human behavior.

Briefly, let us examine a few other examples of motivational issues outside of the realm of advertising and marketing. Why did Susan Smith kill her two children by pushing them into a lake and drowning them? Looking at her background, it was clear that she was molested by her stepfather when she was being raised. Many young women who have had this experience blame themselves, rather than the real offender, which in this case was allegedly the stepfather. This is especially true if the behavior persists—i.e., there are repeated incidents. Because she more than likely blamed herself, she eventually acted out what she believed: She was not the kind of person who deserved to have two beautiful children. The focus here is on the following two motives:

1. Spiritual Survival: She was overwhelmed with guilt because of her past behavior. This is why incest is so devastating and why the results will last a lifetime. She could not forget it. She lived with it every day.
2. OR: Person: Because of the overwhelming guilt, she was unable to see herself or feature herself in the deserving mother role. Most mothers consider their children to be a gift, the most precious thing in their lives. Her guilt and self-deprecation went far deeper than the situational spat that she had with her boyfriend.

What about the "Dear John" letter? This may be a conscious, rational motivator, but it does not explain this extreme situation. After all, there are many people who get "Dear John" letters, and after they adjust to it, they go on with their lives.

Why do people engage in terrorist activities, as in blowing up the World Trade Center in New York or the Federal Building in Oklahoma City? Acts such as these can only be interpreted on the basis of misguided and misdirected attempts at achieving spiritual survival. The people who were involved were religious fanatics, and as we have seen in this book, spiritual survival can often be identified on the basis of fanatic, passionate, and extremist behaviors. The people who did these bombings felt that they had a cause, and that the cause was important enough that they were willing to die for it. Both bombings also occurred on "religious holidays" (the second anniversary of the beginning of the bombing of Iraq, and the first anniversary of the Branch Davidian raid in Waco). The observance of "religious high holy days" is another clue that these were spiritual activities. Investigators and other law enforcement agencies must begin to understand the Spiritual Survival Motive; it will give them much more evidence to move on as well as help them know where to look for suspects.

What about the post office shootings? In recent years the post office has become an emblazened battlefield. When behavioral scientists are consulted, they talk about stress. In fact, we hear a lot of talk about stress today. But as you consider this situation seriously, can you imagine a job that is any less stressful than the post office? Although some of the shootings have been aimed at supervisors, many postal workers are out on the route all day long so they are not really exposed to their supervisors. So just what is happening at the post office?

We do not have the answer. We believe it to be a territorial war, but the chances are better that it is at the level of spiritual survival since it has become a passionate and fanatic war on the part of some employees. Therefore, anyone who approaches this situation without an understanding of spiritual survival and its elements would fail to uncover the real motivations that are involved. If the Silent Side interview method described in chapter 8 were used with selected employees, we believe that the answer would float to the surface. How we would select those employees would depend upon pre-project interviews with management, supervisors, and postal workers at sites where incidents have occurred. Remember, the Silent Side is a diagnostic technique, and it focuses upon the diagnosis of resistance. And today, the post office is a blazing battleground of resistance.

Why would someone buy a $200,000 yacht that they only visit once a year? This is a lot of money to spend on what may be considered a toy. A lot of toys are expensive, but not this expensive. Buying an expensive yacht and only visiting it once or twice a year involves considerable expense, not only in initial cost but in ongoing upkeep. Because it has to be considered unusual and extraordinary to spend this much money on a recreational "toy," the activity has to be classified under the motive of spiritual survival, and the element of renewal and release or perhaps inner peace. For many people, being in or near the water is the only real renewal and release that is meaningful, and since this is their only meaningful quest for spiritual survival, money is no object. A lot of people will not go so far as to buy an expensive yacht, but they will buy a lake-front home or "cottage" for the same reason, and then visit it only two or three times a year!

WAS O. J. SIMPSON GUILTY OR INNOCENT?

During his career, Bryan (1985) worked closely with juries, judges, and lawyers in the process of jury selection. His book, *The Chosen Ones: The Art of Jury Selection*, includes forwards by such distinguished attorneys as Melvin Belli and F. Lee Bailey, with whom he worked very closely. As a medical doctor and an attorney, Dr. Bryan was able to give defense attorneys some valuable advice on getting into the unconscious minds of jurors, both during *voir dire* and during the closing arguments. His formula for doing this was followed very closely by defense counsel in the closing arguments in the O. J. Simpson trial, and virtually ignored by the prosecution. As a result, Simpson was acquitted. Although there may be other reasons for the acquittal, we believe that the most influential factors were the defense attorneys' adherence to the principles described by Bryan and in *Marketing to the Mind*. It was always Bryan's contention that the attorney who used the closing argument to get into the unconscious minds of jurors would win the trial. And he helped many attorneys to win with his methods. Some of his methods may be familiar to those who watched the trial, especially the closing arguments.

Table 13-3
Closing Arguments in the O. J. Simpson Trial

Bryan Method	Simpson Trial Closing Summary
Implant only positive suggestions	Defense: "If it doesn't fit, you must acquit."
Implant suggestions repetitiously	Defense: "If it doesn't fit, you must acquit."
Never implant negative suggestions (they have the opposite effect)	Prosecution: "We could not find evidence beyond a reasonable doubt, but . . ."
Use authoritative references with which everyone is familiar	Defense: Extensive quotes from Bible
Make comparisons between good and evil (spiritual survival)	Defense: Hitler vs. Mark Fuhrman Patriotism vs. racism God vs. the Devil

It is our feeling that the outcome of the trial had multiple determinants, but that the approach taken by the defense in the summary was a powerful assault upon the unconscious mind, using many of the principles that have been described in this book. Most importantly, in the closing argument, Mr. Cochran appealed to spiritual survival throughout, and therefore to powerful emotions. Conversely, the prosecution appealed to reason and rational thinking.

Although this book is not designed to assist attorneys in winning cases, the same principles apply whenever you are addressing people and when you are trying to motivate or persuade them. In no case is this more apparent than in advertising and marketing.

CONCLUSION

Although we always recommend doing the research, some of the examples that have been given in this chapter show that the Silent Side application applies whether or not research is carried out, and it can be applied in a useful framework of human motivation that in turn leads to actionable results! Since human motivation is so pervasive, we can move quickly beyond the area of advertising and marketing and into law enforcement, teaching, entertainment, and many other areas, because, as Krugman (1994) said, "We are learning what people really like and what they don't like."

REFERENCES

Bryan, W. J. (1985). *The chosen ones: The art of jury selection.* Glendale, CA: Westwood Publishing Co.

Fleischman, P. (1990). *The healing spirit*. New York: Paragon House.

Freud, S. (1959). Psychoanalysis and legal evidence. In *Complete Psychological Works* (Vol. 9, pp. 103–109). London: Hogarth Press. (Originally published in 1906–1908)

Krugman, H. E. (1994, November–December). Pavlov's dog and the future of consumer psychology. *Journal of Advertising Research*, 34 (6), 67–71.

Paivio, A. (1971). *Imagery and verbal processes*. New York: Holt, Rinehart & Winston.

Paivio, A. (1978). A dual coding approach to perception and cognition. In H. I. Pick and E. Saltzman (Eds.), *Modes of perceiving and processing information*. Hillsdale, NJ: Lawrence Erlbaum Associates.

Percy, L., & Rossiter, J. (1983). Mediating effects of visual and verbal elements in print advertising upon belief, attitude and intention responses. In Percy and A. Woodside (Eds.), *Advertising and consumer psychology* (pp. 171–96). Lexington, MA: Lexington Books.

Reis, A., & Trout, J. (1981). *Positioning: The battle for your mind*. New York: McGraw Hill.

14

Casino Gambling and Wagering

WHY DO PEOPLE GAMBLE?

Gambling is a clean, wholesome activity and pastime. But sometimes it goes beyond that and becomes an obsession. Today, one estimate states that more money is spent on gambling than on baseball parks and movie theaters (*New York Times*, September 25, 1995). Another estimate states that more money is spent in casinos than on concerts, all professional sports, and video rentals combined.

Gambling is now the fastest growing industry in America, and the *New York Times* article reports it is spreading like wildfire across Iowa. Iowa, which only ten years ago sent a Roman Catholic priest to jail for running a bingo game, has ten casinos across the state. And in a statistic that has caused some alarm, 5.4 percent of Iowans now report a gambling problem, up from 1.7 percent in 1989.

In Iowa, Mississippi, and other states where casino gambling has provided new jobs and new tax dollars, it has also had its impact upon individual suicides, bankruptcies, careers, and broken families. According to the *New York Times*, one professor of commerce estimates that for every dollar taken in by the state in revenue from casinos, three dollars are shelled out by welfare agencies.

There are, however, only a small percentage of addicted gamblers who give casino gambling a bad name. These people are often seen, by outsiders, as the cause of the enormous number of problems that are associated with legalized gambling, especially when referendums are at stake. The negatives are highlighted and given as the rule, not the exception.

Obsessive players who are consumed by gambling are usually unwelcome in most casinos and are well known to management. Their behavior is not the same as the behavior of recreational players and others who play casually or even those who play for high stakes. This is because their motivation is different; hence, their attitudes are different. In this chapter we will look at the internal motives of all types of players, in order to compare behavior.

Casino gambling provides a good illustration of how important it is to know why people do the things they do, so that they may be appealed to at the appropriate motivational level by the savvy marketer. Casino management has always wanted to know this. Gambling and wagering is a highly emotional activity and can only be understood in terms of the unconscious or Silent Side. An appeal to reason and logic will not yield much information on players or on their motives.

We once received a report that had been submitted to us by a psychology professor in a prestigious Ivy League university. She had been retained by one of the larger casinos to study gamblers and their unconscious motivations. Casino management funded this study because they wanted to know how to build loyalty, retain customers, etc. Although this study has undoubtedly faded into obscurity, the conclusions were unforgettable: Serious "gamblers were dominated by their own latent homosexual motives which lead them to want to congregate and assemble in crowded, dark casinos and vicariously touch and rub up against one another." That such a conclusion is outrageous goes without saying. But even if it was not, how could it be of any possible use to casino management in their marketing and advertising strategies? How could they write copy or make their casino more appealing to their audience on the basis of such conclusions? The marketer needs something that he/she can do something with; hence, the Silent Side.

The purpose of looking at gamblers' motivations is so that casino management will know how to appeal to their audience. The marketer needs to know how to establish brand loyalty and unique brand identity in a market that is highly regulated, and where each casino is virtually indistinguishable from the other. Because casino gambling is such a highly emotional activity, it needs to be analyzed strictly in terms of the Silent Side so that those who manage and work in casinos can understand and treat the customers the way that they expect to be treated.

THE EXPECTATION MOTIVE

The major motive underlying any kind of gambling is the Expectation Motive, the belief that one has special powers or qualities, attributes, or characteristics that are unusual and unique and which allow him/her to beat the odds. This is simply an extension of the 90/10/10/90 Reversal Theory (chapter 4) where 90 out of 100 people who lack a healthy perception of the day-to-day world around them believe that they will be discovered or suddenly made rich through some miraculous means, or, in this case, that they have some special gift or quality that allows them to beat the odds.

"Odds" are very rational. In a research project one woman told the interviewer that she had been in the casino with her husband for three days. She finally figured out that, over the long haul, the slots would take her money and she would end up losing it all. In this case, the left brain had won out over the right brain when she discovered that the odds were against her. Her husband, who was still playing, had not yet come to this conclusion. This woman had some experience with the odds, and as a result had undergone some cognitive restructuring. The Expectation Motive could no longer be supported, because of her experience with reality and reason. However, with time the Expectation Motive will return, and she will be back. What will assist her in coming back will be an appropriate advertising and marketing campaign that appeals to this Expectation Motive.

Chapter 4 provided more detail as to the nature of the Expectation Motive. It is clear that it is present in everyone to varying degrees. Table 4-3 in chapter 4 shows how this motive gives rise to the emotion of hope. This motive is much stronger in frequent gamblers than it is in the general population. Even after studying gamblers, it is not known exactly why this is the case. One theory is that many committed gamblers were introduced to the game in one form or another when they were very young. Many such gamblers have been interviewed. One said that his grandmother would take him to the casino when he was eight years old (a very impressionable age), and he had vivid recollections of the bells, lights, whistles, etc. Although he did not quite know what was going on, he could sense the excitement and expectation in the building. It was an exciting place! After he became an adult, he continued to return to the casinos to find the excitement he had found in childhood.

Another gambler told of an abusive stepfather (a common story) who would become drunk and physically abuse him and his brothers and sisters. However, on Tuesday evenings, when his stepfather and his friends played cards, they would drink very heavily and the mood would change. It was much different. Instead of being abusive and hateful, his father would become docile, engaging, and excited in a "friendly way." Actually he was expectant (expecting that he would win). Because of this change in his father's behavior, the young man began to conceptualize Tuesday's behavior. He always looked forward to Tuesday night. He never approached his home in fear, after school, on Tuesday evenings. As a result of these pleasant feelings that accompanied gambling, he became a committed and frequent casino gambler. Over the years, he never really knew if he came out ahead or behind in terms of money. He was seeking a feeling, not a fortune. And he found it in casinos and in other forms of gambling.

More investigation of the Expectation Motive, its origin and its relative strength, is needed, along with investigations of the other motives. Suffice it to say at this point that the Expectation Motive is crucial in any kind of gambling or wagering activity. The casino marketer must deal with the Expectation Motive and the emotion of hope in order to reach the largest segment of the player population.

THE ORIENTATION MOTIVES

A second major group of motives involved in gambling are all the Orientation Motives: person, place, time, and circumstances. This is why alcohol and gambling are closely related. Alcohol is a vital ingredient that assists in disorientation of person, place, time, and circumstances. Although adaptation is the reason why people begin to drink (friends are doing it), change of orientation is why they continue to drink. Many alcoholics are people who just cannot live with themselves, and so they temporarily reorient every evening in terms of OR: Person. Actually, alcohol reorients all levels of personal orientation.

OR: Person

It has already been established that the player feels like a special person, in that he/she has a very strong belief that he/she has some special attribute or characteristic that sets him/her aside from everyone else. The player usually refers to this characteristic as *luck*. The concept of luck arises from the Expectation Motive. For each player, luck is a very personal characteristic that refers only to him/her. For this reason, it is important that the casino make the gambler feel like a special person. To some degree, this has been recognized in the form of perks. Perks, such as free liquor, food, room, board, and transportation promote the gambler's existing belief system—that he/she is a special, gifted person and should be treated accordingly and with appropriate deference.

Casino employees should do the same thing. If feasible, they should be given memory training so that they can recognize the key players by name. When possible, small, individual rooms or special areas should be made available for regular customers, where they may play with a smaller group and feel like they are special. Memberships in "clubs" not only promote loyalty and frequent return, but assist in making the player feel like a special person. The player should at all times be recognized as a special person, as one who possesses this extraordinary talent or asset, so that his/her belief will be reinforced, at least during the time that he/she is in the casino and actively playing. There are many ways of doing this.

Demographics can be established through traditional market research and specific players can be addressed through magazines that they read. Most importantly, communication through personal letters can be undertaken—from casino management to a selected group of players on a periodic basis. This last suggestion, personal contact while the player is away from the casino, is extremely important because it can be highly personalized. However, at the same time, there must be a recognition of the player's need for privacy. With this in mind, it needs to be determined ahead of time if the player would mind having mail sent directly to his/her home or office address.

Because of the OR: Person Motive, a number of possibilities for advertising copy, marketing, and sales exist that would not be evident otherwise. True, all the players are there for the purpose of beating the odds (expectation). Any casino can fill this need. But many players also want to be treated like the special people that they believe they are, since they think that they have this unique capacity to beat the odds. Expectation is stronger than reason, which is another way of saying that emotions are stronger than logic. By keying into the OR: Person Motive, the casino strengthens the Expectation Motive. It needs to be remembered that it was the latter, expectation, that brought the player to the casino in the first place. OR: Person will keep the player there, build further loyalty, and strengthen the Expectation Motive.

OR: Place

In addition to becoming a different person, players also want to change places, temporarily, from the place that they live or work. Actually, they want to be transported into another "reality." By doing this, they come in closer touch with their own Expectation Motive. Casino management needs to make every effort to build a "fantasy island," one that is as far removed from the everyday as possible. There is nothing more distracting, disturbing, and agitating to the player than everyday reality! The casino that more totally removes everyday reality is the one that will have the most brand loyalty. This is a delicate situation. The reality or ambience within the casino must be as close to a total removal from everyday reality as possible. However, it cannot be so far removed that it will interfere with the games themselves. A sensitive, yet critical, balance must be reached.

OR: Person and OR: Place are linked together. This is because the player, in everyday life, is not in touch with his/her Expectation Motive. Ordinarily, players arc not treated like they are special or unusual. The people that they deal with in life do not recognize that they have this special characteristic. But casino management is in a position to recognize it and should. Therefore, the players need to be removed from everyday reality as much as possible and transferred into this special place. This is how the OR: Person and OR: Place Motives work together.

OR: Time

The OR: Time Motive is closely associated with OR: Place. This is because, in establishing a "fantasy island," all references to time need to be removed. Windows are a reminder of day and night, or circadian rhythm. Most casinos know this. Research has been carried out in casinos that had windows, and the effect upon the players was found to be negative. Players simply gravitated away from these casinos over time, but they could not tell the researchers exactly why they did so. They just left and justified their leaving on the basis of some excuse or rationalization.

When casino management looks at the combined affect of the OR Motives— time, place, and person—it should be relatively clear what they need to do in terms of all the following areas: casino design and decor, ad copy, casino ambience, transportation, marketing and marketing plans, media placement, personal contact with players, establishment of brand loyalty, employee training, positioning of food and beverage services, location, and ancillary services (hotels, facilities for children, stores and shops, etc.).

An interesting finding in our casino research was that people who win money in casinos will often prefer to spend it there, rather than take it home. In one location, local retail businesses that thought they would benefit from the new casinos did not, simply because the winners bought their jewelry, food, clothing, souvenirs, and other items from the shops within the casinos themselves, rather than taking the money out. A good study question, in terms of motivation, would be "why is this true?"

OR: Circumstances

This is the weakest of the Orientation Motives. This motive has the least effect upon behavior. The sequence of the Orientation Motives is person, place, time, and circumstances. When a person loses orientation, circumstances is the first motive to be lost and person the last. It is concluded from this that OR: Person is the strongest of the Orientation Motives and that OR: Circumstances is the weakest.

Almost everyone who visits a casino is driven by the OR: Circumstances Motive. The problem is that players who are driven only by the OR: Circumstances Motive will have a very low level of commitment and will probably not return very often, or may visit on the average of two to three times a year, or less. Similarly, these customers do not establish loyalty and have no particular interest in gambling. They can "take it or leave it." They are primarily recreational gamblers and slot players whose driving emotions are unsubstantial and secondary in nature. This level of commitment can be increased. When the ambience of the casino is changed to appeal to the OR: Person, OR: Time, and OR: Place Motives, and to the Expectation Motive, the level of customer commitment will also increase.

THE SURVIVAL MOTIVES

There are two survival motives that are instrumental in gambling and that are often seen in players. They are the Physical Survival and Spiritual Survival Motives. They are much less frequent and much less motivating than the movies that have been discussed above.

Physical Survival

The motion picture *Indecent Proposal* presented the scenario of a couple who had lost most of their income and were facing the imminent loss of their home, property, and everything else that they owned. They had literally no options open to them. As a result, they took what little they had left and went to Las Vegas on a "double or nothing" venture. They ended up with one million dollars, but not from the tables or the slots. Interestingly, and in line with these findings, they did not keep the million dollars, just as players often spend the money that they accumulate from winnings.

Players who are motivated by physical survival are not uncommon. In another study completed by our firm, it was found that 43 percent of the population regularly attending races at a dog track had an annual income below $12,000 and were on welfare. The same figure held up for casinos when they opened their doors in the same area. In fact, a large part of the casino population had merely shifted from the dog track—same church, different pew! These people are living right on the edge in their everyday lives, and wagering at the dog track was just a part of their lives. Casino management might, in their own discretion, discourage the use of Physical Survival Motive as a method of appeal to players. Therefore, in this presentation it is automatically ruled out as an option.

Spiritual Survival

Chapter 4 has given reasons why the Spiritual Survival Motive is the strongest, most durable, and most powerful of all the Survival Motives, and indeed of the entire motivational structure. When a motive is shifted to the spiritual level, the behavior that results from the Spiritual Survival Motive is unreasonable and fanatic and ignores reason and rationality.

Positioning a product or service at the level of spiritual survival is usually desirable, since it is the strongest motive within the Silent Side. But it is only desirable in casino marketing under limited circumstances. This is where casino marketing differs from many other products and services. Two groups of players are motivated to play at the spiritual level: high rollers and "sweats." The major difference between these two groups is disposable income.

High rollers, because of their strength of commitment at the spiritual level, are dedicated to gambling. They also have substantial resources for this kind of activity, and can afford to lose. They usually play quietly, unobtrusively, and often in special semi-isolated quarters. Casino management works hard at keeping these customers, and works the Orientation Motives at all four levels. As a result, high rollers will often demonstrate commitment, dedication, and loyalty to a particular casino.

"Sweats" are the compulsive gamblers. They often do not have the resources to play, but since they are motivated at the spiritual level, emotions dominate reason. They are the true fanatics. They will find ways to play despite the fact that they do not have the resources. Unlike the female in our research, who found out, after three days, that the odds were against her, the sweats never come to this realization. They operate entirely on spiritual survival and therefore their behavior is passionate and fanatical. Passionate behavior is often blind to reason.

Sweats are undesirable, because they often count cards, make the other guests nervous and suspicious, and are generally inconsiderate and rude. They become loud and obnoxious and create an overall feeling of anxiety and agitation, and even fear, with the other guests and with the staff. Most casinos recognize them by name and by appearance and refuse them admission. There have been well-known cases of sweats who have gone so far as to have their appearances changed through plastic facial surgery to gain readmission.

Sweats have subjugated all their motives to spiritual survival. In interviews it was found that they rarely have sex with their partner and have no interest in spending money or any other activity. They are totally dedicated to wagering. The other motives that have been discussed above, Orientation and Physical Survival, have little relevance within this group. Gambling for them is a matter of spiritual survival.

Positioning casino marketing at the level of spiritual survival is not recommended, for the casino runs the risk of attracting sweats and other undesirables. When people commit themselves to gambling beyond the limits of reason, they are generally not satisfied customers and will eventually make trouble for management and for other customers.

THE ADAPTATION MOTIVE

Although adaptation is not one of the strongest motivations in casino gambling, it can be useful in advertising and marketing. An ad campaign directed toward this motive would show happy and satisfied people who visit the casino and the great time they are having.

Adaptation is the motive to do what other people do. Testimonials are one form of appealing to the Adaptation Motive. Showing crowds of happy people who have been to the casino and who have had all kinds of fun will appeal to a target audience, particularly those for whom Expectation Motive is not that strong. Testimonials will appeal even more.

Testimonials from customers in casinos are not hard to find. Since consumers are motivated by emotion, not reason, they generally have to rationalize to themselves their behavior, especially if they have nothing to show for it. Hence, they will say, "Where else could I have had such a good time for $20?" or "The free drinks alone would have cost that much." Because of rationalization and the need to justify, frequent and infrequent visitors to casinos will have to justify the costs or losses to themselves, and they will generally appear satisfied and happy when they pacify themselves with an explanation. Then they will be ready to motivate others with their testimonials. Often testimonials come spontaneously, as when someone hits the jackpot and it is covered by the local newspaper. Employers often complain about this because employee absenteeism shoots up the very next day. This is due to the importance of the 90/10/10/90 Reversal Theory. Also, the traffic to the casinos is proportional to the size of the jackpot!

BUILDING CASINO LOYALTY

Casinos have difficulty in positioning themselves as unique or in building brand loyalty, since, like banks, they all offer essentially the same product. The difficulty is in establishing a unique identity that may be used in attracting new players as well as getting the old ones to remain loyal.

One way to do this is through souvenirs. In chapter 16 souvenirs are discussed as an extension of the experience. Souvenirs are a way of taking the experience beyond the walls of the casino and back to the home or office. Also, since most casino marketing is targeted to impulse, players will often buy souvenirs impulsively and "on the spur of the moment" because they are in an impulse situation. Finally, some large companies have found that when they distribute quality sportswear, outerwear, hats, etc., to their employees to wear casually when off the job, employee loyalty to the company is increased through the pride that they have in wearing the company logo and showing that they are an integral part of the company. Casinos should build on this situation by (1) marketing souvenirs to impulse; (2) merchandising high quality sportswear with logos and other souvenir items; and (3) taking advantage of the fact that many players, if they do win, prefer to spend their money in the casino rather than waiting until they get home. Not only do quality imprinted souvenirs become a profit center, but they also extend casino loyalty beyond the limitations of time and location. The trophy value of souvenirs should not be underestimated!

A second way to build casino loyalty and brand recognition is through specialization. Hospitals have found that the way to stand out in a market where everyone is offering the same product or services is to specialize. One hospital may specialize in emergency room treatment, another in childbirth care, still another in chest pain, etc. Casinos should use the same strategy, especially since health-care and casino marketing are based upon the same basic Silent Side motive: expectation. One casino could specialize in quality entertainment, another in unusual ambience, still another in random prizes and jackpots, and yet another in fine-dining experiences.

SUMMARY

Casino research has discovered various kinds of groups who visit casinos, and their corresponding motives, as seen in table 14-1.

Table 14-1
Types of Consumers Who Frequently Visit Casinos and Their Motivations

Type of Player	Motivations
High rollers	Expectation Spiritual Survival
Budget restrained*	Expectation OR: Person, Place, Time, Circumstances
Compulsive-sweats	Spiritual Survival
Recreational*	Expectation Adaptation OR: Person, Place, Time, Circumstances
Slot players	Expectation Adaptation OR: Place, Time, Circumstances
Big spenders	Expectation Adaptation

*Includes senior citizens

15

Restaurant Marketing

WHY DO PEOPLE EAT OUT WHEN THEY CAN EAT AT HOME?

Most middle-class homes that are built today have kitchens, dining rooms, and an eat-in area. In fact, their kitchens tend to be very well equipped. So why do homeowners have the need to go elsewhere to eat? If consumers were asked why they go out to eat when they can eat at home, the rational and logical response to this question might be:

- So they can have a break
- Convenience
- Actually cheaper (for one or two)
- Doesn't mess up the kitchen
- Don't have to cook after working all day

The reader has heard all of these answers, and more.

Actually people eat out for irrational reasons. The exception may be fast food, which really is convenient and is focused at only one motivational component: physical survival. However, McDonald's has revolutionized the fast food business—at the motivational level—by shifting the reason for dining out from physical survival to spiritual survival: kids, family fun, family values, love, compassion, concern. It is what good parents do with their children, it is the "right thing" to do. As a result, in fast food marketing, McDonald's does better than anyone else, largely because it has directed its marketing efforts at the highest motivational level: spiritual survival.

A CHANGING WORLD

The whole idea of eating out is undergoing a revolution, and has been since 1958 with the introduction of fast food. Before 1958 people could eat conveniently, but they could not expect it to be very fast. The exception was the "Castles and Towers," those little white buildings with turrets and a counter inside. Food was fast, convenient, and greasy. The menu was confined to hamburgers, fries, and a piece of pie for dessert. There was not much in the way of carry out. There was nothing in the way of home delivery. Most of the eating-out experiences were in the area of fine dining, with fast food confined to diners and roadside stands. All of that has changed and is continuing to change.

With the introduction of fast food, people could eat quickly and conveniently. Eventually, the luster of cooking at home began to diminish. More and more, eating at home became either a family or special occasion. Fast food was in. Fast food with carry out was in, too. During the sixties and seventies, there was a gradual shift to a dependence upon fast food, to the point where it is now a fixture in life.

In 1974, Domino's Pizza introduced a novel twist in dining: buy it there, but eat it at home. And it does not even have to be carried out; Domino's can bring it to you in your home. And so the dining experience moves full cycle; from home to restaurant and then back again to the home.

In 1987 Pillsbury began experimenting and trial marketing full-course dinners and desserts that were delivered to the home on demand. These entrees are ordered from a menu that is either faxed or available on a cable channel via one of the information networks. They are microwaved at the customer's door in the van that makes the delivery. The entrees are stored frozen and then prepared in the commissaries. Such commissaries are already in place serving Red Lobster, Burger King, and Pillsbury's other restaurants. Most of the meal is prepared right in the van with a generator, small compressor, and microwave. The driver can be called via a cellular telephone and can be at the customer's home in minutes. Dining at home no longer has to be restricted to pizza. Now customers can truly "have it their way!"

When this system is completed—and it is already in place in some cities—it will further revolutionize the dining experience. Already the attraction of fast food is fading because of the enormous amount of fat in almost all the fast food products. Dining at home and "having it your way" will be the restaurant experience of the nineties. Not only is it convenient, but it is fast, comfortable, and it offers variety. Most importantly, it is personal.

BUT WHAT WILL BECOME OF THE RESTAURANT EXPERIENCE?

The answer to this question is on the Silent Side. Fast food—with the exception of McDonald's—may fade, unless menus are changed substantially. One big problem with fast food is that it is positioned at the level of physical survival (with the exception of McDonald's). But there is a conflict here since people are being told that, for the sake of physical survival, they should not be eating the food that fast food restaurants serve! So where does that leave the fast food industry? Since there are no Spiritual or Territorial or Orientation Motives involved, future problems in the fast food industry are predicted.

Consumers' eating habits are undergoing a revolution. Within the last ten years the Physical Survival Motive has been strongly emphasized and brought into focus. The fast food industry has shown considerable resistance and reluctance to change or adapt to what is known about physical survival. Hardees, Burger King, and Wendy's, as well as others whose specialities are fried everything, may find that they exist in the year 2000, but their multilocations may be cut in half. Too many business travelers have had the unpleasant experience of eating at these places while on the road and then slowly realizing that they have gained unwanted pounds.

McDonald's will remain because it has been marketed at the level of spiritual survival. It is more than food, it is an experience. It is marketed directly to children, who in turn market to their parents. When parents are marketed to by their own children, this phenomenon arouses and creates mild to moderate parental guilt and the parents almost always acquiesce. The family then has an experience, not just a meal. But even at McDonald's, where many changes already have been made in the interest of physical survival, there will be even more extensive changes within the next few years.

The most powerful form of marketing is marketing to the children, who in turn market to the adults. This is a solid example of targeting at the level of spiritual survival and love. A variation of this is "If you love me, you'll buy me that ring, car, CD player, etc." It does not always work, but it is powerful and strong. This is direct marketing to the level of spiritual survival.

The other side of the restaurant experience is fine dining, which will survive because of the motives that it serves. Fine dining is more of an experience than a meal. After all, people can eat at home since most homes are well equipped for serving food. They do not really have to eat out.

Home-served entrees will have an effect upon fine dining, but not nearly the effect that they will have upon the mid-levels of dining. This is because home-served entrees will create an experience also. Showing a couple enjoying a fine-dining experience dressed in casual clothing, perhaps in candlelight and in a romantic atmosphere, could easily move the dining experience from the restaurant back to the home again.

THE MOTIVATIONS INVOLVED IN EATING OUT

The dominant motives involved in the decision to eat out are either convenience (physical survival) or the Orientation Motives. For a female, dining out is an opportunity to change OR: Person for that particular, special, and memorable evening. For a male, the dominant motive is OR: Place.

What does this mean for the restaurant marketer? It means that the upscale dining experience must be positioned as one that is special, unique, and different. The woman and man must be treated like the unique people that they believe they are, or even better, like the ones that they would like to be. This is especially true for females.

Implications for marketing to this particular motive involve ad copy, word of mouth, entrees, staff training, environment (music, interior decor), menus, ambience, specialties, and dress code, among other things. It can readily be seen that all of these components go well beyond the spectrum of what the ad agency can provide, and in some cases (staff training) even beyond the scope of marketing.

In a fine-dining experience a woman tends to focus more on how she feels while she is in this environment (OR: Person). She wants to escape the person that she is, at least for the night. The man will focus on the place itself and be more attentive to the service, the food, and the surroundings. He wants to escape whatever has happened to him on that particular day. Both the male and the female want to change OR: Circumstances, and the more successful the restaurant marketer is in helping them to do this, the more successful the restaurant will be. In addition, OR: Time plays a major role for both the man and the woman, and the food will contribute strongly to this. The more the customers can focus on the qualities of the food—taste, delectability, succulence, tenderness, etc.—the less they will focus on circumstance, time, and the world around them. Alcohol is very influential in changing OR: Time.

The Adaptation Motive plays a small but important role in restaurant marketing. Years ago, some restaurants were known as "the place to go." That is not as true today. A restaurant today has to earn a reputation, and then it will become the place to go. And it gains that reputation by catering on the front end to the Orientation Motives that people bring with them to the restaurant.

SPIRITUAL SURVIVAL IN RESTAURANT MARKETING

Spiritual survival is the strongest motive, and the one that carries the most consumer clout. When a dining experience is positioned at the spiritual level, it is postured as a romantic, ardent, loving, passionate, and amorous experience, not just a place. It is a place where love can be re-experienced, or reborn, and where experiences can be renewed. Basically, this marketing strategy at the spiritual level is simply taking the Orientation Motives to the limit and making the experience permanent rather than transitory or temporary.

TYPES OF DINING EXPERIENCES

Since there are many types of dining experiences, there are different levels of experiences. They are, from the highest level to the lowest level, shown in table 15-1.

When dining at home takes over, the mid-level dining experiences, such as neighborhood taverns, family experiences, cafeterias, etc., will feel pressure since they do not provide intensive motivational experiences that justify the expense and the inconvenience of going out to eat. Family restaurants, heretofore, have tended to rely on coupons and discounts as motivators. Compare these mid-level restaurants to McDonald's, where the primary emphasis is on spiritual survival. Note that in table 15-1, McDonald's is in a category by itself.

Although the cost of eating at home will not be that much cheaper for a couple or a family, the inconvenience of going to a local restaurant will not be worth the difference in the experience. The same motivations may be experienced at home, given the proper ambience, setting, and good food.

SEXUAL SURVIVAL IN RESTAURANT MARKETING

Where does sex fit into fine dining? One well known restauranteur put it very succinctly: sex and dessert go together. Marketing at the level of sexual survival

Table 15-1
Types of Dining Experiences

Dining Experience	Example	Motivation
Fine dining	Generally local, rated 5 star	OR: Person OR: Place Spiritual Survival
Pseudo-fine dining	Marriott, Hilton, chain hotels Upscale neighborhood	OR: Person OR: Place Spiritual Survival
Neighborhood tavern	Bennigan's Applebee's	OR: Person OR: Place
Family experience	Bonanza Western Sizzlin' Chuck E Cheese	Physical Survival Spiritual Survival
Cafeteria & self-serve	Morrison Picadilly Luby's	Physical Survival
Fast food, adult	Wendy's Arby's	Physical Survival
Fast food, family	McDonald's	Physical Survival Spiritual Survival
Castles & Towers	White Tower White Castle	Physical Survival

always involves an approach to gender, impulse, or inhibition. As almost everyone knows, dessert is an impulse item. The diner who has just filled up on salad, appetizer, t-bone, and baked potato will be the first to admit that he/she does not need dessert, no matter how good or tempting it looks. But temptation is the key!

The well known restauranteur who is referenced above said that he found out, long ago, that he always had to have a very attractive woman introduce the dessert cart. This is because women, who are more weight conscious than men, are more likely to forgo the dessert after a huge meal. But men, being less weight conscious, are twice to three times more likely than women to "bite." So how do you usually sell to men at the level of sexual survival (impulse)? The answer is with a beautiful woman. This is sexist by today's societal norms—but it is fact. Very few males can resist. The man gives in and buys the dessert, and the female companion asks for an extra fork so that she can just "see what it tastes like."

SUMMARY

The process of eating is defined as one of the elements necessary to sustain the motive of physical survival. This observation is quite obvious. Eating or dining at a restaurant (physical survival) should not be confused with the total restaurant experience. There is a big difference. The restaurant experience allows a temporary change in orientation at a reasonable price and usually within a convenient 10–30 minute drive from home. The change in orientation is the major motivator, and it is why the customer is willing to pay the price. Poor food, bad service, and other distractions will interfere with the change in orientation and will drive customers away. This is merely a duplication of circumstances that the customer is trying to escape from. Whatever the restaurant marketer can do to assist the customer in feeling like a new and different person will build the business, spread good will, and guarantee customer loyalty. Remember, even a restaurant needs a centralized theme.

Marketing at the level of spiritual survival means including the element of passion. This will intensify all the other motives and increase the bottom line. However, when this position is taken, the marketer needs to make sure that he/she is capable of living up to it, physically. At the spiritual level, customer disappointments can be a lot more damaging and lasting, for spiritual is contiguous with perfection. Not only must the marketer promise perfection, but he/she must be ready to deliver it!

16

Amusement and Themed Attractions

MOTIVATIONAL THEMES

The major purpose of the theme park, from a motivational point of view, is to provide people with an opportunity to disorient themselves in terms of person, place, time, and circumstances and then to reorient them. Although people who visit theme parks cannot verbalize this need, our research has demonstrated that this is exactly what is happening.

Disney says, "Once upon a time is here . . ." Silver Dollar City in Branson, Missouri, says, "You have a great past ahead of you." Both themes speak to reorientation in terms of time (OR: Time).

In chapter 4 it was stated that no one wants to lose his/her orientation; all he/she wants is a temporary change, reprieve, or respite. Proof that people do not want to totally lose their orientation is in their own statements: "I don't want to lose it," or "I wouldn't want to come unglued." When they see a person who has reached an advanced age living in a nursing home with Alzheimer's or senile dementia, they will say, "I just hope I never live that long, that somebody will shoot me before I ever get like that." A major and critical link in the motivational hierarchy that has been presented here is the motivation to remain on track, oriented, and acclimated in terms of who, where, when, and what (person, place, time, and circumstances).

At the same time, almost everyone is looking for a temporary change in orientation in each one of these areas. It was pointed out in chapter 15 that a major motivator in getting people to go out to eat in restaurants is the OR: Person Motive, where there is a temporary change in how they are treated, favored, and ad-

Figure 16-1
Thrill Seekers

(Courtesy of *The Commercial Appeal*, Memphis, TN)

dressed. In chapter 17 it will be pointed out that, for women in particular, buying a new outfit and wearing it allows a change in OR: Person. Cosmetics (chapter 18) are used for the same purpose: to reorient the woman who uses them in terms of the person that she would really like to be (OR: Person).

It should be quite clear that remaining substantially oriented is a major motivation. However, realizing and achieving temporary disorientation, as pointed out by Henry Ford, is also high on the list of personal motivators. Everyone is looking for a new opportunity to change who, what, where, when, and how they are, at least for a brief period of time. This is why weekends are important. The whole purpose of theme or amusement park visitation is to provide a temporary disorientation. This can be done in a number of ways:

- By allowing people to believe that they are someone different than they really are
- By giving them permission to be living at a different time
- By surrounding them with circumstances that are quite different from the ones in which they live
- By creating a totally different environment
- By blocking out present-day reality
- By creating total disorientation of person (with darkness, water, defiance of gravity, etc.)
- By removing the constraints of time

After visitors to a theme park have had the opportunity to experience any one, or all, of these disorientations, they will leave satisfied, and probably return again next year.

On the other hand, if they have the opportunity to experience one or all of these disorientations—plus the opportunity to reorient themselves—then they will leave very, very satisfied and probably return many times that year and the next! All of this will be explained.

EMOTIONAL DEMOGRAPHICS

We have repeatedly stressed the importance of emotional demographics (motigraphics). This is a relatively new term, since little has been known about consumer motivation in the past. Moreover, even less has been done to assess the three-dimensional impact of motigraphics, psychographics, and demographics. However, some things are known. For instance, teenagers are more likely to be entertained by thrill rides than they are by old-time arts and crafts. Similarly, senior citizens rarely stand in line to ride roller coasters and log flumes.

In theme park research, four specific groups surface over and over again in the results of research:

- Thrill seekers
- Second honeymooners

- Extended families
- Senior citizens

Thrill Seekers

Thrill seekers are the group for whom the old amusement parks were originally constructed. They are generally teenagers and young adults, who are typically experiencing an identity crisis in terms of OR: Person. This is a generally accepted psychological theory—that people within this age group are searching for identity and eventually find it after they get an education, marry, and establish a career. Prior to these things happening they are searching for an identity, and one way of doing this is by orienting and reorienting their person (OR: Person).

Thrill rides consist of rides and attractions that are totally disorienting. Usually they make use of gravity by dropping a person 50 or 100 feet, either in a chair, bucket, or perhaps on a train (roller coaster). Sometimes this occurs in darkness, which makes it even more disorienting. A number of these attractions in amusement parks totally disorient the person by taking advantage of disequilibrium. A rocking or twisting ride will disorient the vestibular senses because of a repositioning of the body. In this way when the individual leaves the ride he/she is momentarily totally disoriented in terms of person. This is accomplished by swinging the rider around in a circle, often moving at the same time in an up-and-down motion so that the rider loses equilibrium and becomes disoriented through dizziness. It takes several minutes for the vestibular senses to reorient the person after leaving the ride. The desired outcome is then achieved: temporary disorientation in terms of person, with reorientation following.

It is not unusual for thrill seekers to ride these rides over and over again, keeping "score." The purpose of the repetition is to extend the experience of disorientation and to allow them to compete with their peers. This lets them and their friends know how many times they were able to disorient and then reorient, as if this somehow provides a stronger identity. This means that the repetition part of this cycle is related to the Adaptation Motive.

Disorientation in terms of OR: Person is not exclusive to teenagers. Older persons are sometimes included in the population of thrill seekers. However, younger people make up the largest part of this population, by far.

As stressed over and over again, it is important to know the motives of customers so that rides can be designed, purchased, and placed well. Thrill seekers will often swarm to a theme park when a new ride is introduced, but after engaging in the ride several times, it ceases to be a challenge, and they lose interest in returning. Their identity in terms of OR: Person has been satisfied. The only reason they might return again would be for purposes of adaptation (i.e., to let their friends know that they can do it).

*The Neurophysiological Substrates of Thrill Seeking and
Disorientation*

The motives of thrill seekers and their pattern of disorientation and reorientation were examined briefly in chapter 4. The primary activity of this behavior is fear. The final intent or purpose is to overcome the fear so that they can "feel as if they can conquer anything." In mountain climbing, bungee jumping, parachuting, and in ordinary "hard iron" theme parks, the goal is to overcome one challenge so that the thrill seeker can move on to more challenging and difficult rides. The point at which he/she reaches satisfaction is almost insatiable. This is because, in thrill seeking and in other personal orientation/disorientation activities, there is a good possibility that these activities are addictive in the physical, neurological sense of the word.

Some psychologists believe that true thrill seekers have an imbalance in their brains in the chemical monoamine oxidase, which is a neurotransmitter that plays a role in depression and elation. Zuckerman (1986) believes that the fear stimulated by these activities causes an alteration in the level of this chemical and changes the thrill seeker's mood. But his explanation does not totally account for the real possibility of addiction.

Since thrill seekers and others who regularly seek disorientation often act as if they are addicted, it is very possible that the opioid receptors of the brain are involved. Farley (1986) believes that thrill seekers have a low arousal level, and the feeling of being in danger triggers the reticular activating system in the brain, which in turn stimulates other neuromodulators and neurotransmitters in the rest of the brain. If the opioid receptors are part of this chain, addiction among thrill seekers as well as others who are regularly seeking disorientation may be more easily understood. Consider the illustrations that were given in preceding chapters. One of the major attractions of a casino is disorientation in all four spheres. Isn't it more understandable, then, how many gamblers become addicted? Are they really addicted to gambling, or to disorientation? Or what about the compulsive shopper, or the depressed woman who goes out and buys new clothing?

Remember Henry Ford's statement, "People want to get where they ain't, and then get back home again." Even running away can become addictive and compulsive, because of the effect that it has on each individual, and upon the neurotransmitters of the central nervous system.

Second Honeymooners

The second-honeymooner demographic consists of individuals, generally middle aged (40) and older, who visit a theme park either as a couple or perhaps with one or two other couples. Second honeymooners visit theme parks because of their need for temporary disorientation. However, they are not looking for orientation in terms of OR: Person, like the thrill seeker. This is because their personal identities are usually quite secure at this time in their lives. Their major motivations for making a visit are OR: Place and OR: Circumstances.

Most of the members of the second-honeymooner group are working and in the middle of their careers. Their careers have become competitive and stressful as they face direct challenges from younger, more capable contributors or executives. At home many of them have become bored with each other. Therefore, they look for a different place, a very special place that removes them from the challenge, competition, boredom, restlessness, and all the realities in which they live. They will often drive many miles in a very short time (3–4 days) to find this special place. If it succeeds in disorienting them in terms of place (OR: Place) and in terms of the circumstances that they face on a day-to-day basis at home (OR: Circumstances), they will become loyal and return often.

Theme parks that appeal to second honeymooners should do market research on consumer satisfaction, and the surveys should be constructed around the concept of total and complete satisfaction in terms of OR: Place and OR: Circumstances. This is what consumers of theme attractions are looking for. This will instill and ensure brand loyalty and return visits in the future.

The Extended Family

The extended family is the bread-and-butter demographic of almost every theme park. This is because the major motivation of parents in bringing children to a theme park is spiritual survival. The motives are love, concern, care, togetherness, and passion. These are the strongest motives. This group pursues theme park visitation with fervor and intensity.

The major attractions for this group are rides that are well below the thrill-seeking level. This would include children's rides that are safe and slow moving for children up to age ten and "softer" rides such as log flumes, water parks, or rides through darkness. Thrill seeking takes over after this, generally around ages of 12 to 14. In addition, major attractions for the extended family include musical and comedy shows in which all can participate, having fun and laughing together as a family.

Since this group consists of parents with their children, orientation and disorientation are major issues. Parents, when exercising their responsibility as parents, do not want to become disoriented; they want to remain on track as much as possible. Therefore spiritual survival is the dominant motive that this group brings to the park. Success (in terms of spiritual survival) will mean strengthening family ties as a result of the experience; diminishing the conflict between the parents and the children; increasing love and respect; and increasing understanding of parents toward their children. Attitude surveys for extended family members should be constructed with these outcomes in mind. Brand loyalty and return visitation will occur as a function of how well these objectives are met.

Senior Citizens

There is a demographic crossover between the senior citizen group and the second honeymooners. The senior citizens are often retired. They do not have the pressures of work and other challenges, but they do face the boredom, tedium, and repetition in life in general. Therefore they travel widely, usually in the fall (to avoid extended families) in motor homes, privately owned vehicles, or on bus tours.

Senior citizens are, as a group, increasing in numbers every year because of the changes in life expectancy. They have a great deal of influence, and often have sufficient discretionary income. Although everyone looks forward to retirement years, many senior citizens have found that after a year or so they become restless, disenchanted, and unsettled. As a result, they begin looking for something to do.

Visits to theme parks by this group are motivated at the level of OR: Place and OR: Time. By removing or disorienting senior citizens to place, they are taken out of their everyday circumstances, which is what they are looking for. By removing or disorienting them to time, which is accomplished by going back to another, simpler time, they feel more comfortable, more at ease, and as if they had gone back to a simpler time in their own lives. Many elderly people are not happy with the times in which they find themselves, and often express the desire to be back at a previous time and place in their lives when things were much simpler and made more sense to them. In the real world that they face they feel lost or misplaced.

Senior citizens typically believe that life was simpler when they were being raised; that children had different attitudes; and that people were more kindly and not as self-serving. In disorienting them to time and place, theme park personnel need to understand these motives and needs so they can behave accordingly. To a large extent, senior citizens do not understand why they are treated so rudely in customer service situations, and want to get away to a place where this will not happen.

REORIENTATION AND REVIVAL AT THE SPIRITUAL LEVEL

It should be quite clear that the major motivator for theme park visitation has always been temporary disorientation in terms of person, place, time, or circumstances. If visitors have the opportunity to experience one or all of these disorientations—plus the opportunity to reorient themselves—they will leave very, very satisfied and probably return many times that year. Disorientation and how it occurs has been outlined in this and other chapters. What about reorientation?

One major theme park that requested our services in marketing was staging a closing ceremony every evening at 7 P.M. that was very brief. It consisted of one of the musicians playing "Taps" and the flag being unfurled, usually with the backdrop of a beautiful Pacific sunset. But the overall effect of this closing ceremony was anticlimactic. Visitors had found the disorientation for which they were searching, but there was nothing to guide them through the reality to which they were going to return. They still had to go back to the place, circumstances, and time from which they had been seeking relief. What was needed was a brief reorientation.

The strongest, most visible and emotional way to reorient visitors is through spiritual survival. This is because spiritual survival is passionate. As a result, a closing ceremony was designed that was choreographed and set in an extremely patriotic backdrop or scene. With individual singers and choirs, orchestras, and bands, the music of Sousa was played, flags were waved, and the audience was invited to participate and join in on most of the acts. This was presented as *an American experience*, in which everyone who attended would feel the pride that they had inside them as an American. Having been disoriented from their person, place, heritage, time, etc., during the day, they were now reoriented as Americans in the finest tradition of patriotism, spirituality, and love of country. Patriotism is spiritual survival at its best.

It makes sense that, if people need help in disorientation, they also need assistance in reorienting themselves. Some theme parks do not even attempt this; they simply end the day by announcing over the loud speaker, "Attention all visitors, the park will close in 15 minutes." This is nothing other than a reminder of the grim reality that the visitors face as they head back home. As in any scenario involving spiritual survival, there needs to be a resolution, a climax, and a reorientation. Closure is important to complete the experience.

The importance of reorientation cannot be underestimated. It is a form of resolution. When a person becomes disoriented, even on a temporary basis, he/she is in a highly suggestible and fragile state. To reorient them in terms of spiritual survival—which could be love of family, country, God—is one of the most powerful and lasting positive emotional experiences that people can have. In addition, it is motivating and leaves customers with a feeling that they can take home with them. It has transfer value.

Many people left the closing ceremony, referred to above, with tears in their eyes and wet handkerchiefs. What a time for surveyors to gather information! And what an impact this had upon overall visitor satisfaction, return visitation, and brand loyalty. Not only were the visitors satisfied, but the subconscious was satisfied too.

SOUVENIRS

Souvenirs are always available at theme parks and are a reminder of the experience that the visitor had. But when looking at this in terms of the Silent Side, they are much more than a reminder: they are an extension of the whole experience, and an attempt to apply it to everyday life. Souvenirs, very simply, allow one to extend the disorientation/reorientation experience beyond the confines of the park and that particular day and, hopefully, into the broad expanse of everyday life. Every time they wear the T-shirts or look at objects on their desks or in their homes they are extending the experiences they enjoyed so much into the brief moments of their daily routine. It carries them over from one visit to the next. It also helps them to deal with the reality of everyday life.

REFERENCES

Farley, F. (1986). The big T in personality. *Psychology Today, 20,* 44–52.

Zuckerman, M. (1986). Sensation seeking and the endogenous deficit theory of drug abuse. In National Institute on Drug Abuse, *Research Monograph Series* (Monograph No. 74, pp. 59–70). Rockville, MD: National Institute on Drug Abuse.

17

Fashion Marketing and Merchandising

CONSUMER SEGMENTATION

As in all consumer products, analysis of fashion-buying habits will show that consumers have loyalty to a particular type of product, even though their loyalty is changeable. This loyalty is based on taste, and taste in clothing develops out of the primary motivational structure that was outlined in chapter 4.

In women's shoe research, carried out for a leading importer and manufacturer of women's shoes in the United States, there were three different groups of women that emerged with regard to shoe preference:

- Women whose primary fashion interests were sexual
- Women whose primary fashion interests were career oriented
- Women whose primary fashion interests were in home and family

Women who were primarily interested in sex and sexuality were vitally interested in their appearance. They spend a considerable amount of time dressing, putting on makeup, and "getting ready" to go out, as compared to career-oriented women and women whose interests were in home and family.

Women who were interested in home and family, not surprisingly, wore the least amount of makeup and spent the least time getting ready to "make an appearance." Career-oriented women were in between these two groups.

SEXUAL SURVIVAL AS A PRIMARY MOTIVE IN FASHIONS

The "sexual" group was motivated by the Sexual Survival Motive, and by the Adaptation Motive. Using their own group as a reference point, they would closely analyze women who dressed like they did, assimilate features that they liked, and then attempt to adapt, or be like, those women. They might see these women in magazines, on television, or in real life. All sources served as their models. Women in the sexual group would look at all women, but they would pay the most attention to those women that they perceived to be in their own reference group: sexually attractive, seductive-appearing women.

When marketing to this group of women, shoes, fashions, and some cosmetics items will be more successfully marketed when the message is aimed at impulse, not inhibition. Shoes are but one example. Shoes preferred by this group include medium to high heels, often open at the heel or, if the open heel is out of fashion, a thin strap across the heel. In addition, a low-cut shoe is preferred with the top crossing barely above the toes, making the foot look much smaller. An option would be with toes open. Even when shoes with a strong sexual theme are not available, there are usually variations of this style in a more moderate, low-heel style. If a fashion cycle surfaces where there are no shoes in this particular style, sexually oriented women will be content with another style. But they are usually not happy about it, and will look forward to the end of that cycle and the beginning of a new one when they can buy the kinds of shoes that they want: open, loose, low-cut, and sensual. Women who are sexually oriented prefer style over comfort in shoes. They will not hesitate to let others know this.

It is not always simple to discern someone's motivational orientation. This information was taken from in-depth research that was done with over 100 consumers. However, two findings stood out with regard to motivation in fashion:

1. A woman who is primarily motivated by sexual survival may not necessarily function at that level, although this is where her loyalty will remain. This is where she will direct her primary interest in fashions. For example, even though her primary motivation is sexual, she may function during the day in a career capacity as a nurse, as an executive, or as a mother. The sexual concern is more motivational than demonstrable.
2. A woman who is primarily motivated by sexual survival will, from time to time, change her orientation, although this will always be a temporary change, not a permanent one. This is related to OR: Person, where people tend to want to change their orientation temporarily, but not permanently.

The primary appeal at the level of sexual survival is the product, and its design. Secondarily, the advertising copy and marketing plan can be targeted at this level, if desired. When marketing shoes or other fashions to the impulse level of the Sexual Survival Motive, some of the following suggestions may be considered:

•   Showing a woman with a man in an informal setting

- Showing a woman and a man drinking
- Merchandising impulse items together, in one area
- Merchandising impulse items in recreational and vacation areas (impulse situation)
- Showing a woman in a seductive pose

TERRITORIAL SURVIVAL IN FASHION MERCHANDISING

Women whose primary motivation is career, occupation, profession, or business tend to operate at the territorial survival level. The strongest emotion within the territorial level is security. Other emotions include status, power, authority, intelligence, and competence. These women prefer comfort over style in shoes. The shoes preferred by women who are motivated by territorial survival are conservative in style and in color. Style would include low or medium heels, a closed vs. an open shoe, giving the appearance of comfort and practicality. Generally in women's shoes, the more of the foot that shows the more emotional the shoe.

Ad copy that would appeal to women in this group might consider the following:

- Showing women in formal, business, or political settings, or in sports backdrops
- Showing women in a decision-making capacity
- Showing women who are secure in their situation
- Showing women who have authority in their situation
- Showing women who share authority with men, or have authority over them
- Showing women who know how to get things done

Since the territorial motives belong to the survival group, they are powerful. Advertising at this level will be on target and extremely motivating.

The marketer needs to remember that, for women in this group as well as in the sexual group, the Adaptation Motive is important. In both groups, it is important to use one's peer group as reference, for there is a definite need to adapt and to be like others. The sexual woman looks to other sexual women to see what they are wearing. Likewise, the career woman looks to her peers to discern what is and what is not correct.

THE DOMESTIC GROUP

The third group mentioned above was women whose primary interest and level of motivation are home and family. This is an aspect of the Physical Survival Motive. Women in this group prefer shoes that are flat, often canvas, slip on and off easily, and are comfortable. They show very little interest in style. Color is important, but not primary. The major difference between the women in this group vs. the career and sexual groups is that they are not interested in the Adaptation Motive and care very little about what others are doing or wearing. Their choice of fashions and shoes is based upon what is comfortable. Their choices tend to be utilitarian.

Women in the domestic group have a primary, all-encompassing interest in their children and family, to the point where interests outside the family become insignificant. They spend almost 90 percent of their time in casual shoes and fashions and have little interest in any outside reference group. They read magazines about the home and family and about food and are not really exposed to fashion advertising. They do not conform to the expectations of others.

Consumer groups and their corresponding motivations are summarized in table 17-1.

OTHER MOTIVATIONS IN FASHIONS

For each of these groups in table 17-1, there is one overwhelming motive in fashion design, merchandising, and marketing.

Men have always had difficulty understanding a woman when she says, "I have nothing to wear Saturday night. I may not be able to go." Then the man will look in the woman's closet and see over 40 outfits, and marvel at the fact that she just told him she had nothing to wear!

A major element in fashion design and marketing is the fact that a woman always has the option to become an entirely new and different person by purchasing a new dress, suit, or complete outfit. When she says that she has nothing to wear, what she really means is that she cannot present on Saturday night as the kind of person that she feels she ought to be, since she does not have an outfit to reflect that personality, or persona.

The overwhelming motive in fashion design, merchandising, and marketing should be recognized as the OR: Person Motive. For a female—and to a much lesser extent for a male—the option of becoming a new person, on a temporary basis, is available to her through fashion and what she wears. Research as well as experience in clinical settings with patients, has demonstrated this.

Table 17-1
Consumer Segmentation in Women's Fashions and Shoes

Group	Primary Interest	Motivations	Elements
Sexual	Appearance	Sexual Survival Adaptation	Gender—femininity Impulse expression
Career	Business, career	Territorial Survival Adaptation	Security Acceptance
Domestic	Home, family	Physical Survival Territorial Survival	Nurturing Nesting

Women who become depressed will often seek their own "cure" by going on a shopping spree. They may shop beyond their means and extend the limits of their spending well beyond what is considered reasonable, in an effort to escape depression and become a "new person." Such a change is always temporary. In chapter 4, where the OR: Person Motive was described, it was shown that change in orientation/disorientation is always temporary. Whether in terms of time, place, or person, wherever the consumers go, they always want to return to where they were or who they were.

A major opportunity in fashion merchandising and marketing is to address the OR: Person Motive. The OR: Person Motive is not just applicable to one group, one particular emotional demographic, or depressed persons. The fact is that the ability to "change identity" or personal orientation by putting on a new outfit is a powerful motive shared by almost all women, and it is not unusual for a woman to find a particular identity in the way she dresses, or in a specific outfit she sees.

Marketing to the OR: Person Motive requires that the marketer address change, renewal, revitalization, rejuvenation, and restoration. When this is done, marketing is definitely to the motives and to the mind. This is an example of right brain marketing at its best, since the marketer is going directly for the motive in addition to dealing with external rationalizations.

WHAT ABOUT MEN?

Although men share with women the OR: Person Motive and the need to seek temporary change, it is not done nearly as often with clothing. Instead, when a man becomes depressed he will usually try to change locations, in conformity to the OR: Place Motive. Conversely, women will try and change who they are (OR: Person) vs. where they are. Men's products, such as cowboy boots, jeans, certain types of athletic shoes, underwear, and beachwear, are marketed to men at the level of sexual survival (gender) and are aimed primarily at masculinity.

Labeled clothing (Dockers, Levis, Duck Head, etc.) is marketed to males on the basis of the Adaptation Motive. Business suits, dress shirts, shoes, and ties are marketed to males at the level of territorial survival. Table 17-2 summarizes motivational marketing in men's clothing.

SPIRITUAL SURVIVAL IN FASHION MERCHANDISING

Spiritual survival has been described as the most powerful motive for marketing most products. Although spiritual survival works in fashion merchandising, it can easily be overdone. When the consumer selects fashions, he/she is usually hoping to satisfy the emotions that have been described above: masculinity, feminity, conventionality, security, impulse expression, etc. Therefore, it is always safe to market fashions at these levels, depending upon the particular product to be marketed.

Table 17-2
Marketing Fashions to Men: The Motivational Approach

Fashion Item	Motivational Level	Element
Shirts, ties, suits	Territorial Survival	Security
Underwear, T-shirts, boots, western wear	Sexual Survival (gender)	Masculinity
Casual clothing (label out)	Adaptation	In style, same as peer group
Beachwear	Sexual Survival (gender)	Masculinity

Raising these motivations to the level of spiritual survival can have the effect of increasing brand awareness and intensifying sales. Here are just a few examples of how this might be done:

- Position fashions with love, new relationships
- Show fashions in the context of the family
- Include fashions in advertising that demonstrate significant achievement
- Use creative background of patriotism, love, perfection, career promotion
- Position fashions with unselfish service, giving, loving, finding love, passion, performing a demanding task, contributing, providing, etc.

SUMMARY

OR: Person is a major motive in marketing fashions, where a female can change "who she is" and her whole person, temporarily, with a dress, suit, or gown. Shoes serve the same purpose. Other major motivational categories include territorial survival, physical survival, sexual survival (impulse), and adaptation, depending a lot upon the emotional demographics of the group that is being marketed to.

Men's clothing and fashions are marketed and merchandised somewhat differently, with a major emphasis upon sexual survival (gender-masculinity). Of necessity, "power suits" for both males and females are marketed at the level of territorial survival.

It is possible to raise marketing strategies to the level of spiritual survival. This can be overdone, but if executed correctly, it can have a dramatic effect upon response and upon sales. the marketer always should remember the primary motive of OR: Person. This motive is involved in the effective marketing of fashions, especially in marketing fashions to females. In chapter 18 (cosmetics), the possibility of layering of motives is discussed in detail. It is always desirable to layer two motivational levels together in order to generate a powerful and effective marketing campaign in fashions.

18

Cosmetics Marketing

LAYERING

The decision to purchase, use, and remain loyal to a particular brand of cosmetics is 85 percent emotional and 15 percent rational. Therefore the marketing of cosmetics, face creams, body lotions, and fragrances should consider and address the emotions that are involved. This can be done through a process called *layering*. Layering involves addressing or targeting two motivational levels in the same ad or marketing presentation. This procedure can be used with any product where the marketer is interested in using a three-dimensional approach to marketing and advertising. It is not limited to cosmetics.

Layering works this way. The major motivation to use and purchase cosmetics is OR: Person, but other motivations, such as spiritual survival, are also involved. Another motive involved with cosmetics is sexual survival (gender) where a woman wishes to appear feminine, unique, delicate, soft, fresh, etc. In many cases the marketer will want to focus on just one motivation or level. However, two of these three motivational levels may be layered to create an appeal that is more effective. A third level, the rational level, may then be added to give "permission" to purchase a particular brand or to communicate rationalizations, justifications, excuses, etc., that the consumers may use to justify their purchases.

For example, since the major motivation involved in makeup is OR: Person, the marketer usually wants to remain strongly focused on this motive. This is why many cosmetics advertisements feature a woman alone, as opposed to a woman with a man, or in a crowd. When a woman is featured alone, then the targeted audience may focus on that woman and determine whether or not she is the type of woman that they would like to be. When focusing upon the woman alone, props

are often included, such as upscale cars, places, business settings, etc., to give the
targeted audience some insight into the lifestyle she lives, which is an important
determinant of who she is and whether they would like to be like she is and have
her particular kind of lifestyle.

The second motivational level in our example involves spiritual survival. In
this case, the female might be shown with a man, possibly dining in an upscale
restaurant or enjoying time together in a recreational setting. They have found
love. This is layering. Two motivational levels have been targeted or layered: OR:
Person and Spiritual Survival. To add a third emotional dimension at this point,
such as sexual survival (gender), would cause considerable confusion. This is
because in three-dimensional marketing the third level is logic, which also needs
to be included. Three levels is all that the mind can cognitively handle. More than
three levels would simply result in confusion, disorientation, and possible rejec-
tion of the product. Logic is the third dimension; it allows the customer to give
herself permission to buy and use the product. Some examples of a logical approach to the use of makeup would include price (some drug store brands), long
lasting (many brands), or convenience (Revlon, Maybelline). Logic plays a secondary role in cosmetics, compared to the Orientation Motives. However, the role
that it plays is important.

Another example of layering is seen in marketing flowers and floral products.
The primary motive in sending floral products is sexual survival (gender). Many
women love to receive flowers, especially when there is no particular reason. To
many females, when a man sends flowers, this is an indication not only of love but
of sensitivity on the part of the sender. Many women believe sensitivity to be a
rare trait in a man. Hence, the appeal to gender. A second motivational level can
easily be added in floral products: spiritual survival. Flowers signify love, passion, remembrance and, "thinking of you" at the level of spiritual survival (love).
Therefore, the product can be advertised or marketed at this level. It could be as
simple as "flowers mean love." What is the logic involved in sending flowers?
Often it is an apology, but it could also be a remembrance, event, sympathy, thanks
for a favor, appreciation, etc. As in cosmetics, logic becomes the third dimension
in advertising and marketing floral products.

MAKEUP AND MOTIVATION: THE ROLE OF OR: PERSON

The major motivation involved in the purchase and use of makeup is OR: Person. OR: Person has already been established as one of the strongest Silent Side
motivations and has been shown to be influential in fashions, hosiery, restaurant
marketing, and in various recreational fields. For women in particular, OR: Person plays a serious and ardent role in many facets of their life. For men, OR: Place
usually holds more priority.

Because OR: Person is such an established and durable motive, it should be
taken very seriously. Makeup provides the opportunity for a woman to present

herself, publically, as the kind of person that she really wants to be. She has many options: fresh, fashionable, up to date, conservative, contemporary, creative, smooth, upscale, downscale, sexual-impulsive, sexual-inhibition, etc. The options seem unlimited. Because of all these options, and because this is such a serious, earnest, and sincere endeavor, she is willing to seek assistance in carrying her makeup routine through to a satisfactory conclusion.

Assistance is often found in upscale department stores, where specially trained cosmeticians assist in applying the exact mixtures and textures to the face, skin, eyes, hands, lips, lashes, etc. Women are willing to pay for this assistance since OR: Person is best handled by trained professionals. The brands that provide such assistance are able to sell their products at premium prices since they are, by providing on-site expertise, targeting the market that takes the OR: Person motivation very, very seriously. The women in this market are willing to pay these premium prices for makeup. Literally, money is no object. Brands that provide assistance with OR: Person will always be able to attract the most serious buyers and command the highest premium prices.

OR: Person is dominant, not only with the group that is targeted for service and assistance, but among all the user groups. For this reason, magazines and other advertising and marketing media present women, usually alone, in a variety of settings, with whom the potential user can identify. A woman may scan several hundred such ads, looking at the pictures, until she finds the composite of the woman that she wants to be like. Her final decision often involves brand loyalty and commitment for a lifetime.

SPIRITUAL SURVIVAL

When applied to cosmetics or any other consumer area, spiritual survival involves love, affection, passion, or perfection. Spiritual survival and OR: Person fit neatly together because both motives pursue the achievement of perfection. The stronger the emphasis of the marketer on spiritual survival, the more the interest in perfection. When perfection is emphasized along with OR: Person, the customer is willing to pay more for the product, but will also demand much more. Her demands will include service, consultation, and, among other things, assistance with application and mix.

Spiritual survival also reflects love and passion. In advertising, this may be shown in the form of rescue, or perhaps just happiness in having found the love that she has been looking for. When love and passion (spiritual survival) are emphasized along with OR: Person, this is an example of the layering of motives. Such a presentation will be strong, and each of the motives will have an impact on the viewer or potential user.

Figure 18-1
Cosmetics: Orientation to Person

(Reprinted with permission of Maybelline, Inc.)

PHYSICAL SURVIVAL

A number of cosmetics manufacturers have shown that physical survival is a legitimate approach to the marketing of cosmetics. The two that are the most prominent in this area are Almay and Clinique. Clinique has combined the best aspects of OR: Person, including personal consultation and high price, with physical survival. The physical survival approach emphasizes a nonallergenic ingredient, which appeals specifically to targeted audiences who have had problems with cosmetic allergies and believe that they have overly sensitive skin or who suffer from skin allergies. A number of dermatologists have successfully marketed private label cosmetics through their offices using this same motivational approach: physical survival and an appeal to sensitive skin.

Earlier it has been suggested that attention to issues involving physical survival has increased exponentially in the last ten years. Although at least two cosmetics manufacturers have positioned themselves within this framework, it is believed that there is room for more because of this recent surge of interest in issues that involve the Physical Survival Motive, especially considering the fact that physical survival is one of the most basic motives in the hierarchy.

TERRITORIAL SURVIVAL

An appeal by a cosmetics manufacturer and marketer to the level of territorial survival consists of an appeal to the female who is involved in and committed to her career. Typically, such an appeal will use background props in order to demonstrate the issues of power, decision making, authority, expertise, specialization, and control. When a woman is shown getting out of a helicopter carrying a briefcase, chairing an important business meeting, or running out of a building, the issues of power and territory become obvious. Therefore, in most advertising to career-oriented women, props are all that is necessary. It is not necessary to show another person in the advertising. Showing another woman would only detract from the central character and weaken or dilute the OR: Person Motive, which should always be focused upon as it is the major motivator in cosmetics marketing. To be effective, all that needs to be done is to position the career woman with the obvious symbols of power, and to show that she is secure and confident in her position.

SEXUAL SURVIVAL

Cosmetic products that are marketed or advertised at the level of sexual survival can be aimed at any one of the three sexual components: gender, impulse, or inhibition. Although some people feel that makeup is strictly sexual and worn only for sex appeal, this is not entirely true. Farrell, in his book *Why Men Are the Way They Are*, says that makeup is a major item in all women's magazines since women need to make themselves attractive to receive a man's attention. According to Farrell, what the female gets in return is the security that is offered by a man's commitment. But what Farrell is describing is an appeal to *sexual gender only*. In his analysis of the role of cosmetics, he has completely overlooked any appeals to OR: Person, OR: Place, and territorial or spiritual survival. He has also overlooked any appeals to sexual survival at the levels of either impulse or inhibition (1981). Hence, his approach is too narrow.

The subconscious approach to cosmetics is much more flexible. It involves several different motives: survival, orientation, etc. It does not focus on one motive; however, it does rank these motives, for we have found in our research that the OR: Person Motive is the central theme in cosmetics.

Sexual gender issues involve being attractive, appealing, pretty, charming, and pleasing to a man. A woman wants to fascinate a man so that he will turn his attention toward her. But this does not necessarily connote sex. For example, she may be a business executive who is attempting to fascinate a perspective client with a proposal, or a real estate agent who is listing a property. One would imagine she would not attempt to do any of these things without the appropriate makeup. This is what is meant by sexual gender issues. The marketer, at this level, appeals to a woman's need to be attractive and fascinating to a man or to another woman. This level could easily be used as a second layer in connection with the main motive, OR: Person.

Sexual impulse is, in many ways, the opposite of what has been covered under gender. In marketing to the sexual level of impulse, the vendor emphasizes the alluring, captivating, bewitching, beguiling, and enticing nature of the woman. When cosmetic products are offered and marketed at the impulse level, the issue is sexual seduction of men. There are women who apply makeup strictly for purposes of seducing or alluring a man, and the marketer must determine the nature of his/her target through emotional demographics before positioning cosmetics products at any level. Otherwise, it is easily seen how the sale of cosmetics at this level would be offensive and distasteful to women in other groups.

To determine the nature of the target audience, our firm has developed a scale that measures emotional demographics. We believe that emotional demographics are just as important, if not more important, than social demographics. A periodical may boast that 80 percent of its readers are in management, make over $40,000 per annum, etc. This is great. But the marketer should also know the emotional demographics (motigraphics) that are involved. Are these readers who are in management influenced mostly by territorial motives? What about sexual impulse (seduction of men)? Or what about sexual inhibition? When the marketer knows the answers to these questions, he/she may want to target the marketing approach and message accordingly. When it comes to emotions and the real concerns of the target audience, a shotgun approach will not only miss some of the real emotions, but it could be offensive, dangerous, and completely off course. At best such an approach will cause confusion.

Sexual inhibition is the third element of sexual survival. Many women who are inhibited do not wear any makeup at all. A part of this group believes that cosmetics are used primarily for the purpose of seducing men, and either they are morally opposed to it or, more often, they are just not interested. A large part of the sexually inhibited group are in the "housewife" group that was discussed in chapter 17. These are women whose primary interests in life are home, family, and children. They have no other real or serious interests, even though they may have a career and other commitments in their lives. The housewife group is influenced by the motive of physical survival. So even though some of them may be sexually inhibited or basically disinterested in OR: Person, they will more than likely respond to issues of physical survival. Hence, they often show interest in skin care, the aging process, fragrance, etc., and they could be appealed to at this level.

THE ADAPTATION MOTIVE

If makeup is so highly personalized and unique, how and why would the Adaptation Motive be involved? After all, the Adaptation Motive is the desire to be like other people and we have already stated that makeup is a highly personalized and individualistic item. This is a double-edged sword!

Women who are working in career and management settings need to be and are concerned with the appropriateness of their makeup. They want to be in tune with the situation and with other people's expectations. Therefore, they are always watching other women for relevant and appropriate cues.

Most women watch other women for cues. This is true of almost all women, not just the ones who are involved in careers. This is why women's magazines show pictures of women. Adaptation is a major factor in the sale and use of cosmetics, because women look to other women to help them determine what kind of persona they wish to project. In cosmetics, OR: Person and the Adaptation Motive go hand in hand and complement each other, since the Adaptation Motive involves doing what other people do.

No company knows more about the Adaptation Motive than Mary Kay or Avon. Starting out as door-to-door operations, they found that many women were no longer at home during the day. So the central focus became parties at which the local neighborhood representative introduced the product to a group of women. They also found a large market among career women who sell to each other on the job or at the office—a market that now exceeds home parties. From an emotional viewpoint, this approach is masterful. Not only do women get to observe other women wearing makeup, but they actually get to see where they spend their money. Also, with an expert present, advice is given out and demonstrations are put on for a lot less money than the customer would pay in an expensive department store setting. This is the Adaptation Motive at its best, and it shows how closely this motive is interwoven with the OR: Person Motive.

WHY DO TEENAGERS USE SO MUCH MAKEUP?

It is an accepted fact that teenagers, to the disdain of their parents, generally overdo the amount of makeup that they use. This is easily explained in terms of the unconscious mind. First, teenagers have problems with identity. This was discussed in chapter 16, as we addressed thrill seeking. Since the major motivation in using and applying the makeup is OR: Person, then makeup is a major and primary factor in determining an identity. In most cases, this "identity" will last for a lifetime. Hence, there is a tendency toward experimentation. For a teenager, experimentation means seeking and finding her identity as a person.

Just as important, teenagers are impulsive. Since sex and sexuality are new-found and recently discovered feelings, they do not know exactly how to deal with their impulses. It is not unusual for a parent to say, "You look just like a streetwalker. Go back upstairs and take that stuff off of your face." Part of the reason for the misapplication of makeup is simply a lack of experience. The other part is confusion over how to deal with the onset of sexual impulse, which is still a novelty with most teenagers.

Marketers never address the sexual impulse motive in teenagers, because this is an ethical issue. The whole issue of sexuality and impulse in teenagers is a volatile one, and it would be professionally and otherwise unethical for anyone to exploit this motive with this vulnerable group. Instead the whole concern with identity needs to be left to professionals, who are trained to work with adolescents and know about identity problems.

TARGETING THE MARKET: THE VOLATILE NATURE
OF COSMETICS

The marketer needs to determine the emotional demographics of the target market, especially in such a volatile area as cosmetics. The reason that the cosmetics market is volatile is because it is a highly personalized and emotional product. And it is personalized because of the importance of the OR: Person motivation.

One female who participated in a research study was a medical receptionist and transcriptionist in a one-physician office. The physician's wife, who was from a very wealthy, old, and established family, worked one day a week in the office doing accounts payable and payroll. The receptionist commented on how perfect her makeup was, how it matched her complexion and was perfectly applied. On one occasion she asked the "boss's wife" what kind of makeup she used, but she did not get an answer to her question. The receptionist then realized that it was a question that she should not have asked, because, in her words, "someone of her stature would not want someone beneath her, such as me, wearing the same makeup." The receptionist added that the wife had probably spent many years finding the right "mix." The receptionist then admitted that if she were the one being asked, she would not tell either.

CONCLUSION

Two vitally important motivational issues are involved in the purchase and application of cosmetics and makeup: OR: Person and adaptation. These are especially strong motives (see Typical Motivational Hierarchy, figure 4-7) and account for the strength of the entire market. Because consumers are emotionally committed, the whole market is forceful, strong, and volatile, and consumes millions and millions of consumer dollars.

There are a number of emotions involved in the cosmetics market. The process of layering was introduced so that more than one emotion could be dealt with in a marketing presentation or advertising. Layering involves placing two (but no more than two) relevant emotions into the same marketing presentation and then adding a third dimension: logic. Attempts to introduce more than two emotions and to balance logic at the same time would be confusing and disorienting to the consumer. The process of layering emotions can be used in marketing strategies with almost any product, but is especially effective in the cosmetics market since there are so many human emotions involved in the purchase and use of cosmetics.

REFERENCE

Farrell, W. (1981). *Why men are the way they are: The male:female dynamic.* New York: McGraw Hill.

19

Automotive Advertising and Marketing

HOW TO CHANGE THE ART OF AUTOMOBILE INTO THE SCIENCE OF AUTOMOBILE MARKETING

Under the present rules, auto-marketing campaigns have to be re-invented, over and over again, each time a new spot is created. Under the rules defined by the unconscious mind, although the messages may change from time to time, an automobile can be positioned at one motivational level and left there. An example where this is already being done is General Motors' marketing of the Cadillac. With its emphasis upon perfection and achievement, it has and always will be marketed at the level of spiritual survival. Only the message changes. On the other hand, an automotive product can also be positioned at each motivational level according to the targeted audience and the desired results of the campaign.

Not only are there many different types of automobiles on the market today, but the market is flooded with advertising and marketing gimmicks. Issues involving design, price, style, advertising copy, positioning, sales approach, market share, etc., are debated over and over again. Sometimes it seems as if there is no outcome, because there is no plan or design. This will always happen when there is no methodology, no strategy, or no grand plan behind the marketing approach.

Because of what the automobile represents at the emotional level, there needs to be an appeal to the emotions. At the emotional level, the automobile can represent:

Freedom	Status	Independence	Power
Security	Ownership	Taste	Autonomy
Liberation	Potency	Position	Rank

At the rational level, the consumer has so many choices and ranges of price, that he/she must justify whatever purchase decision is made, not only to himself/herself but also to others. At the rational level some options are:

Price	Economy	Style	Horsepower
Ride	Safety	Engineering	Durability
Features	Service availability		

Motivation and emotion are defined by the Silent Side. Logic and reason are defined by common sense. The job of the creative marketer, engineer, designer, salesperson, and ad executive is to position these two crucial elements together—motivation (emotion) and logic (reason)—and come up with a motivating and credible campaign.

Unconscious advertising allows a scientific analysis of the motivational component, which has not before been available to marketers and manufacturers. The rational side is well known to anyone involved in automobile marketing or manufacturing, and has been used, in fact overused, in attempting to get the consumer to make a decision in a crowded field of foreign and domestic automobiles.

The interesting thing about automotive marketing is that the automobile can be marketed to any level of motivation. In looking at auto sales and advertising, 11 motivational levels are covered. It is then up to the marketer to determine which level will be selected for an effective, three-dimensional marketing and advertising campaign.

THE ORIENTATION MOTIVES

OR: Person

It is an intuitive fact that a person often "becomes" the car that he/she is driving. Each automobile has its own characteristics, based upon the way that it is marketed. For example, at one time movie and television actor Glenn Ford pitched Buick as "the doctor's car." This gave Buick a level of professionalism, status, and authority that could be assimilated by its driver. Classifying Buick as "the doctor's car" is an example of positioning, where the customer can identify with the professionalism of a physician while driving the car. This relates to the OR: Person Motive and is an excellent illustration of how positioning (Reis & Trout, 1981) and the Silent Side complement one another.

OR: Place

As noted in chapter 4, this was the professed motive for Henry Ford going into the automobile business: "Everybody wants to get where they ain't, and when they get there they want to get back home again."

Although OR: Place is not the most powerful motive in the hierarchy, it is a primary motive in automobile purchasing and sales. The automobile can take the consumer across town or across the country, in minutes, hours, or days. The automobile can be used to reorient to place permanently, or temporarily. Most importantly, the automobile is *always available* to allow a temporary change in place, something that is probably taken for granted but can be used as a powerful marketing tool. One respondent told us, "The further west I drive, the smaller my problems get."

OR: Time

There is an antique car market, which has the primary function of carrying people back in time. In one interview, the owner of a classic antique car told us:

We always vacationed at Lake of the Ozarks [Missouri]. It was a special time. We would spend one month out of every year, and the whole family would be together. It was as if all of the cares and worries were left back in St. Louis. One summer I learned to drive there, and it was in a 1951 Ford pickup. I had never been in a truck. When I became an adult I would scour the papers, auto buyer's guides and dealers for a 1951 Ford pickup. When I finally found one it was nothing like the one that I learned to drive on, but I went to work to make it that way in every detail, including color, interior, accessories—*everything!* It took years. But every time I drove that truck it was like stepping right back in time to Lake of the Ozarks, and the feeling of being free of all cares and concerns went right along with it.

When compared to the overall population of potential car buyers, the antique car market is not that large. However, what needs to be recognized here is that a vehicle can become highly personalized and generate human emotions. With this in mind, older model cars have often been positioned alongside new cars because of the emotions that they generate. When the auto marketer, through demographic research, determines his/her target audience, then one consideration might be to have the older car in the background with the new one in front. Although this has been done, it has not been overdone, considering the emotions that can be generated by such a placement or positioning.

OR: Circumstances

As in OR: Place, the automobile can be used to escape circumstances when they become overwhelming, oppressive, or weighty. These escapes are generally temporary in nature, but are necessary to "keep one from becoming unglued." This motive is also taken for granted. Having an automobile sitting in the driveway, parking lot, or garage allows one to *just think* about a temporary escape from circumstances, and that makes it all the more desirable.

SEXUAL SURVIVAL

Automobile marketing can be targeted to any one of the three elements of sexual survival.

Sexual Gender

Some vehicle-marketing efforts are naturally targeted at gender. This could be because of their history, their appearance, or their utility. "Chevy builds tough trucks" is a gender statement (masculine). The Universal model of Jeep (and to some extent, the Wagoneer and Cherokee models) with their square lines, four-wheel drive, and history of military use lend themselves naturally to masculine marketing approaches. Automobiles that emphasize finely appointed interiors can be targeted to the feminine gender level.

Sexual Impulse

There has been a long history of targeting automotive marketing campaigns toward impulse. The best known example was mentioned in chapter 4, when Ford showed the 1966 Mustang with the caption, "we made it hot, you make it scream." Convertibles are naturally and very easily marketed to sexual impulse, directly to men, implying virility, potency, and variety. Since males are the primary car buyers, automotive marketing at the impulse level can rely upon bright colors, low sleek lines, beautiful women in or standing by the car, and a long list of impulse options such as mag or chrome wheels, special tires, chromed engine features, highly technical, multivalved engines, etc. Most of these features are associated with racing and speed, which is in turn associated with impulse.

Sexual Inhibition

Selling a car at the level of sexual inhibition should emphasize the features of control, practicality, safety (although this is primarily physical survival), and pragmatism. To sell a car at the motivational level of sexual inhibition, the emphasis needs to be on how *sensible* the vehicle is, and why it is that way. At this level, there are very few references to romance, fantasy, or whimsy. An automobile is strictly utilitarian. This presentation is very logical and rational.

What would be the advantage of marketing a car at this level, when there are so many "romantic" things that could be said about it? The advantage is that there are many people who are dominated emotionally and motivationally at the level of sexual inhibition, and such a message is appealing to them. Once the marketer has determined the emotional and motivational demographics of the target audience, the size of this market group can be determined. It is believed to be sizable.

PHYSICAL SURVIVAL

Marketing automobiles at this level involves an appeal to safety, security, protection from danger, and fine engineering. Such advertising appeals to a group of people who believe that automobiles are dangerous, that other drivers cannot be trusted to drive safely, and that there is an ever present danger in driving or riding in an automobile. When they are buying a car, safety is their first consideration.

The problem in positioning a car solely at this level is that there are many people who do not believe this, who do not even consider or think about safety when they are driving a car, and who furthermore do not want to think about it. Consider the problems encountered in just getting people to wear their seat belts. Marketing a car at the level of physical survival may be a necessary but not sufficient approach to automotive marketing.

Marketing at the level of physical survival can take one of two directions. The emphasis can be upon engineering, which will appeal primarily to men, or it can be upon safety features, which appeal primarily to women. But if the marketing plan targets safety and engineering features because of the safety of the family and children, this moves the whole approach to the next highest level: the level of spiritual survival. Examples of marketing at this level would be Michelin's "because so much is riding on your tires" and Volvo with its side impact airbag system. The Michelin tire campaign and Volvo are examples of a solid spiritual approach. There is an appeal to the elements of love and family values. Note also the length of time that this type of ad has been running, a typical characteristic of marketing campaigns that are positioned at the level of spiritual survival.

TERRITORIAL SURVIVAL

Marketing an automobile at the level of territorial survival involves an appeal to power, dominance, control, authority, and pride of ownership.

When a vehicle is marketed primarily as a business sedan, it is marketed at the territorial level of motivation. In this scenario, engine features, controls, control (over the vehicle), and horsepower are emphasized. Also emphasized would be anti-lock brakes (as a control feature, not as a safety feature), ride, comfort, and options. Another way to position a car at the level of territorial survival would be to emphasize achievement and the fact of finally having "earned it" or deserved it.

SPIRITUAL SURVIVAL

Spiritual survival is the most powerful motivator, but this does not necessarily mean that it should be used to the exclusion of other motivators, since demographically the motivation to purchase a car exists at all levels in automotive marketing.

When a car is marketed to the emotions at the level of spiritual survival, there are several different routes that can be taken.

First, the car can be promoted on the basis of perfection. In every detail it needs to be shown that the car is perfect, that there has been an unusual amount of attention to detail in order to make it that way. Cadillac's "achieving a higher standard" or the precedent-setting "Standard of the World" are excellent examples of automotive marketing at the level of spiritual survival: perfection.

Second, the car can be promoted on the basis of love or passion, which are two strong emotions associated with spiritual survival. To accomplish this, a loving relationship needs to be demonstrated: love of family; love of wife or man/woman friend; love between an older couple that has been together for years. The possibilities are endless.

A third alternative at this level is right vs. wrong. If it can be shown that the purchase decision relies upon a moral choice—i.e., what is the right thing to do— then there will be a powerful motivating message at the level of spiritual survival. For example, if it is the right choice because of a concern for family safety, then it is a spiritual rather than a physical survival choice, since the primary emotion that is targeted is love.

ADAPTATION MOTIVE

For many years, the Adaptation Motive has been used in selling and marketing automobiles. This is the motive that makes the consumer want to "be like others" whom he/she has known, keep up with them, or in some way have what they have. When a highly credible person like Paul Harvey talks about a particular brand or make of car in a testimonial, then the appeal is to the Adaptation Motive. It is quite likely that the prospective buyer will want to "be like him, and drive that car also."

As pointed out above, testimonials appeal to the Adaptation Motive. So does an appeal to status, achievement, community standing, or a feeling of importance. The example used earlier, where Glenn Ford targeted Buick as "the doctor's car," could work two ways:

"Whenever I drive the car, I feel important, like I'm a doctor" (OR: Person)

OR

"I want to drive a Buick, since that's the car that doctors drive, and they are prestigious people" (Adaptation)

Whatever car a person eventually decides to buy and drive, the label is attached to the outside and is clearly visible to the community. This is similar to the appeal to adaptation that is used in many fashions (Dior, Duck Head, Dockers, etc.) except that vehicle manufacturers have done it for 100 years. Therefore, the appeal to the Adaptation Motive is almost a given for automobiles. Others can see what you are driving!

EXPECTATION MOTIVE

Of all the human motives and emotions involved in automotive advertising and marketing, this one is probably the least applicable. However, an appeal to the Expectation Motive can be useful, especially when people have been led, rightly or wrongly, to have certain expectations about a vehicle. For example, there was a strong rumor circulating about the wind noise in the 1990 Jeep Cherokee Sport models. This rumor or belief surfaced time and time again in focus groups. As a result, the new, redesigned Jeep Cherokee was shown from the inside, parked next to a rushing waterfall, the intent being to change peoples' expectations about the amount of noise that was inside the vehicle. Similarly, a GMC Jimmy was thrown from a bridge with a rope tied to the frame to show that the Jimmy was a "tough truck" and to either create or change peoples' expectations about its durability.

In some ways, the Expectation Motive does not work in favor of the dealership, since people have come to distrust individuals who are in auto sales with the typical stereotype of the "used car salesman." However, this image is changing because of the increase in professionalism involved in selling cars today. As the image changes, the Expectation Motive will no doubt increase in importance.

RATIONALITY AND REASON

It is clear that emotion plays a major role in the overcrowded auto and truck market. But so, too, does reason.

Price, comfort, room, economy, value, and other considerations can "push the consumer one way or the other" when it comes to making a final buy/no buy decision. But initial marketing efforts must target one or more of the emotions that have been discussed in this chapter. The reason is that targeting an emotion, which allows the prospective customer to *personalize* the message, is the only way to cut through the mass of clutter in automotive advertising.

HOW LYNN HICKEY DID IT

Lynn Hickey is America's number one Dodge dealer, the number one used car dollar-volume dealer, and the number seven *Dealer Business/Auto Age* 500 dealer. How did he do it?

We have looked at Lynn Hickey's methods in *Automobile Dealer Magazine*, September/October 1995. Mr. Hickey started in the automobile business in 1961 as a car washer at Dub Richardson Ford in Oklahoma City. In 1970 he took over a Dodge dealership that was planning to sell around 20 cars a month. Last year, that same dealership, which is Lynn Hickey Dodge, sold over 14,000 cars, as *Automobile Dealer* puts it, "just a stone's throw across Route 66 from where Lynn washed cars 34 years ago."

Although Lynn Hickey may not know about marketing to the mind, he knows how to motivate people to buy cars, and he knows how to motivate his salesforce. Therefore, we need to take a quick look at his operation through the eyes of marketing to the mind, just as we looked at the Simpson closing arguments, the Susan Smith case, and other marketing and nonmarketing phenomena. After all, motivation is motivation. If it applies in one situation, it applies in another.

Lynn Hickey has not run newspaper ads in eight years! Newspaper ads, for car dealers, are the ultimate in clutter. Instead, he spends a lot of money using a master pitchman on TV, who does everything from flagpole sitting to being buried alive to getting into a cage with rattlesnakes. Why does this work? See chapter 5, on absurdities.

In addition, there are several other unique and unusual attitudes and procedures that permeate the people and the circumstances at Lynn Hickey Dodge. Let's examine them in terms of how Lynn Hickey Dodge follows our suggested motivational structure, even if it does not know about it.

AT WHAT LEVEL SHOULD AN AUTOMOBILE BE POSITIONED?

Unlike other products discussed in *Marketing to the Mind*, the automobile can be positioned at *any and all* motivational levels. How does the marketer decide upon the most effective level? Motigraphics are determined through market research and were discussed in the three-phase approach outlined in chapter 8. Once the marketer has determined the major motivations that are involved in a particular automobile, these motives can be established and measured in quantitative, large-sample research (phase 2, chapter 8). The results will yield emotional demographics. These same categories can be determined for magazine readers, television viewers, etc., and an exact match can be made in terms of marketing directly to the emotions.

In advertising there have been many examples of overlooking or missing the unconscious emotions and motivations and thus losing out entirely. Perhaps the best example was Schlitz's positioning of beer in the hands of yachtsmen in America's Cup-style racing events. The results were less than anticipated. Because of the cost of advertising today, the marketer cannot afford to make this kind of mistake. And mistakes like this can be avoided if time is taken to establish emotional demographics, targeting the emotions and motives, and then marketing the product accordingly!

Table 19-1
Lynn Hickey Dodge: Motivators

Activity	Description	Motives Involved
Rational Motivator:		
Incentives	Special incentives for salespeople Special financing for customers who have marginal credit	Reward
Emotional Motivators:		
Attitude	Hustle and bustle is choreographed in the scene, creating excitement and action	OR: Time
Inventory control	Just in time for promotions and advertising (when possible)	OR: Time
Special custom	Custom shop that makes the customer's car unique and different	OR: Person
Employee training	Systematic, intense, reinforcement of success	Expectation OR: Person
Traffic control	Customers are routed; if they leave without purchasing, they are interviewed. "Where did we not meet your expectation?"	Expectation
Telemarketing	Customers are contacted after the sale on the phone. "What did we do right?" "Wrong?"	Expectation
Communications	No intercom system to disturb customers while they are in the process of making a very big decision	OR: Circumstances
	Individual 2-way communications for salespeople	OR: Time

Table 19-1
Lynn Hickey Dodge: Motivators (cont'd.)

Activity	Description	Motives Involved
Total orientation	Prospective customers are oriented to the dealership, services, custom shop, financing, etc.	OR: Circumstances
Announcements	The only public announcements made are to welcome new buyers into the Lynn Hickey family.	Adaptation
	Since dealership is positioned as a family, there is an element of spiritual survival.	Spiritual Survival

REFERENCES

Lynn Hickey Dodge, in *Automobile Dealer Magazine*. (September–October 1995).

Reis, A., & Trout, J. (1981). *Positioning: The battle for your mind.* New York: McGraw Hill.

20

Why People Still Visit Elvis and Graceland

BACKGROUND

In 1979, before the official opening of Graceland Mansion in Memphis, Tennessee, yet after the death of Elvis Presley on August 16, 1977, large crowds began to gather in front of the gates at Graceland. At the time, there were no facilities to accommodate these crowds. There were no restrooms, no fast food, and no place to park except on the busy street out front: Elvis Presley Boulevard. A few entrepreneurial merchants eventually added souvenir stores to their restaurants, and the souvenir business went so well that they closed their restaurants and sold only souvenirs and Elvis memorabilia. There are no fewer than 12 souvenir stores in the immediate vicinity of Graceland today.

The crowds kept getting larger and larger. There was no comparison to the number of people who visited Graceland prior to his death. The numbers before he died were so small that there was only one souvenir store, and no other facilities. All of the parking was on the street. But the Graceland phenomenon has grown so much that there are presently around 20 shops, stores, and restaurants in the area; a major hotel with a restaurant; adequate parking for over 500 cars; an RV park; and many other scattered facilities. In addition to touring Graceland Mansion, tourists can go through Elvis's plane, the "Lisa Marie," his tour bus, and a gold record museum.

The Tennessee Commission on Tourism has stated that people come to Tennessee to see three things: Dolly Parton (East Tennessee); Jack Daniels (Middle Tennessee); and Elvis Presley (West Tennessee). This was true, to some extent, before Elvis died. But since his death it has become a major phenomenon. The size of the estate has exploded from $8 million at the time of his death to over $80 million today! Some would say that it has been managed well, which it has. But there is much more to it than that. It is a marketing phenomenon! This phenomenon and the fact that it has demonstrated such longevity is a living testimony to the power of spiritual survival in marketing.

A CASE HISTORY IN EMOTIONAL AND MOTIVATIONAL MARKETING

When our firm established itself as an emotional and motivational advertising strategies firm, it had as its clients, marketers and ad agencies in the Southeast, Midwest, and Northeast. They had questions about consumer emotions and related activities, and about how they could market their products to the emotions. It occurred to the author that the Elvis Presley phenomenon would make an excellent demonstration project, since there were questions about this explosive growth that just could not be answered from a logical or rational point of view. In fact, this phenomenon could be addressed only on the motivational and emotional level. As a result, over 100 visitors to Graceland Mansion were interviewed in Memphis, before the facility was open to the public and before it became what it is today. Many of these visitors came from Belgium, England, France, Canada, and even as far away as Australia. Many sacrificed and saved for years so that they could travel to America. Their primary destination in America was Elvis and Graceland.

WHY DO PEOPLE WANT TO COME AND BE CLOSE TO ELVIS?

The technique used in interviewing these visitors was visualization. This was discussed in detail in chapter 8. The Elvis visitors were brought to a field facility, introduced to the interviewer, relaxed, and shown how to use their "photographic memory." The interviewers often began by asking them to "visualize" the first time they ever saw Elvis, or their first experience with Elvis. Amazingly, many went back, in their mind, to the first time he appeared on the old *Ed Sullivan Show*.

Initially in these interviews the answers obtained were exactly what was expected; rationalizations:

- He was a good man
- He was a good singer
- He loved his mother
- He was just a poor country boy who made it big (the American Dream)
- It's not true that he was on drugs
- Just to pay our respects
- I wanted to feel closer to him, even though he's dead
- It is just hard to believe that he is not with us anymore

There really is not much here that would explain getting on a plane and travelling 6,000 miles to Memphis, Tennessee, to visit a deceased person's grave. There was much more to this than people were able to talk about. For whatever reason people traveled thousands of miles to visit Elvis Presley's grave, it was clear that the answer would only be found in the unconscious mind.

Since our project was addressing a phenomenon that was entirely emotional, it was a demonstration of consumer emotion and motivation. It emphasized the fact that many consumer decisions are based upon emotion, not reason. One fact that needs mentioning, based on the partial list of answers that are listed above, is that people cannot always tell you why they do what they do. The motivation to visit Graceland was never uncovered with questionnaires, market research, or "on the street" interviews, which take place at the conscious level. The motivation to visit Graceland was found in the visitors' unconscious minds.

THE MARKETING OF A KING

The fact that Elvis is believed by some to still be alive; the phenomenal number of impersonators; and the crowds that make pilgrimages to Graceland each year, especially on August 16 (his death) and January 8 (his birth) all point to a major spiritual phenomenon. In fact, it has many of the entrapments that are associated with an organized religion: life after death, resurrection, denial, worship, testimonials, impersonators, pilgrimages, elevation to status of *king*, icons (souvenirs), candlelight vigils, etc. All of this exists and almost all of this occurred after his death.

What was of particular interest in the research was that the respondents, who were from all over the world, were on a pilgrimage. They came to visit "the King" for religious reasons, and this pilgrimage had all the elements of a trip to Lourdes in France or to the Wailing Wall in Jerusalem.

How did the Elvis Presley phenomenon evolve into a great religion and spiritual phenomenon? The answer was in marketing, not rational marketing, but marketing to unconscious. There were three phases in marketing Elvis, which evolved out of the events in his own career.

Phase 1: The Rock Era (1954–1962)

Those who remembered the introduction of Elvis on the old *Ed Sullivan Show* recalled most vividly the cameras cutting him off at the waist, their refusal to show what was going on at hip level and below. Eventually this censure was dropped and what viewers saw, on television, for the first time in their lives, was direct marketing to the motivational level of sexual survival and specifically to the element of sexual impulse. Keep in mind that there are three elements within sexual survival: gender, inhibition, and impulse.

Songs like "Jailhouse Rock," "Blue Suede Shoes," "Hound Dog," and others had the effect of directly targeting impulse and removing inhibition, at least for the duration of the song. On television, inhibition was removed even more as viewers watched "the King" in contortions, distortions, twists, and warps that gave them permission to experience the sexual feelings (impulses) they had been experiencing all along, rather than covering them with inhibition, fear, and secrecy. Elvis had become a rock idol. However, there was no one outside trying to break down the gates to his home in Memphis, and if there were visitors to Graceland, they were very few in number.

Sexual inhibitions were removed while the music was in progress. The fact that Elvis did what he did *in public* and *on television* was almost like giving his followers permission to drop their own inhibitions and guilt and encounter or feel the sexual impulses that they had been experiencing in their lives. In this sense, what Elvis delivered during the rock years (1954–1962) was a new-found sense of freedom, sovereignty, and emancipation.

Phase 2: The Revival Years (1968–1977)

After his marriage and the birth of Lisa Marie, Elvis disappeared for a few years, making very few appearances. When he returned, he had added a vital component to his music: spirituality. At every concert, he would repeat the rock music that had made him famous and that people wanted to hear, thereby removing inhibitions. But then, at the end of the concert, he would close with spiritual and patriotic music. It was as if he had released all the impulses at the beginning of the concert, and then blessed them (spiritually) at the end of the concert. Songs like "Mine Eyes Have Seen the Glory of the Coming of the Lord" and "When the Saints Go Marching In" added a strong element of spiritual survival to every program, every concert. Elvis was on his way to becoming a King. (Not only did he give his audience permission to release sexual impulses, but by the late 1960s he was blessing them!) He took what had started as a curse to many (sexuality) and turned it into a blessing (spirituality).

Just as McDonald's has elevated the Physical Survival Motive to the Spiritual Survival Motive, Elvis elevated sexual survival to the level of spiritual survival. The effect of doing this for any marketer is (1) longevity, (2) consumer loyalty, and (3) revenue.

Phase 3: Death (August 16, 1977)

Elvis's elevation from the sexual to the spiritual level still did not make him "the King." It took one more step: his death. When Elvis died, he very quickly became a *martyr*. A martyr is defined as someone who is busily engaged in a service to humanity but dies during the process of trying to achieve it. Using this definition, there have been only three martyrs in the twentieth century: Elvis Presley, Martin Luther King, Jr., and John F. Kennedy. Some might also add Franklin

D. Roosevelt, but he only marginally qualifies for martyrdom since his greatest contribution was social reform and these reforms were basically in place by the time he died.

When Elvis died (and the reasons that he died are not important for this discussion), he became an instant martyr. The popularity of his music and his recordings grew exponentially. The size of the estate grew. The crowds visiting Graceland grew so that in a very short time it became the most visited destination attraction in the state of Tennessee. It was a sensation and a phenomenon. The annual pilgrimages began. Today, almost 20 years after his death, the average wait for a visitor to enter the grounds of Graceland for a tour can be up to three hours, depending upon the time of year.

WHERE DOES THE RESEARCH FIT IN?

All the conclusions that have been spelled out in this chapter were derived from the research that was conducted on 100 visitors to Graceland. But what may be of interest is how these conclusions were derived. Visitors who volunteered for interviews said they made the long pilgrimage primarily "to be in his presence." They said that as they moved through the halls and rooms of Graceland they felt as if they were "actually with him." They felt close to him, and felt like they understood him better. In a sense, they also understood themselves.

Many of those interviewed were overweight, middle-aged women. They had come to believe, long ago, that sexuality was a curse. For them, Elvis had turned a curse into a blessing. They wanted to see how he lived; touch the furniture on which he sat; see what he did in his spare time; and see if he had really treated his mother in the caring manner that was so widely reported. They strongly believed that when they did this they would become the person that Elvis had allowed or encouraged them to be (OR: Person). They would go through a renewal or a rejuvenation. Even though this renewal did not last very long (souvenirs help to extend the experience), it should be remembered that people wish to achieve changes in orientation only on a temporary, not permanent, basis. This is the foundation for the unconscious.

These mild to moderately obese, middle-aged women appeared to be the most substantial part of Elvis's following. Although they would bring their husbands, it was apparent that the women were instrumental in making the major decision to visit Graceland. When the men were interviewed, they would not talk in religious terms like the women did. Instead, they would repeat the "rags to riches" (rational) theme, how Elvis rose from a poor country boy to become the greatest rock star in the world. This was their primary justification and rationalization for the trip.

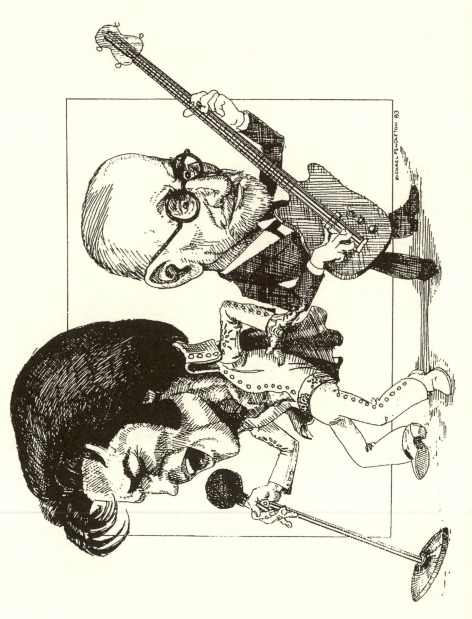

**Figure 20-1
Elvis Presley and Sigmund Freud**

WHO CARES?

Elvis's position as king can only be understood in terms of the three-step sequence that was laid out above and is summarized here:

1. Introduction of rock & roll (removal of sexual inhibition)
2. The blessing of sexuality (elevation of sexual survival to the level of spiritual survival)
3. Death and the achievement of martyrdom

There are many people, including those who will read this book, who could care less about Elvis Presley, Graceland, and his music. That is not the point. The point is that this is an unusual marketing phenomenon that has transfixed tens of thousands of people, worldwide, and that can only be explained by appealing to the unconscious mind, and through subsequent understanding of the Spiritual Survival Motive (right and wrong) in all of its facets. It is motivational and emotional, not rational. The Elvis Presley phenomenon demonstrates the overwhelming importance of spiritual survival in human behavior, specifically in the areas of advertising and marketing and in its overall contribution to the economy.

Does the marketer have to die and become a martyr to make his/her product successful? Of course not! This was an extra touch. Elvis was already on his way to becoming "the King." The point is that he elevated a curse (sex) to the level of a blessing (spirituality) and in so doing he took something that was believed to be wrong and made it right. This is marketing to the unconscious mind. There is a place for it in every product or service that is on the market today, and there always will be. There is no such thing as a product that is totally rational to the point that there is no emotion involved when the consumer makes his/her decision to buy.

TWENTY YEARS LATER

Graceland in Memphis is now the second most visited home in America, following the White House. But it is still an enigma. Why do people come? What are they looking for? How long will it last? The answer to these questions lies in an understanding of spiritual survival—still the most powerful of all the emotions. Rosenbaum (1995) touches on this in a recent article in the *New York Times Magazine*. Each year there is an Elvis conference at the University of Mississippi in Oxford, Mississippi, sponsored by the highly respected and revered Center for Southern Culture. This is not a gathering of Elvis fans and fanatics, but rather of academics and professorial types who are trying to figure out what is going on, almost 20 years later. This year, Rosenbaum attended that conference and summarized it as quite different from the way it was in the past:

This year, the scholars' Elvis has more in common with the one the fans cry out to: the healing Elvis. This is Elvis as racial integrator, as gender liberating sexual healer. The multicultural Elvis is an even grander figure than the one fans conceive of—an Elvis who heals not just personal pain in individual souls but painful rifts in the nation's soul, rifts not only between black and white but between sex and spirituality [emphasis ours]. (p. 54)

Most of this sounds like the academician's Elvis: healer, multiculturalist, integrator, etc. This is a *politically correct* Elvis, and from our own research carried out in 1981, this is not what it is all about. In fact, political correctness was not even in our vocabulary at that time, and certainly not in the vocabularies of those early pilgrims who made the trip, even before the mansion was opened to the public.

We have emphasized the healing of the rift between sexuality and spirituality, between sexual survival and spiritual survival. This is what Elvis did in three stages: when he introduced the "leg wiggle"; then he blessed it; and finally he died for it. The rest is superfluous and excessive, an attempt to invent or devise a politically correct Elvis to justify the ongoing conference each year and the involvement of academics.

An example of the irrelevance of the rest of this is in Elvis as an *integrator*. Rosenbaum himself noted later in his article how few black faces there are at Graceland. In the four hours that he spent there he said that he saw only one black family. He then sets out to defend Elvis lest one assume he was a racist.

African Americans, for the most part, are not interested in Elvis or in what he represents. We have interviewed hundreds of them on this very subject. It is not that they dislike him; it is just that they cannot really figure out what all the excitement is about. After all, blacks had already integrated spirituality and sexuality long before they came to America, and certainly since that time. That integration is apparent in their music, their hymns, their preaching, their homes, and churches. So Elvis really had nothing to offer the blacks, because they had already achieved this integration of the spirit with sex. Elvis is an idol to white people, who have not yet achieved this integration and who are still looking for ways to relieve their guilt. And in order to understand guilt, we must start with and thoroughly understand the motive of spiritual survival.

Graceland stands today as a monument to the motive and reminder of the importance of spiritual survival in advertising and marketing. Graceland is second in visitations only to the White House.

REFERENCE

Rosenbaum, R. (1995, September 25). Among the believers. *New York Times Magazine*, pp. 50–64.

21

Marketing Professional and Nonprofit Services

PROFESSIONAL SERVICES: MEDICAL AND LEGAL

Background

In 1984, right after the FCC lifted restrictions on hospital and medical advertising, two major hospitals in the same city, both church-owned not-for-profit entities, launched their television/radio/print advertising campaigns. One has lasted over the years, while the other had little impact and was eventually abandoned. Based on what the reader now knows about the emotions and motivations that lie behind a marketing effort, here is an opportunity to guess which one was permanent and which was temporary:

Hospital # 1: Commitment to quality
Hospital # 2: A leader in world medicine

One of these statements is rational, the other is grounded in emotion. One worked, the other did not. And although the two hospitals were not exactly equal in terms of budget, size, census, etc., they were close enough for a legitimate comparison.

The reader guessing # 2 is right! Hospital # 1 was making a rational statement that was not based in emotion. Also, when people were asked about the "Commitment to quality" in focus groups, they said that it really did not do anything for them, since quality was the least that they expected from a hospital anyway. At best it was an oxymoron, not required to be expressed when dealing with human life! On the other hand, "A leader in world medicine" has a strong emotional foundation in the Adaptation Motive. The ordinary, unschooled, perspective patient thinks, "If they are a leader in medical advances for the whole world, then that's good enough for me!"

Marketing and Advertising Professional Services

The ordinary individual who is not licensed in medicine has no professional background that would allow him/her to make a technical decision about selecting a physician, or an attorney or any other professional. As a result, logic does not apply in the choice of most professionals. This is a rather ironic and incongruous situation, since the choice of a professional to serve one's needs usually involves a highly personalized service and would be expected to be based upon reason and logic. In fact, often the choice of a physician, attorney, or hospital involves a life-or-death decision.

Because of the seriousness of the decision-making process involved in choosing a professional, and because the average person lacks the knowledge to make an informed decision, all states have had long-standing licensing laws. Licensing laws for professionals—physicians, attorneys, pharmacists, chiropractors, dentists, etc.—are designed to protect the public from charlatans and quacks. In fact, many state licensing laws, in their ongoing effort to protect the public, still prohibit medical and legal advertising, despite the fact that the FCC has ruled such a prohibition is unconstitutional. However, the problem with licensing laws is that they can only enforce minimal standards of practice, and although the consumer does not really know that, notwithstanding licensing laws, the decision to choose a physician or other professional can be open to a wide margin of error.

The fact that the consumer of medical and legal services cannot make a technically informed decision leads to the conclusion that the decision-making process in choosing a professional to provide one's treatment or counseling is primarily emotional. As such, this decision is very similar to choosing most other consumer products and services. In fact, the choice of a physician, dentist, or attorney, and the decision to remain loyal to that professional, is not that much different than the decision to use a particular brand of cosmetics. Both decisions are about 85 percent emotional.

Emotions Involved in Choosing a Professional Service

There are four primary emotions involved in choosing professional services: expectation; adaptation; physical survival (physicians) or territorial survival (attorneys); and spiritual survival. In addition, territorial survival is an issue that often affects the consumer but rarely enters into his/her decision-making process. Territorial survival will be discussed primarily with reference to hospitals and to how it has effected the overall health-care picture. Territorial survival is also a major emotional factor in the choice and use of an attorney, just as physical survival is a major emotional factor in the choice of a physician.

Consumer Satisfaction in Health-care and Other Professional Services

The overall health-care picture is perceived by some as being chaotic. In a recent article in the *Wall Street Journal*, hospitals and attorneys ranked at the very bottom of the order in a survey of consumer satisfaction with the professions. Not only do consumers not know what they want, but they do not like what they are getting from hospitals and attorneys. This creates an enormous problem, since the use of both of these services is almost totally dependent upon the Expectation Motive, or the motivation to trust, believe, and put faith in whomever is providing the professional services. To complicate matters, consumers hear all kinds of horror stories from their government, the media, and their neighbors that relate to medical, legal, and, to a lesser extent, other professional services. Compare this scenario to the gambler with a real strong Expectation Motive who never experiences any kind of a payoff! Eventually, he/she will quit gambling. In health-care and other professional services, the consumer does not have that option. People need professional services—when they need them.

It is at this crucial point that the government steps in and says, "We will come to your rescue." But consumers are not at all sure that this is what they want. Although they have little to go on in the decision-making process, they do not want someone else making the decision for them in such a highly personalized, confidential, and intimate service. One might predict a similar reaction if the government (or anybody else) tried to dictate the use of a manicurist, hair stylist, or any other professional who provided individualized, personalized services. People interpret this as a serious infringement upon their freedom.

The Physical Survival Motive

It goes without saying that the Physical Survival Motive is instrumental in the choice of a physician and/or hospital. When an individual faces a disease or illness, there is an immediate threat to physical survival. At this point, he/she wants to find assistance and overcome this threat to survival.

Twenty to 25 years ago, an era that had been in existence since the beginning of America's history was closed. In this era, threats to physical survival came in the form of serious illness or epidemic disease. Otherwise, the Physical Survival Motive was virtually ignored. People ate what they wanted to eat, smoked, ignored routine exercise, and rarely paid much attention to the whole process of physical survival. The old country doctor was the symbol of the Physical Survival Motive, and hospitals were a last resort. All of this has changed.

Today, people expect results from their doctors and their hospital, and they expect perfection. They have learned that if anything goes wrong, they may have a cause of action and can seek compensatory damages. They also feel that in the pursuit of overcoming any threat to physical survival they have a right to minimal discomfort, immediate service, and limited inconvenience. All of these rational or logical aspects of medical care surround the central motivational issue of physical survival.

Physical survival motivates the individual to seek medical care. But in any situation other than a routine physical, most consumers have little, if any, prior experience with a disease or serious illness. Therefore, when disease or illness strikes, each separate illness is like a new experience that may require a different specialist. The experience that they had in the past does not count. Each time, it is like starting all over again.

The Expectation Motive

In making the decision to choose a physician, attorney, or other professional, the consumer relies heavily upon the Expectation Motive. It may seem ironic that the same motive that inspires or motivates the gambler is the one that influences the potential medical patient.

However, as stated earlier, consumers do not have any technical facts that they can use when it comes to choosing a doctor. This is why the FCC, in the early eighties, ruled to allow physicians to advertise: so the consumer could get some of the facts. Yet, advertising in this case is not really a solution since the consumer remains, for the most part, uninformed. The problem is that the consumer still has no facts on which to base his/her decision, and may even be confused and disoriented by the hype that is created by the media and by advertising. As a result, consumers rely on the Expectation Motive. They are compelled to believe that whatever selection they finally make, they will be taken care of, that the physician will be competent, fair, skilled, and qualified, and that their crisis in physical survival will be successfully resolved.

The Expectation Motive becomes the major motivation in choosing a physician or any other professional. And once the physical survival crisis has been resolved, the patient will generally remain loyal to that physician and resist changing to another, unless the next crisis is outside of that physician's area of specialization. In that case, the patient accepts the physician's referral to another specialist, which leads us to a discussion of the Adaptation Motive.

The Adaptation Motive

The Adaptation Motive consists of doing what other people do. This is the primary source of referral within the health-care community for physicians, dentists, psychologists, chiropractors, and other practitioners. It is also the primary source of referral for lawyers, since the consumer does not have the facts to make an intelligent decision in this field either.

Many hospitals, in their advertising, have tried different approaches, but have reverted to the Adaptation Motive. This makes sense, since the Adaptation Motive was the primary method of patient referral and motivation long before advertising ever entered the picture. For adaptation to work, hospitals maintain a referral list of physicians, by specialty. The patient calls a mnemonic number, such as 1-800-D-O-C-T-O-R-S, and the hospital gives the patient the names of several doctors to choose from. Local bar associations have similar referral services.

In terms of marketing, the hospitals have gone back to something that has always worked. The Adaptation Motive has worked for many years, so many hospitals see no need to change it. Word-of-mouth has always been the best advertising there is, and this is a variation of that form.

Implications for Marketing Professional Services

Summarizing what has been said above, there are three major motives involved when a patient or client is looking for a professional: Expectation Motive; Adaptation Motive; and Physical Survival (in health-care) or Territorial Survival (in law). In addition, Spiritual Survival plays a major role in health-care and in the overall picture of professional services. The role of spiritual survival will be discussed at the end of this chapter under the section that covers marketing in nonprofit environments.

Since expectation is the major motive involved in health-care marketing and in finding a physician, marketing efforts need to revolve around the issue of trust and sincerity. In addition, individuals who market health-care services need to be, whenever possible, appropriately credentialed so that their credibility is unquestioned.

It is not always possible to employ well-credentialed individuals in health-care marketing situations, since individuals with good clinical credentials usually do not want to be involved in selling. But it is becoming easier and easier to do so. This is because there are, more and more, well-credentialed individuals who know the health-care field and who are becoming available. When they are not available to the marketer, what needs to be done is to employ well-credentialed individuals to train those who will do the marketing. This is true for several reasons.

First, health-care, more than any other field, has always emphasized the importance of credentials. Beginning with the physicians at the top of the pyramid down to clerical and maintenance employees, degrees and years of education are usually spelled out for the public to see.

Second, the use of well-credentialed and experienced people in marketing health-care services increases the probability that the Expectation Motive will work in the marketer's favor.

Third, and probably most important, health-care services differ substantially from any other services that are offered for sale to the public. The primary difference is in the ethical obligations and commitments, which are much more arduous than they are in other professions. Unskilled, untrained, and noncredentialed individuals who are marketing health-care services can cause multiple problems for the marketer and for the entire system. Take, for example, the following incident:

A well-qualified individual with a Ph.D. in a health-care specialty was employed by a health-care services firm to market medical services to nursing homes. Although well qualified with experience and with credentials, he had a habit of promising more than the firm that he represented was capable of delivering. In several cases he told nursing home administrators that there would be no charge to the patients beyond what Medicare allowed. Such a practice is a violation of Medicare regulations and is considered fraud and abuse. Had this not been discovered and corrected by the health-care firm, it could have encountered serious problems with the fiscal intermediary for Medicare.

Medicare actively discourages profiteering in enterprises that rely heavily upon Medicare reimbursement. Therefore, a marketing approach that is entrepreneurial, ambitious, and aggressive can cause untold and irreversible damage to a legitimate health-care concern.

In addition to credentials, individuals who market professional services need to display sincerity, trust, frankness, openness, and candor. One of the best ways to determine these qualities is by checking out previous positions a person has held, along with various customer situations he/she encountered and how they were handled.

Because of long-standing traditions in medicine and law that have prohibited advertising in the past, marketing in these professions is still a sensitive and tender issue. Care must be taken to ensure that marketers in these fields fit the mold and conform to the image that the public holds for their doctors and their lawyers.

MARKETING TO THE MOTIVES IN NONPROFIT ENVIRONMENTS

What Makes Nonprofit Different from Profit?

In seminars and presentations we are often asked, "at the motivational level, what's the difference between a profit and a nonprofit organization?" A separate chapter on nonprofit activities was considered, but instead it was decided that it should be included here within a discussion of the professions, medical care, and hospitals. This is because many hospitals are nonprofit. The evolution of this nonprofit status is interesting, and leads to the consideration of the role of spiritual survival.

Many hospitals are church owned and operated. Churches entered the business of health-care long before anyone else did, simply because of the many biblical edicts and injunctions to heal the sick. Therefore, what was an issue in physical survival (healing) became an issue in spiritual survival.

There is one vital difference between profit and nonprofit organizations, and this difference not only evolved from our research but also from years of personal experience. The difference is this: it is much easier to get people to give their money away than it is to get them to spend it. At first, this observation may not make sense. It may even provoke an argument or disagreement. But anyone who has had sales experience on both sides of the fence (profit and nonprofit) will agree with this statement. And the truth of this statement is measured in terms of sales resistance.

Every salesperson who has any experience at all, especially on the profit side, has encountered sales resistance. Rarely are salespeople welcomed with open arms. Instead, the prospect goes through what seems to be a ritual, in which the potential customer raises objection after objection (arising from the rational side) to the product. Many prospects seem to do this even if they eventually intend to buy the product.

In nonprofit activities, the resistance is not nearly as strong or forceful. People seem much more willing to give their money away than they are to spend it. The reason for this behavior, when interpreted against the background of the unconscious and the Spiritual Survival Motive, is rather obvious.

The Role of Spiritual Survival in the Nonprofit Environment

The primary reason that strong resistance is not encountered nearly as often in the nonprofit environment is because most nonprofit activities are based upon the motive of spiritual survival. Very simply, people are willing to put their money where their beliefs and their hearts are. Take, for example, the following list of nonprofit activities and the spiritual issues that they advocate:

Table 21-1
Nonprofit Activities and Spiritual Issues Involved

Nonprofit Organization	Spiritual Issue
National Rifle Association	Gun ownership
Ducks Unlimited	Wildlife preservation
Sierra Club	Conservation/preservation
All church-related hospitals	Healing
Mothers Against Drunk Drivers	Getting drunk drivers off the streets
Alcoholics Anonymous	Sobriety
American Civil Liberties Union	Constitutional rights
Boy Scouts of America	God & country
American Assn. of Retired Persons	Rights of elderly
Teamsters Union	Rights of members

The list is much longer. The point is that when people who are members are asked to contribute their money, they do. They do it because it is something that they believe in, and often their beliefs take the form of passionate commitment. The issues that they hold to be spiritual are at stake and in such cases, giving reasonable amounts of money becomes secondary in importance.

Someone might, at this point, object. The objection is rather obvious: "If it's so easy to get people to give their money away, then why aren't all the churches rich?" After all, if anyone preaches and teaches spiritual survival, it is the churches. There are several ways to address this question:

1. Many churches are rich
2. There are too many churches
3. Not all churches advocate spiritual survival or spirituality.
4. The point of "reasonable" amount of giving is a subjective matter.

The first two examples are obvious and need no explanation. With reference to number three, the churches that are "rich" and have the least difficulty in raising funds are the ones that preach and teach spirituality. On the other hand, churches that advocate social reform and dabble in politics meet considerably more resistance in trying to raise funds. The Southern Baptist church, which consists of people in the middle-to lower-income classes, is right at the top in terms of individual giving. Conversely, the Episcopal church, which ranks within the top five in terms of its members' average annual incomes, ranks 27th in terms of individual giving. The difference? The Episcopal church is a "mainline" denomination, a category that includes Methodist, Presbyterian, and Christian (Disciples of Christ) churches. These churches, which all rank very low in terms of individual giving, are also known to preach a "social gospel" that departs significantly from the message of spirituality that is preached—undiluted—in many of the lesser or poorer denominations. People will give, but it is reasonable to expect people to consider all financial agendas and hence give according to personal ability.

TERRITORIAL SURVIVAL AND THE MOTIVATION TO USE LEGAL SERVICES

Territorial survival is the strongest and single most evident motivational issue effecting the delivery of professional legal services. The motive of territorial survival does not affect the delivery of medical services, except as it is responsible for territorial and "turf" wars between various specialities and subspecialities within medicine. But these skirmishes do not affect the consumer of medical services to any appreciable extent, and so they can, for the most part, be overlooked.

On the other hand, territorial survival is the central motive and theme involved in seeking legal services, along with the Expectation and Adaptation Motives. Usually people seek the services of an attorney when they want to obtain what they believe is coming to them or keep what they already have. This is another way of stating the central core of the Territorial Survival Motive. In terms of motivation, this is the major difference in seeking out an attorney and seeking out a physician: territorial survival vs. physical survival. The other motives remain the same.

There is another issue of territorial survival that is relevant to hospitals. This affects the consumer and has distorted the entire health-care picture, creating chaos and confusion in the overall health-care picture. Hospitals have one mission: the healing and restoration of patients. But over the years, they have assumed another role: teaching. Primarily because of their teaching role, hospitals started competing with one another for what they considered to be the best residents (students) from the best medical schools. To remain competitive, they had to continually upgrade their equipment and their facilities. This is how the territorial wars began.

Although almost everyone believes that hospitals should have the most modern and up-to-date equipment, it should be with the patient in mind rather than the resident. Since many hospitals got caught up in the trap of "doing the right things for the wrong reasons," expenses have mounted. Equipment costing millions of dollars was purchased, even though there were often three or four similar pieces of equipment in the same city, often within one medical center. Services were duplicated. Territorial wars began and took the form of competing to get the best students. The consumer ended up paying the bills.

When advertising was added into the picture, the territorial wars intensified. Costs continued to soar. In the end, the government entered the picture and, at the present time, threatens to take over the whole system—a system that appears to be getting out of control. Because of these territorial wars, which are being fought primarily between hospitals, expenses are largely out of control. Since it is the consumer who ultimately pays the bill, the consumer is ultimately involved in these turf wars that have, in recent years, escalated into major battles.

CONCLUSION

Marketing within professional environments—profit and nonprofit—requires some unique skills on the part of the marketer. The reason that these skills are so vital and indispensable is because of the strength of the emotions involved, particularly the Expectation Motive. Medical and legal services are personal, intimate, and confidential in nature, and as such involve substantial emotional components. Although we may want to think of medical and legal services as being chosen on a rational basis, the evidence shows otherwise. Within these fields, where consumers have no real basis for their decisions, most consumer behavior is emotional, not rational.

22

Marketing Commodity and Business Services

COMMERCIAL AND RETAIL BANKING

Commodity Services

Some services are difficult to distinguish from their competition. How can you tell one bank from another? How do you differentiate an overnight delivery service? A hospital? They are not like restaurants, theme parks, and other activities that have their own character. How can one bank be distinguished from another? Moreover, as governmental regulations, both federal and state, proliferate, all business services become more and more alike, more sterile and less and less distinguishable from one another. Banks appear to be highly standardized.

A small bank in a southeastern state was purchased by a larger bank in the Midwest. The small bank had made a name for itself in small towns after having been in business for almost 70 years. The new owners were concerned that the employees, many of whom were second and third generation employees with the bank, would be restless, unhappy, and uncertain about their future. Since over 80 percent of the bank's business was in small, rural towns, management wanted to retain as many employees as it could. After all, the bank's employees served their immediate neighbors. Management especially wanted to retain those who were on the front lines and who interfaced with the public. The new owners knew that drastic shifts and changes in personnel could create insecurity, uncertainty, and indifference in the bank's customers.

The new management contacted an ad agency. Together they devised an ingenious plan. Since the new name for the combined bank was Community Bank, the ad agency decided to do a feature article each week on an individual employee and to spotlight that employee in terms of what volunteer work he/she did in the community. The results were phenomenal.

Not only did the community respond, but many customers said that they had never even thought about their teller or their loan manager as a member of the community. And of course the employees were overwhelmed with the response from the community. In a real and impressionable sense, customers saw them as the neighbors and friends they actually were, not just as familiar faces. There were volunteer fire fighters, police deputies, EMTs, child care workers, disaster relief assistants, and all kinds of public-spirited citizens working in the bank. No longer was the bank just talking about being a neighbor . . . it provided evidence!

In many cases, the organization distinguishes itself with its people. There is something different about a Federal Express courier and a Wal-Mart associate. They may both be friendly, greet you, and act like they are happy that you are there or doing business with them. This is one thing that makes these organizations stand out. And the answer is often found in employee training, not in marketing. In this case, training makes the difference.

The Community Bank example is just one of the things that a bank can do to stand out from the others. But rather than copy another method or strategy, consider a strategy unique to the individual case. The best place to start is with the unconscious mind.

The Unconscious of Marketing Banks and Financial Institutions

When banks commission studies involving consumer attitudes and motivations, they usually get the same results, over and over again. When customers are asked why they bank at First National, the typical answer is that it is "convenient." And yet, subsequent studies have shown that these same customers drive past two, three, even six other banks to get to "their bank." Could convenience be a real reason, or just a rationalization?

The table that follows is an example of what an "unconscious mind" banking study might reveal if carried out on retail customers. The major motivations involved in banking are expectation, physical survival, and territorial survival.

As noted in chapter 3, money can be subsumed in either the territorial or physical survival categories, depending on how much money one has. If a person does not have much money, then money becomes an issue within physical survival. If a person has a lot of money, then it becomes a territorial issue. The two major elements within territorial survival regarding banks and money are (1) leveraging and (2) asset accumulation. Also, the more money a person has, the more others are prompted to "come after it," either legally or illegally. A third territorial issue becomes one of "holding on" to what one has already accumulated. The physical survival issue, for the individual with little or no assets, becomes one of "hanging on."

Table 22-1
Motives, Features, and Benefits Involved in Commercial and Retail Banking

Motivation	Corresponding Feature	Corresponding Benefit
Expectation (Trust, accountability, reliability. Knowing the bank will be there when you need it.)	Attitude of employees Loan policy	Feeling that one will be taken care of if and when the time comes
Physical Survival (Safety and security)	Accuracy and account-ability Size of banking insti-tution	Feeling of safety Security
Territorial Survival (Accumulating and hold-ing on to assets)	Business acumen	Feeling (by the commercial customer) that his/her needs are understood

In a recent study of several rural banks in the Southeast, an interesting phe-nomenon was found. In a number of small, rural villages where there was usually only one bank, there were a few customers who would come to the bank, perhaps every two or three months, to "see" their money. The banker would oblige them by getting "their money" out of the safe and showing it to them, per their request. This is an excellent illustration of the primary motive involved in banking, the Expectation Motive. These older rural customers had begun using the bank reluc-tantly following the closure of many banks in the Great Depression. They lacked a strong expectation or trust. They were not at all sure about bankers and "city folks." Consequently they demanded to see their money from time to time, since they were not really sure they could entrust it to someone else's care. Although this practice may seem to be pedestrian or "folksy," the purpose that it serves is not substantially different from the toll-free number that is available to most investors today, where a complete and up-to-date accounting is available at any time, 24-hours per day, and is just a telephone call away.

As in medicine, law, professional services and gaming, the Expectation Motive plays a major role in banking and investment services. This means that the cus-tomer is motivated primarily by trust, because he/she puts his/her money into the hands of people that he/she does not know. For many people, trusting their money to someone else is like trusting their life.

If the motive is expectation, then what are the benefits? Basically, they differ from one banking institution to another, and this is why studies are carried out. But we might expect that they would be similar to the benefits that were involved in health-care and in choosing an attorney: security, trust, confidence, reliance, and belief. All of these benefits together spell faith, and that is the essence of banking. Because of their expectations, customers, both retail and commercial, put their faith in the banking institution and they believe that it will come through when and if they need it. They "trust."

How Banks Strengthen the Expectation Motive

The benefits of faith have been conveyed to the customer in many different ways, over time. The immediate visibility of the bank's safe is usually part of every banking room. The image of solid, concrete, and substantial buildings, with architecture in the Greco-Roman tradition, conveyed the image of trust and rock-hard foundation. But in the Great Depression, many banks that looked that way did not make it, and a lot of those buildings will survive today. Unfortunately for some they may serve as grim reminders of an earlier time and bank closings.

There is, of course, more to banking than a building. This is where training comes in. Although the image of rock-solid stability is important, today a bank's image is in its employees. There has been a long-standing tradition that bankers should look, act, and dress conservatively, and this certainly fits in with the whole scenario of instilling faith and the image of stability in customers. But this can also be carried too far; representatives of the institution can become so "professional" that they are unreachable and untouchable. At this point, the customer's faith begins to waiver.

What is needed in dealing with customers' fulfillment of the Expectation Motive lends itself to a well-structured, ongoing, and consistent campaign that is aimed at bolstering faith. Components of the Expectation Motive are best addressed by including:

- We are there when you need us
- We won't let you down
- We will find a way or make one
- We are on your side
- We want to be your partner in business
- Our people make the difference

Not all these statements can be made without qualifiers, which is what makes it so much more challenging to conduct an effective marketing campaign. However, the statements are put forward for the purpose of giving the reader some idea as to what it takes to bolster faith. Faith—the Expectation Motive—is the major motivation involved in customer banking. As a result, it must be dealt with and answered. The best way to do that is through a consistent, repetitious campaign.

Since faith involves believing in something, the bank must present something in which to believe. This is accomplished through those who represent the banking institution and how they present themselves. It must be presented by the employees. In chapter 14 it was explained that the person who has strong expectations believes that he/she is "special" and deserves special treatment. That is what helps to explain habitual gamblers. Whether or not the customer gets this treatment depends upon the people in the bank, and how they are trained. If they do not get this treatment, then the customer's Expectation Motive is weakened and their "faith" becomes shattered.

An example of how faith can be shattered is when a customer is coldly and directly informed by a clerk in a store that his/her credit card has been refused—no reason, no excuse, no explanation, let alone sympathy. Then when the customer calls the bank, a recording tells him/her that "your business is very important to us, please hold, because all of our agents are busy right now." Such an approach, used by many banking institutions today, is a direct assault on the Expectation Motive. Often when a card is refused it is a technicality or sometimes an error, but the customer's expectations are weakened. Proper handling of this unfortunate "error" by the institution's personnel could help to prevent the loss of a customer. Addressing the problem personally could help lessen the damage to the Expectation Motive.

There are two major appeals to the Expectation Motive. First is the way that the bank itself is presented (an image). The second appeal is the way that the people who represent the bank present themselves. Each of these campaigns must target the Expectation Motive directly, which is the major motivation in the choice of a bank and in the decision to remain loyal to a banking institution.

HOW SOME BANKS HAVE INTENSIFIED THE EXPECTATION MOTIVE

Since the Expectation Motive is almost "everything" in banking (and you can take that to the bank), let us look at what some banking institutions have done in order to increase or strengthen the Expectation Motive in their customers, both retail and commercial:

- Have live people answer the telephone; refuse to install computer answering systems.
- Provide instant accessibility to senior officers.
- Provide on-site conference rooms for customers in branch banks and other banks around the state, opening these rooms to the customer for private meetings with his/ her clients or customers.
- Provide "kiosks" or on-site one-person offices around the state, with fax, computer, on-line services, and telephone and data services, similar to airline clubs in airports, so that customers may conduct their business when out of town.
- Provide holiday parties for commercial customers.

- Sponsor backyard barbecues, picnics, or other get-togethers for retail customers, so they can feel like they are "part of the family."
- Sponsor trips for retail customers, at advertised discounts (these are especially effective for senior citizens).
- Intensify employee-training procedures at all levels.
- Intensify customer service-training procedures at all levels.
- Intensify customer expectation and trust through advertising. Use ad copy that lets the customer know that the bank will "be there."
- Use ad copy that lets the customer know that the bank "understands" his/her situation, where he/she is and where he/she is coming from (empathy).
- Provide electronic (PC) banking for customers who want to "see their money" at any time, day or night, on their computer.
- Provide extended hours (already being done by most banking institutions).
- Establish specialized banks for specialized business services. For example, the commercial customer needs to know that his/her business is "understood." Examples are high tech banks for the software/hardware industry, health-care banks, attorney banks, etc.
- Emphasize the credentials of banking personnel, since expectation and trust are the major motivations that are involved. As in health-care, the consumer needs to know that bankers are experts, and that they are well qualified to do what they are doing because of their background and their training.

Physical and Territorial Survival

Both Physical and Territorial Survival Motives are involved in banking. People want to maintain their assets (physical survival) as well as increase their assets (territorial survival) whenever they can. The banking institutions know this, intuitively.

In a very general way, the retail customer deals with banking and financial matters in terms of physical survival. Conversely, the commercial customer deals with banking in terms of territorial survival. Bankers need to know that the two different types of customers are coming from two different backgrounds. The assumptions are different. The retail customer wants to hold on to what he/she has. The commercial customer desires to use leverage and take risks to increase what he/she has. Each group has to be reached at its respective level. The different motives will dictate ad copy and creative and marketing strategies.

Although banking services deal with the three motives previously discussed (expectation, physical survival, and territorial survival), banking can also be positioned at the level of spiritual survival. When this is done, the appeal becomes more powerful.

These examples represent a very slight change in focus—from a focus on money and business (physical survival and territorial survival) to a focus on family values, love, and permanence, which are the essence of spiritual survival.

Table 22-2
Benefits Associated with Motives in Banking and Financial Transactions

Physical Survival (Retail Customers)	Territorial Survival (Commercial Customers)
Security and safety	Security and safety
Convenience	Leverage
Helpful personnel	Understanding personnel
Availability of assets	Expansion, growth
Conservative outlook	Less conservative outlook
Immediate access	Future access
Cash	Accrual
Long term	Immediacy and urgency
Limited services	Service intense

Table 22-3
Examples of Positioning at the Level of Spiritual Survival

Graphic	Message
Newborn baby in father's arms	First State is with you from cradle to college
Family in front of new home	Your family needs a partner to make sure that all your plans work out
Newlyweds	First State at every turn in the road

COMMERCIAL PRINTING, OFFICE SERVICES, AND OVERNIGHT DELIVERY, ADVERTISING BUSINESS-TO-BUSINESS SERVICES

In most business-to-business interactions there are primarily four Silent Side motivations that come to bear. In order of their importance they are:

1. Orientation to Time (OR: Time)
2. Territorial Survival Motive
3. Adaptation Motive
4. Expectation Motive

Most people would think that there are very few or limited emotions involved in business-to-business operations. This is largely because businesses appear to screen out emotion or pretend that emotion does not exist. Executives wear subdued colors; emotional language and behaviors are ruled out of meetings and in general emotional undertones are ignored. Psychologically, this is simply a form of denial. In fact, business-to-business endeavors are very emotional. What happens when a customer goes over to the competition?

Orientation to Time

Perhaps the most salient issue involved in business-to-business relationships is the issue of orientation to time. Almost everyone in business faces deadlines and cutoff dates. But since most jobs are too complex and difficult to carry out alone, everyone needs help. What evolves in business is a complex network of contractors and subcontractors who rely upon each other to compress time frames and meet impending deadlines. These are the specialists who perform their special "task," and allow their "customer" to meet schedules as well as the "final customer's" expectations. Essentially they are asking for a reorientation of time.

Most of us can remember when we were in high school or college and term papers were required in certain courses. Almost without exception, everyone waited until the weekend before the deadline to do the research and complete the paper. Many were up all night the evening before the paper was due. This same form of procrastination carries forward into business and permeates the workplace at all levels. Of course, in business much of this is due to an overloaded commitment schedule. As a result, the services that are requested by businesses from other businesses are to provide assistance with meeting deadlines, compressing time, and performing minor miracles with regard to orientation to time.

The well-known example for this model is the success of overnight delivery. Overnight delivery service is the demonstrated ability of one company to compress time. Federal Express dramatically changed the expectations of government agencies, businesses, courts, and even individuals by delivering overnight. The entire definition of what could be expected and when to expect it was altered with overnight delivery. What often took days was shortened into hours. By 1984 the word FedEx had become a verb in the English language, and people came to expect immediacy and punctuality in the workplace. By 1990, the hours were again shortened to minutes by the general acceptance in most offices of the telephone facsimile or fax machine.

In the workplace, the goal may not always be to shorten time frames, although this is generally true. In the case of many governmental agencies and bureaucratic organizations, it appears that the object may be to extend time as opposed to compressing it. Cynically, some would say that this is due to the inability or unwillingness of many government bureaucrats to make a decision because of security (territorial survival). Either way, the most important motive in business is the reorientation to time.

Territorial Survival

By definition, territorial survival is made up of the day-to-day struggle between competitive forces that do battle with one another over territory. That territory may consist of listings, clients, patients, sales, accounts, etc. Every day, tens of thousands of accounts fall into the hands of someone's competition, and the territorial war is either won or lost, depending upon which side one is on. The emotions associated with the acquisition of or the loss of territory are associated with the Territorial Survival Motive.

Territorial survival applies to corporations and to individuals. In chapter 17, when types of women were described in fashion research, the career woman was seen as one who was primarily driven by the Territorial Survival Motive. To the extent that one is driven by a career or a job, they have territorial motivations. Benefits associated with territoriality include security, prestige, rank, money, status, and identity. As Eric Fromm, a well-known psychoanalyst has observed, the majority of Americans shake hands and identify themselves not in terms of who they are, but in terms of what they do for a living.

Loss of territory involves the loss of all these benefits. This is why territory is jealously guarded, and why it is one of the primary motives in a business-to-business environment. Territory is one of the four survival motives. For many people, loss of territory means loss of survival.

The Adaptation Motive

Consultants who sell their services to business are aware of the fact that most businesses will not buy services that have not been proven. In this sense, they will not take risks or "go out on a limb." This is because of the delicate issue of territorial survival or, in a more primal sense, the issue of survival itself.

Many businesses have a "me too" approach to the services that they buy. The first question asked is "who have you done business with?" This is the Adaptation Motive at work. For this reason, consultants often specialize in a particular field: health-care, banking, automotive, engineering, etc. This takes the risk out of buying a service or product.

The Expectation Motive

The Expectation Motive, which plays such an important role in banking and health-care, plays a role, but only a minor one, in the business-to-business environment. This is because of the unwillingness of most businesses to take risks and to operate on the basis of faith and trust. Many businessmen consider themselves "hard nosed," practical, down to earth, and pragmatic. They pride themselves on not taking risks or plunging into the unknown without charts and diagrams. This is the way many operate, at least in business. As we have shown in some of the preceding chapters, it is not always possible to do this. Only when a person has all of the facts at his/her fingertips can he/she operate without the motive of expectation. In business, no one has all the facts at his/her fingertips, even if he/she has a wealth of experience. Hence, business people operate on the basis of the Adaptation Motive, relying upon the experience and recommendation of someone else rather than experimenting with expectation, which is more risky. However, since those business people are human, and humans rely heavily on the Expectation Motive, it still comes to bear. It occurs especially when one's guard is down, which tends to happen in high pressure situations.

INSURANCE

The success of the insurance industry is based upon the concept of life insurance and the whole idea that a person can do something for his/her family long after he/she is gone, thereby assuring and ascertaining that long after he/she dies, love will live one. As seen in chapter 4, a vital part of spiritual survival is the refusal to accept the end. Life insurance, more than any other business product, is based totally upon the motive of spiritual survival—hence, its overwhelming success.

The basic assumption that the buyer of life insurance makes is that "I would never be able to live with the thought of my family not being provided for after I'm gone." The notion of living with the thought affirms the motive of spiritual survival, the idea that even after one is gone, the guilt will haunt them forever. Life insurance is insurance against that ever happening.

Men are much better prospects for life insurance than women, simply because they have come to believe, over the years, that, should they die, their money may serve as a partial if not adequate replacement for their absence. On the other hand, women, especially those who are mothers, do not believe that anything or any person can easily replace them if they die. Therefore, they are more reluctant to even consider such an event and, as such, are poorer prospects for insurance. In terms of the possibility of a sudden ending, men who are fathers and women who are mothers conceptualize much differently.

Since life insurance is based almost entirely upon the motive of spiritual survival, it is one of the most successful industries in America. Other forms of insurance are based upon other motives. Health and hospitalization insurance is based upon physical survival; business insurance upon territorial survival and expectation; and disability insurance upon expectation and physical survival. But most companies that sell these different kinds of insurance either started out with life insurance or else were eventually led to include it in their underwriting portfolio.

In chapter 20 the Elvis phenomenon was explained to further illustrate the concept of spiritual survival. This is the only "logical" explanation for why people still visit Elvis and Graceland. Similarly, the close connection between the life insurance industry and the Spiritual Survival Motive leaves little doubt of the power of spiritual survival and its inclusion at the very bottom of the motivational hierarchy, or the most powerful of all motives.

SUMMARY

Most industries encompass a wide array of types and sizes of manufacturers. The printing industry serves as an example of business-to-business operations that are commodity based, exhibiting both service and manufacturing attributes. There are many other similar examples in business. This apparently dual role complicates the motivation picture; however, it is still understandable.

Imagine a large commercial printer. It competes with other large commercial printers. Presumably they all have similar, if not the same, equipment on which to manufacture (print). What separates or distinguishes? What makes one printer "better" than the others? As seen in banking, but for different reasons, it is probably the service that is provided by the employees. Clearly the Expectation Motive, the Physical Survival Motive, Territorial Survival, and Orientation to Time come to bear. The motives are the same, but the customers' benefits differ. When the customers' expectations are met, when time is compressed to meet the customers' schedules, when they can take home their profits and increase market share, then all of these motives are satisfied.

23

The Features and Benefits of Three-dimensional (Silent Side) Marketing

SPIRITUAL SURVIVAL

One very basic, yet powerful motive introduced in this book was spiritual survival. It is the foundation for all of the other ten motivations. It is based on the principles of right and wrong. Since it is an abstract concept, it is difficult to describe. Hence, the chapter on why people visit Graceland was included to demonstrate how spiritual survival is useful in predicting activities that are lasting and how it causes people to act in situations that may not be explained by any other definition. Some readers may interpret this in a concrete way: "Well, I haven't gone to Graceland and never will, so what's spiritual survival have to do with me?" This is missing the point.

Since just about every child before the age of seven has some kind of an experience with death, the child's only choice is to make an age-appropriate (concrete) interpretation about death. That interpretation involves the discovery that "it can happen to me" and that life is not permanent. But there is something else that is permanent, and that is the life of the spirit. Just as physical survival is attained by eating, drinking, exercising, bathing, etc., spiritual survival is attained by doing the right thing and avoiding the wrong thing. Specifically, Fleischman's ten elements of spiritual survival have been included in chapter 4 to help clarify this complex motive.

Spiritual survival is a very complex issue, and not everyone has the same concept of right and wrong. Although these right/wrong concepts may be universally shared in childhood, values become more diverse and change with age. Aging or maturing is a process that causes diversity, and introduces the "shades of gray" between right and wrong. What happens is that the priorities in the motivational hierarchy (figure 4-7, page 64) get shifted around by the vicissitudes of life for the individual. When this happens on a personalized level, right and wrong become relative. This shifting takes place in one or more of several different ways:

1. Most values and standards are *learned* in childhood, and psychologists agree that learning is the way that children realize the difference between right and wrong. However, if parents have inverted or shifted the survival motives in the pyramid, then they will probably pass this on to their children.
2. A person can shift blame at the spiritual level. This involves simply pointing the finger at someone else and saying "It's his fault, not mine" or "She made me do it; it's not my fault." By shifting blame under certain circumstances a person can rationalize (conscious) almost any behavior, including homicide, theft, infidelity, etc. That behavior then shifts from the wrong side to the right side.
3. Dissociation in childhood may occur, where a child encounters trauma and simply removes his/her mind from the incident and learns to do this on a regular basis whenever trauma or discomfort is encountered. In later life, alcohol may become an aid in helping the person to dissociate. Sometimes adults who have been involved in homicide swear that they are innocent: "It was like having a force step out of my body, and I watched it, but I didn't participate. I was there (at the crime scene) but I'm innocent."
4. Adaptation has already been discussed. It is one of the strongest motivators in the hierarchy, next to spiritual survival. A person's values are clearly affected by the values of his/her peers, at any age. Values at the level of spiritual survival can and usually do change on the basis of who one associates with on a regular basis. Many studies have been carried out in social psychology that attest to the strength and importance of the Adaptation Motive (Sherif and Hovland, 1961; Orne, 1962; Rosenthal, 1966a, 1966b).
5. The importance of the Expectation Motive has been discussed. People can change their values when "things don't work out"—for example, the lady in the casino who decided, after three days, that the payoffs did not warrant the time that was spent (chapter 14). A classic study in social psychology that attests to the importance of this motive and consequent change in values is *When Prophecy Fails* (Festinger, Riecken, and Schachter, 1956). In this study, it was shown that although some people will change their values and beliefs on the basis of the failure of their expectations, others will hold firm regardless of what happens.

WHY THINGS ARE NOT ALWAYS THE WAY THEY ARE SUPPOSED TO BE

The five above methods or techniques of shifting priorities within the motivational hierarchy help to explain how and why things go wrong, why values get changed and how spiritual survival and other motives get either displaced or replaced. Some concrete and specific examples of how this happens follow:

*   A person becomes a cocaine abuser and begins stealing and burglarizing to pay for drugs. This is an example of OR: Person (drug abuse and drug effects) taking priority over spiritual survival (right/wrong).

- A broker begins siphoning money from his customers' accounts to pay for his "rich and famous" lifestyle. This is an example of the priority of territorial survival (greed) over physical survival (security).
- Child molesting: sexual survival takes priority over spiritual survival, physical survival, adaptation, and most of the other motives.
- Insider trading: territorial survival (greed) over physical survival (security).
- Political favors and kickbacks: territorial survival (greed) over physical survival (security) and spiritual survival (patriotism and lawful order).
- Philandering: sexual survival (impulse) over spiritual survival (family values).
- Inability to hold a job: OR: Place (disorientation) over physical survival (security).
- Credit card abuse (e.g., a woman preoccupied with OR: Person overspends on clothing and shoes): OR: Person (ego) over physical survival (security).
- Drug or alcohol abuse: OR: Person (disorientation) shifted to number one position in the motivational hierarchy.
- Speeding and reckless endangerment: OR: Person, OR: Place (disorientation), or sexual survival (impulse) takes priority over physical survival (security).
- Smoking: adaptation (imitation) takes priority over physical survival (health), which is why so many people smoke.
- A compulsive gambler begins siphoning money off of the books at work in order to "stay in the game." Expectation (luck) over territorial survival (job or career) and spiritual survival (right vs. wrong).

These examples may assist in the understanding of motivation from the point of view of when things go wrong. Criminal behavior, bizarre behavior, and many kinds of disordered behavior can be explained on the basis of this shifting of the priorities within the motivational hierarchy, which was explained in chapter 4. Attempts at correction and reversal need to be aimed at *why* and *when* such a shift took place. However, in looking at criminal behavior alone in the United States, such a task would be so enormous and so overwhelming that it simply could not be accomplished. The alternative is to take people who have shifted their values and priorities and who are dangerous off the streets.

In many areas, the knowledge of motivation will assist us in understanding why people do what they do. Law enforcement officials, when confronted with a crime, place priority on establishing the motivation. Without the motive, they cannot solve the crime. Teachers work with motives to improve learning. Sales people often intuit their customers' motives to give an effective presentation and close. Marketers are in the same situation: they need to know the motives.

Consumer behavior is not disorderly. It is orderly and normal, as opposed to the pathological and abnormal conditions that were described above and that are caused by "shifting" of priorities. The hierarchy that was described in chapter 4 describes the way things *ought* to be. It is the normal state of affairs, which is what the marketer and the advertising executive need to know and understand since they are attempting to reach humans. The shifting and re-ordering of motives within the hierarchy should be left to the police, the psychologists, and the psychiatrists.

THE ROLE OF COLOR AND EMOTIONALITY IN CONSUMER BEHAVIOR

Color has, for many years, been recognized by marketers as having a crucial role in emotion. Psychologists have also recognized this, and color plays a major role in psychological testing. In some tests that are used for personality assessment, the subject's response to color is a strong indicator of how he/she handles his/her own as well as other people's emotions and emotional situations.

Color can often be a determining factor in sales and marketing. Marketers are well aware of the role of color in labeling, automotive choice, fashions, interior design, etc. People in seminars almost always ask, "What is the role of color in motivation?" It is difficult to associate color and motivation as it has been described in this book. For example, color cannot be directly associated with OR: Person or OR: Place, since these motives encompass a whole host of activities. If a woman wants to temporarily escape from depression, defeat, or discouragement and she is motivated by OR: Person, she will probably not buy a black or a gray dress. But what color will she buy? To some extent, it depends upon what she is escaping from and, more importantly, the type of a woman that she would like to become.

On the other hand, color can be closely associated with some of the motivations that have been introduced here. Sexual impulse is frequently associated with the color red, which is hot. Similarly, territorial motives (career and business) almost always come in blacks or grays. This is because of *masking*. Masking involves covering hot emotions with a thin layer of rationality, logic, and reason. Masking takes place in business, in legal and judicial situations, and in other environments where territorial motives are prominent. Masking requires that we cover our emotions with reason, hence, the dull and muted colors of gray and black. Imagine a federal judge riding around in a yellow car (taxicabs excluded)!

Spiritual issues are often associated with white, clear (diamonds), or sparkle. Silver and gold are strongly identified with perfection and stability.

There are many different colors associated with physical survival, because a big item within this category is food. Since people do not consume foods that are colored blue, that color is usually not recommended in the packaging and labeling of foods. However, a wide range of other colors is available and often used, such as green for vegetables, orange for citrus, red for meats, etc. If the physical survival issue is health, injury, or wellness, the color white is often used, signifying sanitation and the defeat of germs and bacteria, which are believed to be the major causes of disease.

The Expectation Motive, when it concerns casinos and gaming, involves bright colors associated with glitz, sparkle, glitter, twinkle, and glow. Golds, silvers, and yellows are part of the advertising approach for the gaming industry. Inside the casinos colors play a secondary role to the glimmer and glitz of the signs, slots, mirrors, etc. All this is done for purposes of disorientating the customer (OR:

Person, Place, Time, and Circumstances), and it is very effective.

Further research needs to be carried out on how color is associated with the motives on the Silent Side that are described for the first time in this book.

USE OF THREE-DIMENSIONAL (UNCONSCIOUS) MARKETING TO BUILD A PREDICTIVE MODEL

One of the major goals of science is prediction. Having data that allow prediction of the future help one from repeating the mistakes of the past. How does the unconscious-mind methodology expedite prediction?

Several studies have been carried out in our research that separate the "quitters" from the "stayers." These studies have been done in universities and on job sites. No one wants to invest a lot of money in recruiting, advertising, and training people if they are just going to drop out and never "make good." Prediction allows the identification of these "quitters" and helps to distinguish them from those who will stay.

- Jane Ramirez, the human resource manager at a 500-employee plant interviewed over 40 applicants for the controller position. She finally selected Raymond Tagmier, who had excellent references, test scores, etc. Within six months he embezzled over $25,000 from the company. How could the screening process have predicted this?
- William Latimer, the dean of academic studies at a well-known college, noted that over a five-year period GPAs were lower and more students were quitting before getting their degree. How could he improve on the quality and stability of applicants through the student selection process?

Scenarios such as this, taken from actual research that has been carried out, emphasize the importance of prediction. The decision to embezzle money, quit school or a job, or move to another location is almost always an emotional, not a rational, decision. Use of various modifications of the Silent Side methodology will help marketers, human resource managers, and others identify the emotional factors that cause these bizarre, spontaneous, and unpredictable behaviors:

- Emotions, motivations, and memory are all targeted in a singular approach or strategy.
- Most consumer decisions are based on emotion rather than reason.
- Emotional decisions are critical in areas that have little or no rational reason for purchase.
- Our research includes the right side of the brain through a unique visualization method. This is generally considered to be the emotional, motivational, intuitive side.
- Three-dimensional marketing can be applied in any area, since even "rational" products and services have emotional components.
- There are only 11 motives in the unconscious, which allows the marketer to base his/her decisions and strategies upon a limited number of people. This does not mean that conclusions can be drawn about the conscious side from this same limited group of people.

- Individual differences are not part of the unconscious. Characteristics like IQ, attitudes, beliefs, eye color, height, and weight all differ from one person to another. Conversely, the unconscious is more like the bodily organs, where everyone has the same structure, more or less: one heart, one brain, two eyes, two ears, ten fingers, etc. There are 11 motives and this structure does not differ from person to person. However, the priorities will vary.
- The unconscious targets three areas simultaneously: memory, emotion, and motivation.
- The difference between what people say, what they want the marketer to hear, and what they really mean is sorted out and becomes clear in three-dimensional marketing and advertising.

THE BENEFITS OF THREE-DIMENSIONAL MARKETING

The benefits of three-dimensional marketing are many and, perhaps, can be best summarized in a list format:

- Three-dimensional advertising and marketing is *wholistic*. It deals with the whole or entire person, including intelligence, emotions, motives, feelings, logic. It does not try to slice off or isolate the person or use approaches that often end up insulting the consumer's intelligence or missing out on motivation.
- Ad copy, marketing strategies, and other persuasive attempts are aimed directly at consumer motivations, causing them to act.
- Three-dimensional marketing complements rational, logical thinking and accommodates it, rather than offering it as an alternative.
- In the unconscious, there is only one marketing strategy: personalization. This strategy works at all demographic levels and knows no language or cultural barriers. Personalizations can be combined with rationalizations, with mnemonics, with absurdities, or they can be used alone. When personalizations are used, motivation is aroused and memory is enhanced, as long as the personalizations are product related (e.g., Michelin's "so much is riding on your tires").
- Three-dimensional advertising and marketing improves recall and retention of what was seen and heard, primarily through personalizations and secondarily through absurdities.
- Creative people and ad executives do not have to re-invent the wheel over and over again for each new client or campaign. They simply decide which motives are involved in the product or service, and focus on that motive or motives.
- Consumers end up getting what they want, instead of what the marketer or people who are surveyed think they should have.
    - Visitors to casinos get the kind of treatment that they feel they deserve—because of their belief that they are "special" and therefore merit special treatment.
    - Restaurant and fine-dining customers get the "experience" that they have been looking for, not just a good meal.
    - Visitors to theme parks have the opportunity to escape and "lose themselves," and then to "find themselves" again.
    - Patients feel that they can *trust* their doctors (and clients, their lawyers), which is what they have really been looking for all along.

- Car buyers get what they want (emotionally) in a car, since they are going to have to live with it for several years. This also applies to home buyers.
- Women have the opportunity to apply cosmetics and buy fashions that will "make them over" into the person (or persons) that they really want to be. They have options.
- Consumers can make more intelligent decisions, since they rely on all three dimensions rather than one, or none.

- Since three-dimensional advertising focuses on motivation and emotion, it gives the client everything he/she needs to establish brand loyalty toward a company's product or service.
- Three-dimensional advertising, which uses an in-depth approach, can assist a commodity business (one which has a difficult time distinguishing itself in the marketplace) to stand out and be noticed.
- Three-dimensional advertising provides the foundation and structure for marketing and advertising plans.
- Three-dimensional advertising and marketing yield many benefits (other than advertising and marketing) to the user, including:

Employee training	Customer service	Hiring
Interior design	Exterior design	Prediction
Interviewing	Product design	Packaging
Labeling	Motivation	Ad copy

- A marketer can establish emotional demographics for his/her product, and then match these emotions with corresponding emotions of people who read a particular magazine or who watch certain TV programs, etc.
- Because the unconscious presents a new diagnostic method for marketers, research directors, and anyone else who needs to know about human motivation, it has numerous applications and opens the door for advances in the whole area of motivation. This is because it is the only method that we know of that addresses the question *why*.
- The study of the unconscious is the method of choice for uncovering and exposing consumer resistance to products and services.

CONCLUSION

Marketers often feel that when they commission a market research study they keep getting the same information back over and over again, or the information they they get is "missing something." This is because the information they usually get is *descriptive* rather than *explanatory*. It describes the sample and all its characteristics, but it does not explain why consumers make the decisions that they do.

Marketing to the Mind offers the marketer 11 simple, brief, and yet comprehensive motives that explain consumer behavior in all its facets and in many different areas. These emotions account for the many benefits that consumers perceive when they purchase a product or service. They explain what has not been explained before: why consumers do what they do.

Explanation is vital in any scientific endeavor, simply because it leads to the next step: prediction. Once the marketer knows why his/her customers do what they do, he/she can talk about what they will do in the future. And what they will respond to, purchase, or buy into. And what will bring them back again. And perhaps most important of all, what they want. The secrets of the unconscious mind are the single most powerful tool that a marketer can hold in his/her hands.

REFERENCES

Festinger, L., Riecken, H. W., & Schachter, S. (1956). *When prophecy fails*. Minneapolis: University of Minnesota Press.

Orne, M. T. (1962). On the social psychology of the psychological experiment: With particular reference to demand characteristics and their implication. *American Psychologist*, 17, 776–83.

Rosenthal, R. (1966a). *Experimenter Effects in Behavior Research*. New York: Appleton-Century-Crofts.

Rosenthal, R. (1966b). Teacher's expectancies: Determinants of pupils' IQ gains. *Psychological Reports*, 19, 115–18.

Sherif, M., & Hovland, C. (1961). *Social judgment: Assimilation and contrast effects in communication and attitude change*. New Haven: Yale University Press.

Selected Readings

Berkowitz, L. Social motivation (1969). In G. Lindzey & E. Aronson (Eds.), *The hand-book of social psychology* (2nd ed. pp. 50–135). Reading, MA: Addison-Wesley.

Buck, R. (1988). *Human motivation and emotion* (2nd ed.). New York: Wiley and Sons.

Fennell, G. (1989). Action vs. attitude: Motivation makes the difference. In D. W. Schumann (Ed.), Proceedings: *Society for Consumer Psychology*. Knoxville, TN: University of Tennessee.

Fennell, G. (1975, June). Motivation research revisited. *Journal of Advertising Research, 15,* 23–28.

Lazarus, R. S. (1991). *Emotion and adaptation.* New York: Oxford University Press.

Percy, L. (1991). Understanding the mediating effect of motivation and emotion in advertising measurement. In Copy Research, *The new evidence, proceedings of the eighth annual copy research workshop.*

Rossiter, J. R., & Percy, L. (1987). *Advertising and promotions management.* New York: McGraw-Hill.

Rossiter, J. R., Percy, L., & Donovan, R. J. (1991). The place of motivation in Rossiter and Percy's theory of action for advertising. In M. Lynn & J. M. Jackson (Eds.), *Proceedings for the society for consumer psychology.*

Rossiter, J. R., & Percy, L. (1991). Emotions and motivations in advertising. In R. H. Holman & M. R. Soloman (Eds.), *Advances in consumer research, 18.*

Name Index

Subject Index

About the Authors

RICHARD C. MADDOCK is a psychologist licensed in Tennessee and Arkansas. He is in private practice, and is also the President of Tel Video Productions, Inc., in Memphis. He holds a Diplomate in Psychology (Administrative), is a member of the American Psychological Association, and is listed in the National Register of Health Service Providers in psychology. He has carried out over 25 years of research in psychology, with over 40 professional publications and papers. With coauthor, Richard L. Fulton, he has produced a number of workbook-video presentations, one of which, *The Silent Side of Communications*, won the Crystal Award for Excellence in Communications in 1995. He is also an adjunct professor at Arkansas State University and regularly conducts lectures and workshops for businesses and universities on the principles and practices of marketing to the mind.

RICHARD L. FULTON is president of a 140 million dollar division of a 1.5 billion dollar printing and digital services corporation, headquartered in New York City. Also, he is Vice-President of Tel Video Productions, Inc., in Memphis. He has held several senior management positions in industry and has had his own private management consulting firm. Previously published in trade journals, he has co-published several management training modules with Dr. Maddock.